Developing Data Migrations and Integrations with Salesforce

Patterns and Best Practices

David Masri

Apress®

Developing Data Migrations and Integrations with Salesforce: Patterns and Best Practices

David Masri
Brooklyn, NY, USA

ISBN-13 (pbk): 978-1-4842-4208-7   ISBN-13 (electronic): 978-1-4842-4209-4
https://doi.org/10.1007/978-1-4842-4209-4

Library of Congress Control Number: 2018966512

Managing Director, Apress Media LLC: Welmoed Spahr
Acquisitions Editor: Susan McDermott
Development Editor: Laura Berendson
Coordinating Editor: Rita Fernando

Cover designed by eStudioCalamar

Cover image designed by Freepik (www.freepik.com)

Distributed to the book trade worldwide by Springer Science+Business Media New York, 233 Spring Street, 6th Floor, New York, NY 10013. Phone 1-800-SPRINGER, fax (201) 348-4505, e-mail orders-ny@springer-sbm.com, or visit www.springeronline.com. Apress Media, LLC is a California LLC and the sole member (owner) is Springer Science + Business Media Finance Inc (SSBM Finance Inc). SSBM Finance Inc is a **Delaware** corporation.

For information on translations, please e-mail rights@apress.com, or visit http://www.apress.com/rights-permissions.

Apress titles may be purchased in bulk for academic, corporate, or promotional use. eBook versions and licenses are also available for most titles. For more information, reference our Print and eBook Bulk Sales web page at http://www.apress.com/bulk-sales.

Any source code or other supplementary material referenced by the author in this book is available to readers on GitHub via the book's product page, located at www.apress.com/9781484242087. For more detailed information, please visit http://www.apress.com/source-code.

Printed on acid-free paper

To Nancy,

Who continues to fill my life with joy and laughter, each day more than the last, and for whom my love grows in kind, each day more than the last . . .

Table of Contents

About the Author

David Masri is a technical director with Capgemini Invent, a Salesforce global strategic partner, and is the data strategy and architecture lead for their Salesforce practice. He has more than 20 years of hands-on experience building integrated ERP (Enterprise Resource Planning), BI (Business Intelligence), e-commerce, and CRM (Customer Relationship Management) systems, and for the past five years has worked exclusively with the Salesforce platform. David holds more than ten professional certifications, including seven Salesforce certifications, the PMP (Project Management Professional), and Google's Data Engineer Certification. He has been involved in dozens of Salesforce migration and integration projects and has used that experience to run numerous training programs for aspiring integration/migration specialists.

David is a lifelong New Yorker, born and raised in Brooklyn, New York, where he currently lives with his loving wife, Nancy, and their kids, Joey, Adam, and Ally. When he is not fighting with his kids to get them to do their homework, he takes what little time he has left to sleep.

About the Technical Reviewer

Jarrett Goldfedder is the founder of InfoThoughts Data, LLC, a company that specializes in data management, migration, and automation. He has significant experience in both cloud-based and on-premise technologies, and holds various certificates in Salesforce Administration, Dell Boomi Architecture, and Informatica Cloud Data. Jarrett's chief goal is to improve productivity by reducing repetitive tasks, and is confident this book will do the same.

Acknowledgments

There is an old Jewish saying: "Who is wise? One who learns from everyone." It's really brilliant in its simplicity and truthfulness. Throughout the years I have learned so much from so many very smart people. It's a strange thing that when you learn from so many people, their knowledge accumulates in your head, ideas and concepts merge, and—somehow—in an almost magical way, they coalesce into a unified, consistent, and rational structure that allows you do amazing things. It's impossible to list everyone whose ideas have somehow made its way into this book, but I appreciate and thank all of you.

I do want to use this section to thank the people who I know have had a direct effect on the ideas in this book, as well as those who have had a direct impact on its production.

To my parents, Joe and Alice Masri: You raised me with the proper values and discipline, instilled confidence, financed my education, and encouraged me to pursue a career I would enjoy. One never really understands how much parents sacrifice for their kids until you have your own. Thank you! I love you!

To my uncle, Ezra Masri: You introduced me to the world of professional services and consulting. It was under your guidance that I grew from a relatively junior developer into a true professional. And though I always had a passion for working with data, it was under your tutelage that I went a bit integration crazy. Thank you!

To Brennan Burkhart, Kenny McColl, and Derek Tsang: You introduced me to Salesforce and trusted me to work on your largest accounts. It was during my time with RedKite (now part of Capgemini Invent, where I am currently employed) that I formulated most of the patterns and practices discussed in this book—and then implemented. Brennan, Kenny, and Derek really fostered a fun environment, conducive to self-betterment, process improvement, and, more importantly, a culture of holding oneself to the highest of standards and delivering work of the highest quality only. I have made so many lifelong friendships here. Thank you!

To Eric Nelson, Richard Resnick, and Gireesh Sonnad: Rich and Gireesh founded Silverline, and put in place this really great objectives and key results (OKRs) system that encourages not only profession growth, but also personal growth. Eric was my manager during my short tenure at Silverline, and it was with his encouragement that I decided to pursue authoring this book as of my OKRs. It's really no surprise that Silverline won Glassdoor's top spot as 2018's (Small & Medium) Best Places to Work. Thank you!

To my technical reviewer, Jarrett Goldfedder: When deciding on a technical reviewer, I wanted someone who not only knew data and Salesforce, but also I wanted someone with whom I have not worked, who would see this content for the first time, and who came from a very different background than my own. I met Jarret a few years ago. We spoke for maybe 20 minutes and have not spoken since—that is, until I reached out and asked him to be the technical reviewer for this book. He agreed enthusiastically and I couldn't be happier that he did. For the past seven months he has worked tirelessly to ensure everything in this book is factually correct and has made countless recommendations for improvements. Thank you!

To the great team at Apress, Rita Fernando Kim, Susan McDermott, and Laura Berendson: I thank you for your guidance through the publishing process. You have made this an incredibly enjoyable journey.

To my awesome team of team of volunteer peer reviewers: These are a good friends and close colleges who graciously agreed to read early drafts of this book and provide feedback. This group of amazing people comes from all parts of Salesforce Ohana and from various roles—from administrators to architects, from data integration specialists to team leads, from product mangers to alliance mangers. Their feedback was invaluable in ensuring the book was understandable regardless of background or experience level. Thank you!

Anuraag Bhadana	Don Koppel	Manan Doshi
Astha Panchal	Gary Nackenson	Miriam Vidal Meulmeester
David Deitch	James Roberts	Robert Masri
Ben Prescott	Jay Rivard	Sarah Huang
Brendan Riera	Jennifer Slominski	Vincent Ip
Derek Tsang		

To my wonderful wife, Nancy, to whom this book is dedicated: You allowed me to skirt my duties as a husband and I appreciate all your active encouragement. I could never have done this without your support and love. Thank you! You have my love always!

And, of course, to our three children, Joey, Adam,[1] **and Allison:** For ten months I spent nearly every Sunday locked in my office working on this book, rather than spending time with you. You tolerated my sarcastic "I'm writing a book! Why are you complaining about having to write a book report?"–type comments. Thank you! I love you guys so much and, although I don't say it as often as I should, I am so very proud of you!

To Lilly: Born to us just as this book is going into production. You added an additional level of pressure to finish writing before your arrival. You have brought a new energy into our home and we are all so excited to have you as part of our family.

---

[1]Adam, Shhh! Don't tell mom, but this book is really dedicated to you.

Introduction

The *Economist* recently declared, "The world's most valuable resource is no longer oil, but data."[1] The reason data are so valuable is because data can be turned into information, and information is power—or so they say. Is this true? Is all information power? The truth is, information is only powerful if it's *actionable*, and that's exactly what the Salesforce platform does. If designed properly, it takes your data and turns it into actionable information and makes that information available anywhere in the world. Actionable for the sales reps reviewing their accounts or planning their day. Actionable for the marketing assistant building a list of campaign targets. Actionable for the product manager reviewing common complaints to decide which features to add to the next release. Actionable for the executive planning next year's budget.

Salesforce is a great platform, but to get the most out of it, we want it to be the go-to place for all customer information. This means we may, for example, have to migrate our account and contact data to Salesforce, and then integrate it with our order processing system to bring in ongoing sales and status data. As the Salesforce platform grows more powerful, it also grows in complexity. Whether we are migrating data to, or integrating data with, Salesforce, it's important to understand how these complexities need to be reflected in our design.

When we are performing data migrations, we generally think of moving data to a new home—taking it out of one (legacy) system, moving it to another, and then turning off the legacy system because the data now live in their new home (in this case, Salesforce), where it will be maintained going forward. Salesforce becomes the new source of truth for that data. We often think about data migrations as a one-time process: We move our data and we are done.

When we are building data integrations, we are building an automated data movement that runs regularly. The source system remains the data's "home"; we are only surfacing its data in Salesforce. Maybe we are pulling the data in real time; maybe we are

---

[1]Anonymous, "The World's Most Valuable Resource Is No Longer Oil, But Data," https://www.economist.com/leaders/2017/05/06/the-worlds-most-valuable-resource-is-no-longer-oil-but-data, May 6, 2017.

loading only the updated records once a month. Regardless, we know we must maintain the code long term, watch it, and handle errors properly.

There are so many common misconceptions about data migrations and integrations. One is that data migrations and integrations are two very different things. Another is that data migrations are somehow easier to build. A third is that data migration code is a one-time run, throwaway code.

The data migration and integration tracks of a project are often viewed as the riskiest part of the project—and for good reason. They can be incredibly complex and full of nuanced details. I have seen so many projects be delayed for months because of poorly designed integrations or migrations that, really, were not designed at all.

This book aims to dispel these myths and reduce the risk of failure by teaching you how to design and build low-maintenance, high-performing data migrations and integrations with Salesforce. The book covers the patterns and best practices needed to build migrations and integrations the *right way*.

Who This Book Is For

This book is written primarily for data migration and integration practitioners working with the Salesforce platform. However, anyone involved in a Salesforce implementation project will most certainly benefit from it, whether they be a Salesforce administrator, developer, or a project manager. One caveat: Although I review these topics, this book assumes some basic knowledge of working with data and Salesforce.

How This Book Is Structured

When I was deciding to write this book, I knew that if I was going to write it, I was going to provide you with new content. I absolutely did not want simply to rehash information that is available online. At the same time, I didn't want to do you a disservice by ignoring all the great resources and information available online. I resolved this issue through the heavy use of footnotes. I often introduce a topic, explain just enough for you to understand its importance and context, then include a footnote to provide you with further reading options, should the topic interest you. I also collected all these resources and made them available to you in a consolidated list in Appendix C.

Chapter 1 of this book lays the foundation of working with data by reviewing the fundamentals of relational databases. This positions us to understand more fully how Salesforce's data engine is architected (Chapter 2), and then we move on to working with the Salesforce application programming interfaces (Chapter 3), and get our hands dirty loading data using the Apex Data Loader.

We then learn exactly what it is that makes for a good data migration or integration, as described by the six attributes (Chapters 4 and 5). Chapter 6 expounds on how to meet these six attributes with actionable best practices. We then take this knowledge and perform a full end-to-end, real-world data migration (Chapter 7). Now that we have some real-world experience, Chapter 8 helps us by describing how to deal with error handling and performance tuning.

Chapters 9 and 10 cover migration and integration patterns, and is followed by a discussion of real time-integrations in Chapter 11. We then wrap up the core of the book with a library of reusable transformation code (Chapter 12) and a discussion of frequently asked questions (Chapter 13).

Last, there are three appendices. Appendix A covers the basics of data cleansing, and I walk you through an algorithm for detecting duplicates in data. Appendix B is a quick reference guide of the core concepts covered in this book. And, as already mentioned, Appendix C is a collection of resources for further reading.

Downloading the Source Code

To download the source code for this book, go to `www.apress.com/9781484242087` and click the Download Source Code button to take you to the book's GitHub repository.

Contacting the Author

You can contact me on LinkedIn (`https://www.linkedin.com/in/davidmasri/`). Please feel free to reach out. (Let me know you've read my book as part of your intro message. I'd love to hear your feedback!)

CHAPTER 1

Relational Databases and Normalization

In today's world of big data, it's easy to forget just how much of the world's systems run on relational databases. But the fact remains, relational databases still dominate the data space.[1] There is good reason for this: They work incredibly well, particularly when dealing with structured, well-defined data.

As the Internet became prevalent, the need to scale up and big became more common. People began to think about alternatives to relational databases to make scaling easier; thus, the "NoSQL" movement was born.[2] During the mid 2000s, there was a mini-war of sorts between the Structured Query Language (SQL) and NoSQL camps that resulted in NoSQL being turned into an acronym "Not Only SQL," as opposed to simply "No SQL," and people agreed to use the best tool for the job. Well, *duh*! Every mature data engineer already knew this. For decades, relational database engineers have been denormalizing their data strategically for a variety of reasons (usually performance ones), and I doubt there is a single proponent of NoSQL who would recommend that you migrate your 2GB Microsoft (MS) Access Database to Hadoop.[3]

---

[1]Matt Asay, "NoSQL Keeps Rising, But Relational Databases Still Dominate Big Data," `https://www.techrepublic.com/article/nosql-keeps-rising-but-relational-databases-still-dominate-big-data/`, April 5, 2016.

[2]With SQL being the primary language of relational databases, NoSQL is meant to mean "no relational databases."

[3]If you don't know what Hadoop is, don't worry about it; it's not important for this discussion.

© David Masri 2019
D. Masri, *Developing Data Migrations and Integrations with Salesforce*,
https://doi.org/10.1007/978-1-4842-4209-4_1

Putting aside the Salesforce multitenant architecture[4] and focusing on how we, as users, interact with Salesforce, Salesforce looks like it has a relational data model, and many people think it is a relational database, but there are some very important differences. I spend the remainder of this chapter reviewing the fundamentals of relational databases. Chapter 2 examines how Salesforce differs from them. If you feel confident in your knowledge of relational databases, feel free to skip the next section.

What Is a Relational Database?

A relational database is a digital database that's structured based on the relational model of data as proposed by Edgar F. Codd during the early 1970s.[5] When data are stored in this model, it's said to be *normalized*. The goal was to model a data store so that, intrinsically, it enforces data integrity (accuracy and consistency). Codd created a set of rules for "normalizing" a database. The following is a simplified set of these rules categorized by the level (form) of normalization. Each level builds on the lower levels, so third normal form includes all the rules of the first and second forms, plus it adds an additional rule:

1) First normal form

    a. Data are stored in tables of rows and columns.

    b. A column always stores a single piece of data, and all values in that column of that table represent the same attribute.

    c. There are not multiple columns to store repeating attributes. (For example, you can only have one column for "Phone Number" even if a person has two.)

---

[4]*Multitenancy* refers to the architecture technology used by Salesforce and other cloud systems to allow for individual customer systems (orgs) to share infrastructure and resources. It's an analogy to a building with many tenants. Every tenant has their own private space, but they also make use of the building's resources. If you are interested in the details of Salesforces' multitenant architecture, see Anonymous, "The Force.com Multitenant Architecture, `https://developer.salesforce.com/page/Multi_Tenant_Architecture`, March 31, 2016.

[5]For more information, see William L. Hosch, "Edgar Frank Codd," Encyclopaedia Britannica, `https://www.britannica.com/biography/Edgar-Frank-Codd`, August 19, 2018.

2) Second normal form

    a. Each table has a key that uniquely identifies each row. [This is called the *primary key* (PK)].

3) Third normal form[6]

    a. Storing data that can be calculated based on data that are already stored is not allowed.

    b. All columns in each row are about the same "thing" the PK is about.

Let's walk through an example. Look at the dataset shown in Figure 1-1, which are modeled as a single table. How many of the previous rules does this data model follow?

CodeName	SecretIdentity	Power1	Power2	Power3	Skill1	Skill2	Skill3
Spider-Man	Peter Parker	Spider Sense	Climb walls	Super Strength	Chemistry		
Hulk	Bruce Banner	Super Strength			World Leading Expert on Gamma Radiation		
Iron Man	Tony Stark	Iron Suit			Engineering	Heavy Artillery	Gamma Radiation
Punisher	Frank Castle		asdf...		Martial Arts	Light Artillery	

Figure 1-1. Superheroes dataset

1) First normal form

    a. Data are stored in tables of rows and columns. *Yes.*

    b. A column always stores a single piece of data, and all values in that column of that table represent the same attribute. *Yes, the powers columns always have columns and the skills columns always have skills.*

    c. There are not multiple columns to store repeating attributes. *No. We have three columns to store power data (Power1, Power2, and Power3) and three columns for skills (Skill1, Skill2, and Skill3).*

---

[6]If you get to third normal form, you can say your data are "fully normalized," even though there exist fourth and fifth normal forms, which are not discussed here.

2) Second normal form

    a. Each table has a key that uniquely identifies each row. [This is called the *primary key* (PK).] *Maybe. We could argue that CodeName or SecretIdentity uniquely Identifies each row.*

3) Third normal form

    a. Storing data that can be calculated based on data that are already stored is not allowed. *Yes. We have no derived columns.*

    b. All columns in each row are about the same "thing" the PK is about. *No. This is a tricky one. On the surface, it looks like the powers and skills columns are about the superhero, but in reality, they are their own "thing" that the superhero happens to know. Take "Chemistry," for example. It has nothing to do with Spider-Man. It's its own thing that Spider-Man just happens to know. That column represents the association (or relationship) of "Chemistry" with Spider-Man.*

Great! Now let's look at a partially normalized model of these same data (Figure 1-2).

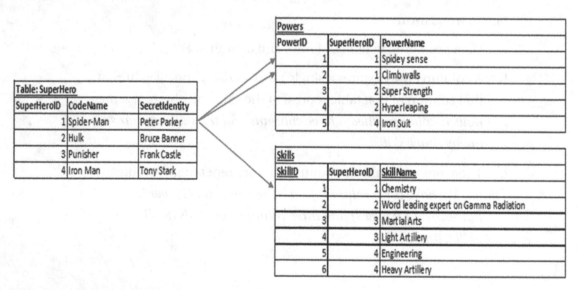

Powers

PowerID	SuperHeroID	PowerName
1	1	Spidey sense
2	1	Climb walls
3	2	Super Strength
4	2	Hyperleaping
5	4	Iron Suit

Table: SuperHero

SuperHeroID	CodeName	SecretIdentity
1	Spider-Man	Peter Parker
2	Hulk	Bruce Banner
3	Punisher	Frank Castle
4	Iron Man	Tony Stark

Skills

SkillID	SuperHeroID	SkillName
1	1	Chemistry
2	2	Word leading expert on Gamma Radiation
3	3	Martial Arts
4	3	Light Artillery
5	4	Engineering
6	4	Heavy Artillery

Figure 1-2. *Superheroes dataset partially normalized*

First, notice that we are now following most of the rules of normalization. (In fact, we are following all except for rule 3b). To get our data, we need to hop from one table to the next and search for corresponding Ids in the other tables. For example, if we want to get all the data pertaining to Spider-Man, we start at the SuperHero table and find Spider-Man's record. Note the PK of "1." Then, move right (following the arrows) to the Powers table and Skills table, and find the records where SuperHeroID equals 1, and voila! We have all of Spider-Man's information.

Some Basic Vocabulary (Also used by Salesforce)

- **Primary key, or PK**: unique identifier for a row (or record).

- **Foreign key, or FK**: a field on a record that contains an Id that refers to a different record (may or may not be on a different table). The SuperHeroID field in the Powers table is an example of an FK.

- **Relationship or joins**: when one table refers to another (or itself) by use of an FK; the tables are said to be "related" or "joined" via that key.

- **Self-related or self-joined**: when one table has an FK that points to another record in the same table; the table is said to be "self-related." For example, if we had a table called People that had a field called Father that contained an Id of a different "People" record, this would be a self-relation. Salesforce, by design, uses lots of self-relationships.

- **Parent and child**: the relationship between two tables. When the records in the table with the FK point to another table's PK, that second table is called the *child*. The table with the PK is said to be the *parent*. So in Figure 1-2, the SuperHero table is the parent of the Powers and Skills tables (the *children*).

- **One-to-many relationship**: when a parent can have more than one child record; this is called a *one-to-many relationship*. A superhero can have many powers. So, the SuperHero table has a one-to-many relationship to the Powers table.

- **One-to-one relationship**: when a parent can only have one child record; this is called a *one-to-one relationship*. This kind of relationship is rarely used because we could simply combine the two tables into a single table.

- **Many-to-many relationship:** when a parent can have more than one child, and the child can in turn can have more than one parent. This relationship type will be further explained in the next section.

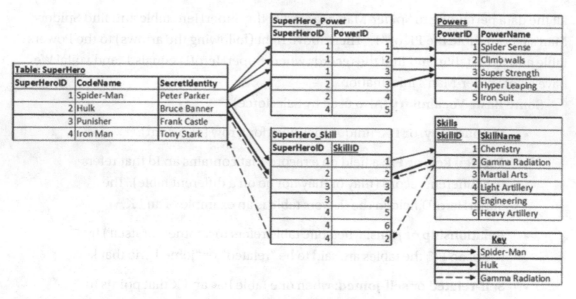

Figure 1-3. *The superhero dataset fully normalized*

Let's take this a step further and fully normalize our data, as shown in Figure 1-3. Here we create two new tables, SuperHero_Power and SuperHero_Skill. By doing this, we resolve the issue we had earlier with rule 3b. Previously I stated: "On the surface, it looks like the powers and skills columns are about the superhero, but in reality, they are their own "thing" that the superhero happens to know. . . . That column represents the association (or relationship) of 'Chemistry' with Spider-Man." The indication of Chemistry in Figures 1-1 and 1-2 represents not Chemistry, but the *relationship* between Chemistry and Spider-Man; Spider-Man knows about Chemistry. So, we create a table to be representative of the relationship by use of a *junction table*[7] (again, this is Salesforce terminology). The SuperHero_Skill junction table has a one-to-many relationship with the SuperHero table and a one-to-many relationship with the SuperHero_Skill table. These two relationships together define a many-to-many relationship between superheroes and skills. By creating this junction table, we added a huge benefit. We can now start at the Skills table and move from right to left. Following the dashed arrows in Figure 1-3, we can start at the Gamma radiation record and find all the superheroes that possess that skill.

---

[7]These are also often called *intersection tables.*

The key thing to understand is that when your data model is normalized properly, the data model itself enforces your data integrity (accuracy and consistency), making it impossible to run into data integrity issues. Consider the following scenarios:

1) Suppose we wanted to add a description to the Powers table (what is Hyperleaping?). If we were working with Figure 1-1, we would need to add three columns, one for each Power column, and then we would have to find all the cells that have the same power and update the description of each of them. Furthermore, there is nothing enforcing consistent naming of powers! Both Iron Man and The Hulk know about gamma radiation, but in Figure 1-1 they are called different things!

2) If a new skill is now available but we don't have a superhero to which to associate it, Figures 1-1 and 1-2 have nowhere to store that data, because in these models, skills and powers can exist only when in relation to at least one superhero.

3) In Figures 1-1 and 1-2, we have no way to enforce the consistency of powers and skills. As you can see in Figure 1-1, someone fat-fingered ("asdf . . .) a power for The Punisher.

It's easy to follow this line of thought and come up with another 10 or 15 such examples, even with this very simple data model. If our data are not normalized properly, we have the potential to create *data anomalies* anytime we modify data (be it via an Insert, Update, or Delete). The important thing to remember is that anytime we have data that are duplicated, or stored in the wrong place, this creates the potential to have conflicting versions of information.

Entity Relationship Diagrams

Entity relationship diagrams (ERDs) are the standard for diagraming relational data models (Figure 1-4). Entities (tables) are shown as boxes with table names up top and the fields listed underneath. The relationships between tables are represented with lines joining the tables, with the endpoint denoting the relationship type: a cross for one and a "crow's foot" for many. In addition, if a field is a PK or an FK, it is indicated as such to the left of the field name.

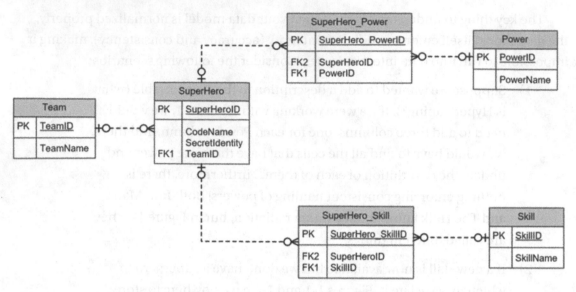

Figure 1-4. *A traditional ERD*

Trading Write Speed for Read Speed

Let's consider one more scenario. Suppose we want to retrieve all the information we have on Iron Man. Which data model do you think would return the data the fastest? It's clearly the model used in Figure 1-1. All the data is right there on one row! With Figure 1-3, we need to do a bunch of joins and searches. This performance boost only works for very select cases. It won't work if I want to find all superheroes with a particular skill, for example. But, if it's important that you be able to get superhero information incredibly fast, denormalizing may be a good option.

This is not to say that we must sacrifice our data integrity to get the performance boost needed. It just means that we can't rely on our data model to enforce our data integrity. We can write code that monitors for updates to a skill or power name, and then updates automatically all the places that exact name is used. So, we are essentially trading the time (and processing power) it takes to update data to get a boost in read time, and we are no longer sacrificing our data's integrity.

There is nothing wrong with denormalizing data strategically, as long as we understand the consequences and deal with them appropriately, or are simply willing to accept the data anomaly.

Summary Tables

A common way to do get a performance boost by strategically denormalizing is to use summary tables. Suppose you are tasked with generating a report at the end of each day that includes a bunch of key performance indicators (KPIs). The SQL code to generate these KPIs is very complex and, as volumes increase, it takes longer and longer to generate a report each day. You decide to add code that updates the KPIs in real time as new transactions come in. You then brag to managers how they no longer have to wait until the end of day to see their KPIs. They can now view them at any time instantaneously! After you are done bragging, you start to worry that if something goes wrong, your KPIs won't be updated and they will get out of sync with the transactions (a data integrity issue!). So, you code a batch job to recalculate the KPIs after hours and fix any issues. Problem solved!

Structured Query Language

SQL (sometimes pronounced "*ess-cue-el*" and sometimes pronounced "*see-qwel*") is a language used to work with data in a relational database. SQL can be broken into sublanguages as follows:

- **Data Definition Language, or DDL:** This is the part of SQL that is used for modifying the data model itself—in other words, for adding or removing fields and/or tables.

- **Data Manipulation Language, or DML:** This is the part of SQL that is used for working with data or performing what are commonly referred to as *CRUD operations*, where CRUD means Create, Read, Update, Delete.

- **Data Control Language, or DCL:** This is the part of SQL that is used for managing data security and permissions.

In 1986, the American National Standards Institute (ANSI) declared SQL the standard language for all relational databases. This ANSI version of SQL is called ANSI SQL. Of course, this did not stop the big database companies from adding their own features and producing their own dialects of SQL. (Microsoft (MS) has T-SQL; Oracle has PL-SQL.) In general, ANSI SQL runs on any relational database, and if you know one dialect, you can write code in another without too much difficulty, but they are by no means compatible. If you to want to migrate from one database to another, don't expect things just to work.

Relational Database Management Systems

By definition (Thank you, Edgar Codd), for a database to meet Edgar's standards, it must be an electronic one, which means that software is needed to manage it. A relational database management system (RDBMS) is the application that manages the database. It does things like manage data storage, process SQL, return requested data, perform updates and deletions, enforce security, and so on.

RDBMSs all have a SQL interpreter that, when given SQL code, first assembles a query plan, then executes that plan to return the data requested. RDBSMs are very good at finding the fastest approach to pull the requested data.

The Binary Search Algorithm

The binary search algorithm, also called the *half-interval search,* has been proved mathematically to be the fastest way to search a sorted (ordered either alphabetically or numerically) list. Basically, we keep cutting the list in half until we find whatever it is we are looking for. Take a look at Figure 1-5, four "seeks" to find one number out of 20 may not seem very fast, but it scales up very quickly. The list length can double with every additional seek! So with just 30 seeks, you can find a single record within a list of 1,073,741,824 items. With 35 seeks, that number increases to 34,359,738,368; with 64 seeks, 18,446,744,073,709,600,000 !

Sorting is a computationally intensive, slow process. To make use of binary searches but not lose all the speed gains made by having to sort lists, RDBMSs maintain indexes. Indexes are nothing more than sorted lists.

We can choose to physically store the data already sorted, but a table can only be sorted physically in one order. When we physically store the data ordered, we create what is called a *clustered index.* Going back to our superhero example, if we want to search on either the superhero name or the secret identity, we want two indexes.[8] We can create one clustered index on superhero name and one regular index on secret identity. The RDBMS will sort the table physically by superhero name, then will create a new "hidden table"—an index with just two columns: SecretIdentity and SuperHeroID (the PK). The "index table" is sorted by secret identity.

---

[8] I say "want" because we could always choose to search the whole list unsorted. Also, we should always index our PK (most RDBMSs do this for you).

But wait! We are duplicating data! This is a violation of our normalization rules! This is okay because (1) the RDBMS does it without us knowing about it and (2) indexes are not really part of our data model. Of course, this means that anytime we update data, the RDBMS also has to update the indexes,[9] which takes time and processing power. This is another great example of trading write speed for read speed.

If we are doing a search on a field that is not indexed, the RDBMS query engine determines whether it's faster to sort the table and then do a binary search, or simply to scan the whole table.

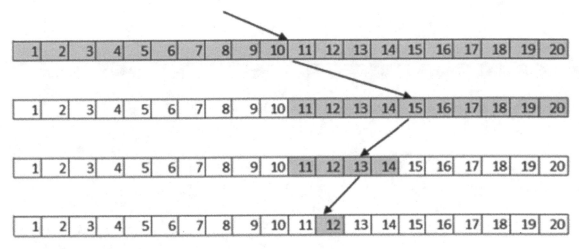

Figure 1-5. *A binary search for the number 12 in a sorted list of numbers*

Summary

In this chapter we covered the general theory behind relational databases, the fundamentals of relational data modeling, and why people normalize data. We also examined how we can trade write speed for read speed, and why some people may choose to model their data in a denormalized way. Last, we learned about binary searching—the algorithm behind every major RDBMS in existence. We are now set up perfectly for Chapter 2, in which we learn how Salesforce differs from traditional RDBMSs and why.

---

[9]Even if our index is clustered, the RDBMS must first find the proper location to insert the data, as opposed simply to writing it at the end of the file, as it would if there was no index.

Summary

CHAPTER 2

Understanding Salesforce's Data Architecture

People often view Salesforce's data engine as a relational database with a web service layer wrapped around it for performing CRUD operations, but this view is wrong—or at least incomplete. As we learned in Chapter 1, it's perfectly normal (and good) to denormalize our data strategically for a needed performance boost. Salesforce takes this a step further. It not only denormalizes the data, it also encourage developers to continue this pattern of denormalization. The question, then, is how far from Edger Codd's vision can we go and still consider our data model normalized? I would say that Salesforce is way past that line. I searched quite a bit for an official statement from Salesforce stating that it's not a relational database, and this is the best I could find:

> At the heart of all conventional application development platforms beats a relational database management system (RDBMS), most of which were designed in the 1970s and 1980s to support individual organizations' on-premises deployments. All the core mechanisms in an RDBMS—such as its system catalog, caching mechanisms, query optimizer, and application development features—are built to support single-tenant applications and be run directly on top of a specifically tuned host operating system and raw hardware. Without significant development efforts, multitenant cloud

© David Masri 2019

D. Masri, *Developing Data Migrations and Integrations with Salesforce*,

https://doi.org/10.1007/978-1-4842-4209-4_2

database services built with a standard RDBMS are only possible with the help of virtualization. Unfortunately, the extra overhead of a hypervisor typically hurts the performance of an RDBMS.[1]

I think the reason Salesforce doesn't come out and say that it's not a relational database is twofold:

1. Its object model is relational in the sense that the objects are related to each other via the use of keys, so technically it is relational (it uses relationships), it's just not by Codd's definition. Saying its nonrelational will cause confusion.

2. There is an Oracle database[2] (an RDBMS with a non-normalized data model) buried deep down in its architecture. In the same article quoted previously, Salesforce states: "At the heart of Force.com is its transaction database engine. Force.com uses a relational database engine with a specialized data model that is optimal for multitenancy."[3]

Regardless, it's not important how Salesforce's data engine/model is classified. What *is* important to know is how it's modeled so that we can extend it (with custom objects) and interact with it properly. Because the closest thing to Salesforce's data engine/model is a traditional relational database and RDBMS, we will use that as our point of reference.

Salesforce Database Access

Salesforce is an "API (Application Programming Interface) First" company. This means Salesforce made a decision that any functionality added to the system must first be exposed via an API, then Salesforce's own user interface (UI) must use that API to perform the function. So, anything we can do via the Salesforce UI can also be done

---

[1]Anonymous, "The Force.com Multitenant Architecture," `https://developer.salesforce.com/page/Multi_Tenant_Architecture`, March 31, 2016.

[2]Recently, Salesforce's relationship with Oracle hasn't been great, and there are rumors that Salesforce is moving away from Oracle. If this is the case, Salesforce will probably build their own database engine. Regardless, the RDBMS is so abstracted away it should not impact us.

[3]Anonymous, "The Force.com Multitenant Architecture," `https://developer.salesforce.com/page/Multi_Tenant_Architecture`, March 31, 2016.

via an API.[4] Salesforce's APIs are all HTTP (Hypertext Transfer Protocol) based and are exposed as SOAP (Simple Object Access Protocol) or REST (Representation State Transfer) web services. This includes the data APIs. (I discuss the various APIs and how to use them in Chapter 3).

In general, when working with an RDBMS, if we are on the same network [either a local or over a virtual private network (VPN)], we connect directly to it over TCP/IP.[5] If we need a web service layer we can implement one (it's becoming more common for database vendors to provide web service layers as a product feature). If we want to work with Salesforce data, we have no choice. We must go through the UI or its APIs.[6]

SQL vs. SOQL and the Data APIs

As discussed in Chapter 1, SQL is the standard for querying a relational data. Salesforce has a custom language that looks a lot like SQL called *SOQL*, which stands for Salesforce Object Query Language. We can pass SOQL to the Salesforce APIs to get our desired record set. The following list presents the key differences between SQL and SOQL:

1. SOQL is a query-only language. It can't be use it to insert, update or delete data. (We examine data modification in Chapter 3.)

2. With SQL, we can (and must) specify the Join criteria. With Salesforce, Joins are attributes of the data type. For example, the Salesforce Contacts object has an AccountID field. As part of that field definition, Salesforce knows that it joins to the Account object, so we don't have to tell it to do so. This may seem like a nice feature, but in reality it's a huge limitation. Because of this, we can join only on Id fields—only on predetermined joins—so we can't join on derived data or other non-Salesforce Id fields (such as a date field).

---

[4]There is still a bit of legacy stuff that is not available via the API from before Salesforce made this decision.

[5]TCP/IP = Transmission Control Protocol (TCP) and the Internet Protocol (IP).

[6]Even if we are writing Apex code, all data access is routed through the Salesforce API. See Anonymous, "Apex Developer Guide," version 44.0, https://developer.salesforce.com/docs/atlas.en-us.apexcode.meta/apexcode/apex_dev_guide.htm, n.d.

3. When selecting from a Parent object, we can only join one level down. For example, we can join from Account to Contact, but not down another level to a child of Contact (a grandchild of Account).

4. When Joining up, we can only go five levels up—for example, from Case ➤ Contact ➤ Account ➤ Owner (this is four levels).

5. We can't Join from a child to a parent and then back down to another child—for example, from Contact ➤ Account ➤ Account Note.

Listing 2-1. Example of a SQL Account-to-Contact Join

```
1. SELECT
2.     c.id
3.     ,c.FirstName
4.     ,a.Name as AccountName
5. FROM Contact c
6. Join Account a on a.id=c.AccountID
```

Listing 2-2. Example of a SOQL Account-to-Contact Join

```
1. SELECT
2.     Id
3.     ,FirstName
4.     ,Account.Name
5. FROM Contact
```

Notice in the SOQL query, we can reference fields on the Account object because the join is defined by the Account field. We don't have to specify the join criteria. We simply use it as shown.[7]

---

[7]The full SOQL documentation can be found here: https://developer.salesforce.com/docs/ atlas.en-us.soql_sosl.meta/soql_sosl/sforce_api_calls_soql.htm.

DDL vs. Metadata API

If we want to modify our data object structures in Salesforce programmatically, we can use the Metadata API.[8] There is no Salesforce equivalent to DDL. Of course, we could also make our changes directly in the Salesforce UI via the Setup menu, similar to using an RDBMS UI.

Data Types for Type Enforcement and UI Rendering

One of the rules of normalization is that all data in a row pertains to the same thing (see Chapter 1). This disallows for storing data on a record that's sole purpose is for UI rendering, which makes sense. Good data people understand that their data will outlive the systems used to access it. Traditional thinking is that data layer and UI should be independent, and that when we build our data layer, we should focus on data concerns (integrity, performance, and so on) and not worry about presentation.

Salesforce ignored this completely and created its own set of data types that has a dual purpose:

1. Data-type enforcement

2. UI rendering

For example, Salesforce has data types such as CheckBox and Email. Check boxes are always displayed in the UI as a check box and e-mail messages are always displayed as hyperlinks and include proper e-mail format validation. We examine all the Salesforce data types later in this chapter.

Picklists vs. Reference Tables

Salesforce makes use of a data type called *Picklist* to replace small "type" tables, as well as a multiselect picklist to replace one-to-many relationships to small "type" tables. This data type allows us to select from a predetermined list of values.

Data that should be stored in a related table are now stored in a single field. In the case of a multiselect picklist, values are stored in a delimited string, which violates the "only one piece of data per field" normalization rule.

---

[8]The Metadata documentation can be found here: https://developer.salesforce.com/docs/ atlas.en-us.api_meta.meta/api_meta/meta_intro.htm.

Lookups and Master Detail

As mentioned earlier, all relationships (joins) in Salesforce are an attribute of the data type. Salesforce has two relationship data types: Lookups and Master Details. In addition, Lookups and Master Details fields act as relational database FK constraints, which enforces our data integrity.

Storage Costs

Being a cloud system, one of the things Salesforce charges us for is data storage (disk space). To make storage cost easy for us to calculate, Salesforce counts most records as 2KB in size[9] as opposed to using actual disk usage numbers. This practice gives us a financial incentive to denormalize our data. If, for example, we have a parent table with 100 records and a child table with an average of three records per parent, we need 800KB (100 × 2KB +3 × 100 × 2KB = 800KB). If we denormalize it, using a multiselect picklist instead of a child table, we only need 200KB (100 × 2KB)—a 75% savings in storage!

Rollups, Formula Fields, and Views

There is no Salesforce equivalent to an RDBMS data view.[10] Salesforce has Formula fields and Rollup fields. These are fields on the object that are calculated. They are similar to MS SQL Server's or Oracle's Computed Column data type.

Generally, Rollup fields are stored physically on the object (for performance purposes, which is in violation of the normalization rules). Formula fields are calculated at runtime and are discussed in the next section.

---

[9]There are some objects that Salesforce gives us for free—meaning, they don't charge any storage for them. You can find the list of objects that **do** count as storage here: https://help. salesforce.com/articleView?id=admin_monitorresources.htm&type=5.

[10]SQL views a basically stored SQL that can then be queried by name, using SQL as if there were a table.

CRUD Fields

Every object in Salesforce has native CRUD[11] fields that are system maintained.
Salesforce refers to these as *Audit fields*.

These fields are

- CreatedById

- CreatedDate

- LastModifiedById

- LastModifiedDate

- SystemModStamp[12]

Triggers, Validation Rules, Workflows, and Process Builders

Most RDBMSs have data trigger functionality. Salesforce also has triggers that are written
in Apex (Salesforce's proprietary language). It works almost exactly like RDBMS triggers,
firing when data are inserted, updated, or deleted. Like RDBMS triggers, Salesforce
triggers can run either before or after the action (before insert, after insert, before
update, and so on) and can stop the action from taking place (based on some custom
validation code).

Salesforce also has workflows and process builders, which are like triggers, but are
designed to be written by Salesforce administrators using clicks, not code.

Validation rules are simple triggers used for validating data at the time of saving
(or updating through the API). If a rule is violated at the time of update, an error is
thrown. They are also designed to be written by Salesforce administrators using an Excel
formulalike language.

---

[11]Remember, CRUD stands for **C**reate, **R**ead, **U**pdate, **D**elete.

[12]When is SystemModStamp different from LastModifiedDate?: https://help.salesforce.com/
articleView?id=When-is-SystemModStamp-different-from-LastModifiedDate&language=en_US&type=1

Record Locking

As with an RDBMS, Salesforce locks records when they are being modified, to prevent two people from updating the same record simultaneously, which would result in a conflict. Salesforce does not block users from viewing the data in the UI while updates are in progress. If we click the Edit button while looking at a record, Salesforce documents the record's "Last Modify Date" at the time of the click. When we click Save, Salesforce checks the date again. If it matches, Salesforce knows no changes occurred since we grabbed the record and allows the save to go through. If it differs, Salesforce knows someone else changed the record while we were editing it and displays an error. (This is generally referred to as *optimistic locking*.[13])

We want to avoid situations in which we have an object that is regularly updated via the API and requires users to spend a long time on the edit screen. I've run into an issue when users would spend hours updating a proposal via the Salesforce UI before clicking Save. Every day at noon, a batch process would update every single record in that object. Users who started working before noon and ended after noon would lose at least an hour of work because Salesforce would not allow them to save. Needless to say, they were not happy.

One would expect that if we are updating a single record, only that record would get locked, but this may not the case. Keep in mind that if we have cross-object formula fields or rollups, Salesforce persists that data on the object in which the field resides, and those records get locked as well. In addition, triggers, workflows, and process builders can also cause locking on other objects and records. Last, even if we have no Formula fields, rollups, triggers, workflows, or process builders, Salesforce *still* often locks parent records when children are being updated. I'm not sure why this is,[14] but Salesforce puts out a cheat sheet[15] so we can better understand when locking will occur.

---

[13]For a good explanation of optimistic vs. pessimistic locking, see Anonymous, "Optimistic vs. Pessimistic locking," https://stackoverflow.com/questions/129329/optimistic-vs-pessimistic-locking.

[14]I suspect it's because Salesforce uses inverted indexes. If they do, this would certainly require locking of the parent when a child record is updated. I know for a fact that Salesforce uses inverted indexes in Einstein analytics.

[15]Salesforce, "Record Locking Cheat Sheet," http://resources.docs.salesforce.com/194/0/en-us/sfdc/pdf/record_locking_cheatsheet.pdf.

In Chapter 3, we examine a few techniques to avoid record-locking contention, and there is a more in-depth discussion along with performance tuning in Chapter 8.

Indexes

Unlike an RDBMS, Salesforce creates indexes for us, although we can contact Salesforce support if we need custom indexes created. Salesforce automatically indexes the following field types:

- PKs (Id, Name, and OwnerId fields)

- FKs (lookup or master-detail relationship fields)

- Audit dates (described earlier)

- External Id or unique fields

Salesforce Data Types

As discussed previously, Salesforce data types have a dual purpose: data-type enforcement and UI rendering. We briefly examined some of Salesforce's data types, but now let's review each of them in detail.

Unless otherwise specified,

- Every data type has the option to be set as a required field

- Custom field API names are always suffixed with "__c"[16]

- All strings are stored as Varchars, so there is never any extra space padding—neither at the beginning nor end of the string—even if we type in extra blank spaces purposely

---

[16]Note that the API name is like a database field name; it can be referenced in code. Because Salesforce fields are also used for UI rendering, they also have a label attribute. The label is what is displayed next to the field when it's being shown in the UI. We don't have to worry about changing label values because they are generally not referenced in code, so changing them won't break anything. This is not the case for API names.

I am focusing on things you need to know for interacting with Salesforce data via the API. I am intentionally leaving out some details that are relevant only to Salesforce administrators or developers who are responsible for building out the Salesforce UI.

Lookups/Master Detail

As discussed earlier, all relationships (or joins) in Salesforce are attributes of the data type. The two relationship data types are Master-Detail relationship or Lookup relationship. In both these cases, we add the field to the child object and specify the parent object as part of the setup. Salesforce then enforces the referential integrity of the field and allows us to use the join in our SOQL queries as well as do other things like add a related list (in other words, a grid that displays child records) of child data on the parent record's page.

As of this writing, we can have a maximum of two Master-Detail fields per object and a maximum of 40 relationship fields (Master-Detail + Lookup) per object.

Lookup Relationship

With Lookup relationships we can configure the field to be required—in other words, it must always have a value to be saved. If we don't choose to make it required, we can then choose either to allow or block the parent from being deleted if a child record exists. If we allow the parent record to be deleted while a child record exists, and a user deletes the parent, Salesforce clears out the parent field on the child records, leaving them parentless.

We cannot create Rollup fields based on Lookup relationships.

Master-Detail Relationship

Master-Detail relationship fields are always required. When deleting the parent of a Master-Detail the deletion cascades down automatically and deletes all child records. There are also settings to control the security of the child record based on a user's access to the parent record. Master-Detail relationships allow us to create rollups on the parent object summarizing data of its children.

Last, there is an option to "allow reparenting of child records. This means the default is *not* to allow reparenting—meaning, once the child record is created, we must select a parent (because it is required) and then it can never be changed.[17] If you are building an integration to Salesforce in which the source system owns the relationship, I advise that you allow reparenting. Let the source system do its job and own the relationship rules.

Record Types

Record types are a special kind of lookup relationship used to control page layouts and security configuration. For example, if we have two types of accounts (Schools and Companies) and we want a different set of fields to be displayed depending on which record is being displayed, we would create two record types for the Account object (Schools and Companies).

When we add a record type to an object, Salesforce creates the RecordTypeId field for us. It's a lookup to the RecordType object and is always required.

Fifteen- and 18-Character Ids

All Id fields are stored as a 15-character alphanumeric, case-sensitive string. Because so many systems are not case sensitive, this made integrating to Salesforce a pain. To ease our pain, Salesforce added three additional characters (calculated), making it an 18-character case-insensitive string. These Ids can be used interchangeably in Salesforce. If you use the 15-character Id in a case-insensitive environment (MS Excel or an RDBMS configured to be case insensitive) you *will* run into problems with invalid data joins or lookups. I recommend always using the 18-character Ids.

Salesforce Ids are unique across the org[18] (not just within the object), with the first three chars indicating the object type. For example, any Id that starts with 001 is an Account; 003, a Contact[19]:

Example of a 15-character account Id: 0016A00000PBUBV

Corresponding 18-character Id: 0016A00000PBUBVQA5

---

[17] A user can't change the parent but an Admin can change the setting after the field is created, even if there is already data in it, then change the parent.

[18] A Salesforce instance if referred to as an organization or org for short.

[19] Standard Field Record Id Prefix Decoder: https://help.salesforce.com/articleView?id=Standard-Field-Record-ID-Prefix-Decoder&language=en_US&type=1

AutoNumber

Salesforce AutoNumbers are really number fields and should probably be called *autoincrement fields* because Salesforce allows us to add a text prefix to it or include date parts. The increment portion must be a number (see Figure 2-1).

Substitution Variables in Display Format

{0}	Required	**Sequence number:** One or more zeros enclosed in curly braces represent the sequence number itself. The number of zeros in the curly braces dictates the minimum number of digits that will be displayed. If the actual number has fewer digits than this, it will be padded with leading zeros. The maximum is ten digits.
{YY} {YYYY}	Optional	**Year:** Two or four "Y" characters enclosed in curly braces represent the year of the record creation date. You can display two digits (for example, "04") or all four digits (for example, "2004") of the year.
{MM}	Optional	**Month:** Two "M" characters enclosed in curly braces represent the numeric month (for example, "01" for January, "02" for February) of the record creation date.
{DD}	Optional	**Day:** Two "D" characters enclosed in curly braces represent the numeric day of the month (for example, "01" to "31" are valid days in January) of the record creation date.

Examples

Display Format	Sequence Number	Formatted Number	Comments
{0}	1 250 5000	1 250 5000	No formatting. No leading zeros.
{000}	1 250 5000	001 250 5000	With leading zeros padded to three digits.
{000000}	1 250 5000	000001 000250 005000	With leading zeros padded to six digits.
{YYYY}{MM}-{0}	1 250 5000	201801-1 201801-250 201801-5000	Four-digit year and month used as prefix to number.
PO# {00000000}	1 250 5000	PO# 00000001 PO# 00000250 PO# 00005000	Prefix with "PO# " (including space).

Figure 2-1. *The Salesforce screen explaining the AutoNumber formatting options*

When creating an AutoNumber, we can set the initial starting number as well as choose to populate all existing records. AutoNumber fields are system maintained and cannot be updated.[20] They are always unique. (If we have duplicate values in a field, we can't change that field to an AutoNumber.)

AutoNumbers can be configured as External Ids, which are discussed in Chapter 3.

Check Box

A check box is the Salesforce equivalent of a bool (or Boolean), but it always displays as a check box on screen layouts and reports. Internally, it's stored as zeros or ones (where 0 = False and 1 = True), and when we export the data, it exports as zeros and ones. When loading data (via the API), it also accepts the string values True or False.

When creating check boxes, Salesforce forces us to choose a default value of either Checked or Unchecked. There is no option for Required; Salesforce check boxes are always required. If nothing is selected, it uses the default value. With Salesforce, a check box is a true boolean field; it allows for only zeros or ones, which can mean True/False or Yes/No.

With most RDBMSs, a Boolean data type, unless disallowed explicitly, allows for NULL values. So, in truth, we could have three values: 0, 1, or NULL. If we decided to use a check box to represent our bool, a NULL will look like a zero (or False, because it's unchecked). But what happens when a user clicks Save? Do we leave it as a NULL or set it to a zero? These are two very different things. A zero represents "No" whereas a NULL represents "I don't know," and they look exactly the same. Suppose we had a check box on a (computerized) medical form for "Allergic to Penicillin." What do we do if we don't know the answer? I have always disliked check boxes for this reason. It's nice that Salesforce does away with this problem for us.

Currency

Currency is a number field that represents money. We can specify the number of decimal places. When displaying currency, it is shown with the currency symbol based on our Salesforce orgs' configured currency type.

---

[20]We can change the data type to Text, update the values then change the data type back to an AutoNumber (and set the starting value to what it was before we changed it to text).

If we have multicurrency enabled, when we create a Currency field, two fields are created—one for the currency value and one for the currency type [International Standards Organization(ISO) Currency Code], and Salesforce displays the appropriate currency symbol next to the value. Salesforce also creates conversion rate tables to store conversion rates. Every user can be assigned a default currency, so if they want to view summarized data, Salesforce converts the values to users' currency setting and then summarizes the data. If your org is using multicurrency, I advise you to read up on this feature.[21]

Date

Salesforce Date fields store dates only, without timestamps, and are not subject to time zones. This field type is ideal for things like birthdays, which don't change with time zone.

Date/Time

Salesforce Date/Time fields store date and time data in UTC[22], but when displayed, it's always displayed in the user's configured time zone. When interacting with date and time via the API, the UTC data are always used. So, when we send data to Salesforce for insertion, we need to send the UTC time. When pulling data out, the UTC time is returned.

Most middleware/exact transform load (ETL) tools (including the Salesforce data loader) that have Salesforce connectors have built-in features to perform time zone conversions for us. Unfortunately, there is no standard way the various tools implemented this, and it's up to us to read the documentation for the tool being used.

SOQL allows querying Date and Date/Time fields using relative keywords, such as Yesterday, Today, Last_Week, and so on.[23]

---

[21]You can start here: `https://help.salesforce.com/articleView?id=admin_currency.htm&type=5`.

[22]The official abbreviation for Coordinated Universal Time is UTC. This abbreviation arose from a desire by the International Telecommunication Union and the International Astronomical Union to use the same abbreviation in all languages. English speakers originally proposed CUT (for "coordinated universal time"), while French speakers proposed TUC (for "temps universel coordonné"). The compromise that emerged was UTC.

[23]For a complete list, see: `https://developer.salesforce.com/docs/atlas.en-us.soql_sosl.meta/soql_sosl/sforce_api_calls_soql_select_dateformats.htm`.

Time (Beta)

The Time field is currently in beta (and will probably be in general release by the time this book goes to publication). It stores time without a date and does not adjust for time zone. We can load data formatted as HH:MM using the 24-hour format or HH:MM AM/PM using the 12-hour format.

E-mail

Salesforce e-mails are strings with a maximum length of 80 characters. Salesforce validates that e-mails are in a valid format (SomeWord@Domain.top). E-mails are displayed as hyperlinks, can have uniqueness enforced, and can be configured as External Ids.

Geolocation

Geolocation fields are used to store longitude and latitude and can be used to calculate distances.

Name

Just about all native Salesforce objects, and all custom objects, have a Name field. This is the text that is displayed at the top of a record when viewing it in the UI. Names are always required. For custom objects, we have the option to configure Name either as a string, with a maximum length of 80 characters, or as an AutoNumber. For native objects,[24] there is a lot of variation. Let's look at some examples.

- Account is a string (255).

- Opportunity is a string (120).

- Activities use the Subject field [string(255)].

---

[24]Native objects are objects that are standard to Salesforce; they are sometimes called *standard objects*. Custom objects are object created by Salesforce users or developers. For a complete list of salesforce native objects, see `https://developer.salesforce.com/docs/atlas.en-us. object_reference.meta/object_reference/sforce_api_objects_list.htm`.

- Cases use CaseNumber (AutoNumber).

- Contacts uses a formula field that concatenates the various parts of the contact's name (FirstName, MiddleName, LastName, and Suffix) and is limited to 121 characters, which is the combined length of the concatenated fields.

If you have questions about Salesforce standard object name field definitions, refer to the Salesforce Standard Object Developer Documentation.[25]

As you can imagine, when a Name field is calculated (as with cases and contacts) the field is read only.

Number

Numbers are numeric fields. When defining the data type, we must specify the length of the number and how many decimal places it can have. The maximum total characters (not including the decimal point itself) is 18. So, for example, we can define the number with 16 long to the left of the decimal and two to the right (16 + 2 = 18).

The decimal length is only enforced via the UI (not by the API). If we have our number defined as 5,2 (#####.##) and we enter 36.123 via the UI, Salesforce rounds the number to 36.12. If we load 36.123 into the same field via the API, Salesforce saves it as 36.123 (and displays it as 36.12[26]); it does *not* throw an error.[27]

Numbers can be configured as External Ids and have the option to be enforced as unique.

Percentage

Percentages are similar to numbers, but they display with the percent symbol. When interacting with percentage fields via an API, always use the decimal value—in other words, load in 0.2 as opposed to 20, for 20%).

Unlike numbers, percentages cannot be configured as External Ids nor can they be enforced as unique.

---

[25]https://developer.salesforce.com/docs/atlas.en-us.api.meta/api/sforce_api_objects_list.htm.

[26]This can affect calculations that use the field, causing lots of confusion.

[27]Infuriating.

Phone

Salesforce phone data types are nothing more than strings with a length of 40. If entering data through the UI, Salesforce formats the phone number (adding the parentheses and hyphens) and saves that formatting with the data. When phone numbers are exported via an API, they are exported with the formatting. When loading data through an API, we must format the data ourselves prior to loading it or it won't be formatted, even when viewed in the UI.

Picklist

Picklists are Salesforce's equivalent of drop-down lists and are stored as strings with a length of 240 characters. We configure the available list values at the time of creation and can change them at any time. We can also configure our picklist values to be dependent on a previous picklist selection to create things like a type/subtype or category/subcategory hierarchy.

Unlike a traditional "combo box," when entering data into a picklist through the UI, a picklist does not allow for free text entry. There is no Salesforce equivalent to a combo box.

When removing a value from the set of picklist options, we can either delete the option or deactivate it. If we choose to delete it, Salesforce asks us to select a valid value to replace all records that have the old value with the new valid one. If we choose to deactivate a value, Salesforce leaves the records as is, but does not allow any new records to be created or updated with the deactivated value through the UI because it's not available for selection.

When loading data into a picklist field through an API, if we load a value that does not exist, that value is created automatically as an inactive value and the update/insert succeeds.

We can configure a picklist to be restricted. This action implements validation at the API level, so instead of creating a new inactive value, Salesforce blocks the update and throws an error.

If you are building an ongoing integration to Salesforce that is pushing data to a picklist field, I recommend you *do not* set the picklist to restricted. This allows the source system to control the values in the list.

Multiselect Picklist

Multiselect picklists are the Salesforce equivalent of list boxes and are exactly what you would expect: a picklist with the option to select more than one value. Everything discussed in the previous section on picklists also applies to multiselect picklists.

All values in a multiselect picklist are stored as a single string, with the individual values separated by a semicolon. This is also how we have to load data into Salesforce when using an API. For example, if we want to update the Color multiselect picklist field, the value we pass looks something like this: Red;Blue;Green;Purple.

Note   Salesforce stores the list values in the order they are configured in the Picklist setup, *not* in the order they are loaded. So, when exporting the data from Salesforce, it may not come out in the same order in which we inserted it.

Text

Text is a string that is displayed as a single line with a maximum length of 255 characters. If we include an ASCII line feed [Char(10)] in a text field, the UI only displays the first line, but all the data are saved in the field.

Text fields can be configured as External Ids and have the option to be enforced as unique.

Text Area

Text area is a string that is displayed as a multiple-line text box with a maximum length of 255 characters. Line breaks are represented by ASCII line feeds: Char(10).

Text Area (Long)

Text area (long) is a string that is displayed as a multiple-line text box with a maximum length of 131,072 characters. Line breaks are represented as a ASCII line feed: Char(10). Yes, the total data storage for the record still only counts as 2KB.

Text Area (Rich)

Text area (rich) is a string that is displayed as a multiple-line text box with a maximum length of 131,072 characters and it allows for limited HTML formatting.

We can load HTML tables into rich-text fields, which is a great way to save on storage. I once needed to store "hours of operation" for 500,000 offices (Accounts). If we went with a child object that contained an average of five records per office, that equates to 2.5 million records, at 2KB each, which adds up to 5GB of storage just for that one data point. Of course, this severely limits our ability to report on these data, but the client said, "We don't need reporting on that. We just need to see it when looking at the record." See Figure 2-2; it's not bad!

Office Hours

Day	Start	End	Lunch
Monday	8:00	17:00	12:30 - 1 Hours(s)
Tuesday	8:00	17:00	12:30 - 1 Hours(s)
Wednesday	8:00	17:00	12:30 - 1 Hours(s)
Thursday	8:00	17:00	12:30 - 1 Hours(s)
Friday	8:00	17:00	12:30 - 1 Hours(s)

Figure 2-2. *HTML table of office hours in a rich-text area field*

You can find a list of supported HTML tags at `https://help.salesforce.com/articleView?id=fields_using_rich_text_area.htm&type=5`.

Text Encrypted

Encrypted text fields are just like text fields, which are stored encrypted at rest (single line; maximum length, 255 characters). They have some special security features, a masking feature, and a whole bunch of limitations with regard to sorting and searching. From an API perspective, we treat them just like any other data type. Everything is done for us behind the scenes.

Salesforce has a product called Salesforce Shield[28] that can be used to encrypt other data types as well as file attachments, and has a bunch of other features. Discussion of Salesforce Shield's Platform Encryption feature, other features, and third-party competing products are out of scope for this book. But, from an API perspective, just like the Text Encrypted data type, even when using Shield or a third-party product, we should be able to treat encrypted fields just like we would if the data were not encrypted. Everything is done for us behind the scenes.

URL

URLs are text fields (single line; maximum length, 255 characters) that are displayed as and functions like a hyperlink. When we load data into a URL field, if we forget to include the protocol (the http://), Salesforce adds it for us. But what if we don't want to use HTTP? Perhaps we want HTTPS or FTP. In this case, we must specify it when loading in the data.

Formula Fields

Formula fields are calculated at runtime and can include references to parent objects. For example, we can create a formula on the Contact object that references its parent Account (Account.Name). These types of formulas are referred to as *cross-object formula fields*. Formula fields are always read only and are exposed via the API when exporting data.

Because formula fields are calculated at runtime, the record's audit information is not changed. This means that if we updated an Account name and we have a formula on our Contact object, the contact's field (LastModifyDate) is *not* updated (nor is the (SystemModStamp) field), even though the data on the object have changed.

Rollups

Rollups are similar to formula fields in that they are used to expose calculated data in real time. The key differences include the following:

1. Rollups are created on the parent object and "roll up" (summarize) data from its children. A formula field either references itself or its parent objects.

---

[28]See https://www.salesforce.com/products/platform/products/shield/.

2. Rollups work more like triggers because they are recalculated based on an update action, then stored physically on a parent object if possible. Some rollups may be nondeterministic because they include data that are time based; so, effectively, they are always changing. These types of rollups are calculated at runtime. When we create a rollup, Salesforce decides for us whether the rollup is deterministic or nondeterministic. There is nothing special we need to do for this.

3. If the rollup is deterministic, when a record is updated, Salesforce updates SystemModStamp but *not* LastModifyDate or LastModifyBy.

4. Rollups can only be created on Master-Detail relationships (not Lookups)

Owner Id

Owner Ids are lookup relationships to the user object and are used for security. Depending on how security is configured (for the object in question), Salesforce may or may not add this field. Often, people use the Owner field for things, such as like Sales Representative or Account Executive.

Address

Addresses aren't a data type[29]; they are a special UI construct that combines the following five fields:

1. Street

2. City

3. State

4. Postal code

5. Country

---

[29]See https://developer.salesforce.com/docs/atlas.en-us.api.meta/api/compound_fields_address.htm.

Users can't create new address field groups, but they can use the ones created by Salesforce on the Account and Contact objects. Of course, users can create four new fields and display them separately in the UI.

Note that Street is a text area, so if we have multiple lines, we need to separate them with an ASCII line feed: Char(10). If we have four lines in our source system and we want to load them to the Contact BillingStreet field, we can do something like that shown in Listing 2-3 to combine them[30]:

Listing 2-3. Combining Multiple Address Fields into a Single Multiline Field

```
1. Select
2.     Coalesce(Street1,")
3.     +Coalesce(char(10)+Street2,")
4.     +Coalesce(char(10)+Street3,")
5.     +Coalesce(char(10)+Street4,")
6. as BillingStreet
7. From tblAddress
```

In this way, if Street2 is NULL, when we add it to Char(10), the combination becomes null and Coalesce[31] returns an empty string. By doing this, we don't have to worry about having weird combinations of street lines populated (like Street1 and Street3 populated, but not Street2 and Street4). There are no extra blank lines in our address.

Revisiting our Superhero Data Model

Revisiting our superhero data model from Chapter 1, we can use the Salesforce native Account object for Team and the native Contact object for SuperHero, and we replace the Powers and Skill tables with multiselect picklists (see Figure 2-3).

---

[30]The example is shown in T-SQL, which is MS SQL Server's dialect of SQL. Note that all SQL examples in this book use T-SQL

[31]Coalesce is a T-SQL command that returns the first non-null values in a parameter list.

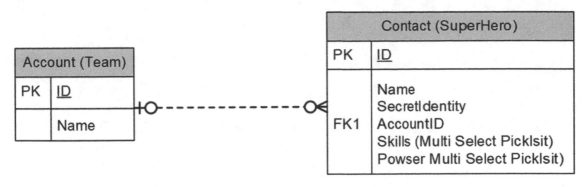

Figure 2-3. *Salesforce ERD*

Summary

Great! We now have a solid understanding of the rationale behind how Salesforce models its data and how it differs from a relational database. We also learned that Salesforce is an API First company, and all external interactions with Salesforce data must go through its APIs. We learned the differences between SOQL and SQL, and, last, we did a deep dive into each of Salesforce's data types.

We are now ready to move on to Salesforce's data APIs, to learn about the various tools we can use to interact with those APIs, and—yes—to do our first data load!

CHAPTER 3

Working the Salesforce Data APIs

As mentioned in Chapter 2, Salesforce is an API First company, and hence has quite a few APIs.[1] It has APIs for working with data, interacting with chatter, streaming, viewing and modifying metadata, and even for creating your own custom APIs. So, of course, the way we migrate data to Salesforce, or integrate external systems with Salesforce, is via the APIs. The APIs with which we are primarily concerned are as follows:

- **The SOAP API** is used for interacting with Salesforce data over SOAP. You can insert/update/delete in batches of 200 records in a single call synchronously. When exporting data, you can export up to 2,000 records in a single call.

- **The Bulk API** is used for interacting with large volumes of data over REST (by uploading and downloading zipped .csv files) in batches of up to 10,000 records in a single web service call. These batches can be processed serially or in parallel, but they always run asynchronously. You can monitor your batch jobs in the Salesforce UI by going to Lightning or Salesforce Classic:

  - **When using Lightning**, click on the gear in the upper right hand corner of the screen and select Setup, then on the side bar, select Environment. Then, under Jobs, select Bulk Data Load Jobs.

---

[1]For an overview of these APIs, see `https://trailhead.salesforce.com/en/modules/api_basics/units/api_basics_overview`.

© David Masri 2019

D. Masri, *Developing Data Migrations and Integrations with Salesforce*,
https://doi.org/10.1007/978-1-4842-4209-4_3

- **When using Salesforce Classic,**[2] click Setup, then on the side bar, select Jobs, then select Bulk Data Load Jobs.

- **The REST API** is used for interacting with Salesforce data over REST, one record at a time, synchronously.

In general, if we are doing batch (extracting or updating "batches" of data) integrations or data migrations (which are batch by definition), we use the SOAP or Bulk API. If we are working with record-level data (in other words, building a web or mobile app that works with Salesforce data at the record level), we work with the REST API. The two primary reasons for this are performance and API call limits. The SOAP and Bulk APIs let us push or pull data from Salesforce in batches, so if we are doing batch updates, they tend to perform better and use less API calls.

API Limits

Salesforce strictly limits the number of API calls that can be made to a Salesforce org during any rolling 24-hour period. The number of calls your org is allocated is based on how many licenses you have, and the license type.[3] Keep in mind that they are API call limits *not* record limits, so if we make a Bulk API call to update 10,000 records, that counts as a single API call. Keep these limits in mind when building your migrations and integrations as you don't abuse them. But, if you code things in a reasonable way, you'll rarely have a problem.

On occasion, I have been in a situation in which I was migrating lots of data to Salesforce and couldn't use the Bulk API for technical reasons (discussed in later chapters). I had to open a ticket with Salesforce to give us a temporary extension to get through our migration. It's good to know that Salesforce can and (in general) will do this for you for a data migration, but don't expect them to do this for prolonged periods to support a poorly built integration.

---

[2]Note that for the remainder of this chapter, all step-by-step instructions will be for the Lightning UI.

[3]For more information on API limits, see https://developer.salesforce.com/docs/atlas.en-us.salesforce_app_limits_cheatsheet.meta/salesforce_app_limits_cheatsheet/salesforce_app_limits_platform_api.htm.

Third-Party ETL Tools and Middleware

There are lots of really great examples of how to use these APIs by writing code using various languages on the Salesforce's developer web site,[4] so I don't cover that here (and raw code is not the focus of this book anyhow). For the most part, we will be building our integration and migrations using middleware or an ETL tool that has built-in API wrappers (or adaptors) for connecting to Salesforce and interacting with the APIs. So even if we are using the Bulk API, we can connect our middleware or ETL directly to the data source and not have to worry about exporting data to .csv's and zipping them. The middleware or ETL does this for us. The primary exception to this are cases of building real-time integrations, but even then there are lots of options that can do the job using middleware, without needing to write raw code to interact with the APIs directly.

As mentioned in Chapter 2, ETL stands for extract transform load, so ETL tools are, in general, very visual platforms that enable the movement and transformation of data. Middleware is designed to sit in the middle of your organization and facilitate all sorts of data movement, as well as things such as replication, data cleansing, monitoring, and other data services. Most middleware (including the ones we will discussed shortly) include an ETL tool.

The following discussion includes some of the most commonly used data tools in the Salesforce world, and it is not—by any means—exhaustive. My aim is to demonstrate the breadth of options available for interfacing with Salesforce (and to give you a starting point in the tool selection process). None of the following is meant as an endorsement of a specific product. When choosing a data tool, I recommend that you start with the ETL or middleware tool that best fits your (or your organization's) current skill set, even if it's not described in the following sections. If you are in an MS shop, you should probably look at SQL Server Integration Services (SSIS); if you are an Informatica shop, that's where you should start. The next thing you should be looking at is other connectors (adaptors) that you may need (for the other applications/databases with which you need to integrate). Regardless of the tool you choose, because all of them hit the same APIs, the Salesforce connectors in them are quite similar. In addition, all the patterns and practices discussed in the coming chapters apply equally to each of them.

---

[4]Sample Java and C# code can be found at <Emphasis FontCategory="NonProportional">https://developer.salesforce.com/docs/atlas.en-us.api.meta/api/sforce_api_quickstart_steps_walk_through_code.htm.

Apex Data Loader

The Apex Data Loader is a free utility provided by Salesforce. It's great for testing the SOAP and Bulk REST APIs under various configurations, as well as doing one-off updates and exports. I do not recommend it for a full-blown data migration or integration because of its lack of features as an ETL tool, not because of any limitations in working with the Salesforce APIs.

Later in this chapter, we walk through installing the Apex Data loader, connecting to Salesforce through it, and performing a few simple tasks.

Informatica

Informatica (`https://www.informatica.com/`) has been in the middleware and ETL space for a long time and is very common in the industry. Informatica Cloud specifically is widely used for Salesforce integrations (`https://www.informatica.com/products/cloud-integration/connectivity/salesforce-connector.html`).

SQL Server Integration Services (SSIS)

SSIS is MS's enterprise ETL tool, as part of its SQL Server Database platform. Because its built on the MS platform, it makes it very easy to use for anyone with an MS background, and it includes the ability to embed native C# code if you need to do things that are not part of its native tool set. It also allows you to write or buy custom components for it. SSIS does not have a native Salesforce connector, but you can buy one for a relatively low price. If you already have a[5] SQL Server license, SSIS comes free with it, so this becomes a very powerful low-cost option.

Third-Party SSIS Salesforce Connectors[6]

- **KingswaySoft**: `http://www.kingswaysoft.com/products/ssis-integration-toolkit-for-salesforce`

---

[5]After (exhaustively) discussing this with the Apress editors, it was determined that you (the reader) are most likely pronouncing SQL as "sequel," as opposed to "ess-cue-el," and that it should be written as "a SQL." Of course, if you are reading this and pronouncing it "ess-cue-el," I should have written it as "an SQL," but I didn't, so that would make it (and me and the Apress editors) wrong. So, don't do that. Thank you.

[6]All of these have a free developer version.

- **TaskFactory**: `http://pragmaticworks.com/Products/Task-Factory/Feature/Salesforce-SSIS`

- **CozyRoc**: `https://www.cozyroc.com/ssis/salesforce`

Azure Data Factory

Azure is part of the MS suite of cloud products; Data Factory (`https://azure.microsoft.com/en-us/services/data-factory/`) is its cloud-based ETL service. MS recently released a new version of its Salesforce connector (`https://docs.microsoft.com/en-us/azure/data-factory/connector-salesforce`). Azure Data Factory also allows for the hosting and running of SSIS packages in the MS cloud with our having to spin up a virtual machine (VM[7]).

MuleSoft

MuleSoft (`https://www.mulesoft.com/integration-solutions/saas/salesforce`) is another common middleware with a Salesforce connector. MuleSoft was recently acquired by Salesforce,[8] and at the time the purchase was made, Salesforce announced that it was building a new integration cloud.[9] At the time of this writing, not much is known about what Salesforce's new integration cloud will look like, and I don't want to speculate, but I think it's safe to say that MuleSoft technology will be used in some way. Regardless, I can assure you that all the patterns and practices discussed in this book still apply.

DBAmp

DBAmp (`https://forceamp.com/`) allows you to create a SQL Server linked server that connects to your Salesforce org. (I wouldn't classify it as either an ETL tool or middleware.) You can then interact with Salesforce data from within SQL Server by passing in SOQL code. It has stored procedures for replicating data down to SQL Server, including metadata. So if, for example, you add a column to an object in Salesforce,

---

[7]You can also host your SSIS packages in Azure SQL Server Database running SQL Integration Services.

[8]See `https://www.mulesoft.com/press-center/salesforce-acquisition-completed`.

[9]See: `https://www.salesforce.com/products/integration-cloud/overview/`.

DBAmp adds that column to the local table. (Note that some middleware such as Informatica Cloud have a similar feature.)

Don't make the mistake of thinking that if you use a tool like DBAmp, then you don't have to know anything about the Salesforce APIs. If you make this assumption, you'll be in for a world of pain. For example, if you write SQL joining to Salesforce linked tables in SQL Server, DBAmp downloads all the data then performs the join locally. (Just as SQL Server would for any linked server.) DBAmp also has a set of stored procedures for updating Salesforce data.

If you are used to working with stored procedures or simply want a tool that makes it easy to report on Salesforce data locally, and you are an MS SQL Server shop, you should look at DBAmp (but, again, you still need to use proper patterns and practices).

Relational Junction

Relational Junction (`http://sesamesoftware.com/relational-junction/salesforce-integration/`) runs as a service on either a Windows or a Unix/Linux server. It replicates all Salesforce data down to a local database, supporting a wide range of databases (Oracle, SQL Server, Azure, MySQL, PostgreSQL, DB2, Informix, and Sybase). Like DBAmp, it also replicates the data structures for you dynamically. So if you add a field to an object in Salesforce, for example, Relational Junction adds those columns automatically to the database. Relational Junction also allows you to update the local copy and flag records with an action flag (I = insert, U = update, D = delete, R = restore delete). Relational Junction then pushes those updates to Salesforce.

Dell's Boomi

Dell's Boomi (`https://boomi.com/solutions/salesforce/`) is cloud-based middleware and an ETL tool that has been gaining popularity recently in Salesforce circles.

Jitterbit

Jitterbit (`https://www.jitterbit.com/solutions/salesforce-integration/`) provides a free Salesforce data loader, so it has also gained some popularity.

dataloader.io

aataloader.io (`https://dataloader.io/`) is a free, Web-based ETL utility provided by MuleSoft.

Scribe

Scribe (`https://www.scribesoft.com/solutions/crm-integration/salesforce/`) is another piece of common middleware with a Salesforce connector.

Open Database Connectivity Drivers

There are a few Salesforce ODBC (open database connectivity) drivers on the market that interface to Salesforce APIs. I recommend avoiding them because the Salesforce APIs don't line up well to standard ODBC functionality and you end up having all the limitations of the APIs plus all the limitations of the ODBC protocol, and you have no way of knowing what the ODBC driver is doing behind the scenes. For example, what is it doing when I send it 500 Insert statements? Will it attempt to use the Bulk API? What batch size will it use? Will it make 500 API calls? These ODBC drivers tend to abstract too much, which makes them difficult to manage. If you simply need to export data without any complicated joins, perhaps an ODBC driver may work for you, but at the time of this writing, I don't know of any ODBC drivers on the market that meet the needs of moderately complex or large-volume data migration or integration.

The Salesforce Recycle Bin and Data Archiving

Before we dive into API operations, let's examine how Salesforce handles deletions and archiving of activity data.

The Salesforce Recycle Bin

When you delete a record in Salesforce, it does a kind of soft delete. It flags the record as deleted and hides it from users and the system as a whole (for example, it's not used in triggers, rollups, formula fields, and so on). If you want to view (or restore) the record, you can simply check the Salesforce recycle bin.[10] When using the API, you can query (using SOQL) for records where "IsDeleted=1" (note that all Salesforce objects have this field).

Salesforce's recycle bin autoempties when it fills up (its capacity is 25 times your org total storage space). Salesforce autoempties the oldest records. Although Salesforce claims to autoempty records that are more than 15 days old, I have seen older data in the recycle bin, so I am unsure of the exact cutoff time, or even if there is an exact time. If you combine this feature with the user's ability to empty data at will, you end up with a situation in which you can't rely on the IsDeleted flag to identify newly deleted records with confidence (and that may need to be processed by some integration job). We look at other, more reliable methods to identify deleted records in Chapter 9.

It's also important to note that even when records are in the recycle bin, Salesforce still maintains referential integrity on them, so they can still cause all the locking issues discussed in the previous chapter! What's worse is that, even if you empty the recycle bin, because of locking issues, Salesforce merely tags the records for cleanup, hiding them from the recycle bin UI, but they are still visible by the API. It can take up to three days[11] for data to be physically deleted and to free you from your locking issues!

Data Archiving

Salesforce archives Events automatically that are more than a year old, and archives Tasks that are more than a year old and are closed. These two objects have a IsArchived field that indicates whether the record is archived. Like the IsDeleted flag, you can query the Salesforce API (using SOQL) for archived records by using "IsArchived=1".

---

[10]For information on viewing and purging the recycling bin, see `https://help.salesforce.com/articleView?id=home_delete.htm`.

[11]I got this "three-day" time frame from a Salesforce support rep when working through an issue that I could not delete a record with no child objects and nothing in the recycle bin because of a "DELETE_OPERATION_TOO_LARGE:Cascade deleting too many records." error. I have no way to verify the three-day time frame, but Salesforce officially says the deleted records blocking cascade delete issues are "working as designed." For more information, see `https://help.salesforce.com/articleView?id=000149021&type=1`.

API Operations

For whatever reason, probably because they were targeting less technical users, Salesforce did not use the API method names when creating the Apex Data Loader operation buttons (see Figure 3-1). If you look in the Salesforce API documentation,[12] you will not see a method called Insert; it is called create(). Nor will you see a method called Export; it is called query(). When third-party vendors started creating utilities to work with Salesforce data, they tended to use the names used by the Apex Data Loader. This is also the language used in the industry, so we will continue to use that language here, but note you will find some variation in the names, depending on the middleware or ETL tool you decide to use.

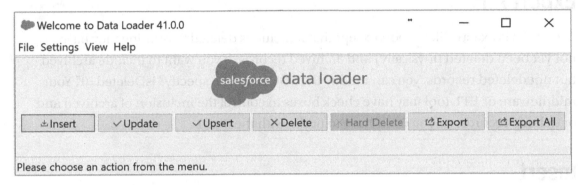

Figure 3-1. *The Apex Data Loader*

The following sections review the most common API operations. These operations should cover all you need to code any data migration or to build even the most complex Salesforce integrations. The REST, SOAP, and Bulk APIs each support all of them. Not all the tools discussed in the previous section support all the operations described here. When choosing middleware or an ETL tool, be sure to confirm it supports all the operations you need (and at least the SOAP and Bulk APIs).

Note that even though you pass the data in batches of records, and they are processed in batches, records can "error-out" individually. So, if you upload a batch of 200 records to be inserted, it's possible that 198 rows insert and two fail. Each row is processed independently (it's not a transaction with rollback). The exception to

---

[12]API-supported calls can be found here: `https://developer.salesforce.com/docs/atlas.`
`en-us.api.meta/api/sforce_api_calls_list.htm`.

this (each row being processed independently) is if there is a trigger that works on the whole batch at once (the trigger code acts as a single transaction). It this is the case, then you can have the entire batch fail because of one bad record.

Export

Export is your basic export data operation that passes in a SOQL query. Most middleware and ETL tools have a built-in SOQL builder to abstract this completely. A good utility allows you to override the generated SOQL and write your own. Export always excludes deleted and archived records.

Export All

Export All is exactly like Export except that it includes deleted (assuming they have not yet been deleted physically) and archived records. If you want to include archived but not deleted records, you can modify the SOQL code to specify "isDeleted=0". Your middleware or ETL tool may have check boxes to control the inclusion of archived and\ or deleted records, so you don't have to fiddle with the SOQL.

Insert

Insert is your basic create-new-record operation. The API returns the Ids of the newly created records, and either success messages or error codes and messages for rows that failed.

Update

Update works exactly as Insert does except it updates existing records rather than inserts new ones. To use Update, you must pass in the Salesforce Ids of the records to be updated. If you don't have the Ids, you first have to perform an export to get the Ids, then you can push the updates using the Ids.

Upsert

An Upsert is a combination of insert and update in a single call. If the record exists, Salesforce updates it; if not, Salesforce creates it. When using Upsert, you must specify on which field the match should be made. By doing so, Salesforce knows whether it should do an update or an insert. This field must be specified as "External Id" (see Chapter 2 for the data types can be defined as External Id). You don't have to have uniqueness enforced on the External Id used, but if two matching records are found, the row will error. Salesforce created External Ids especially to be used as a joiner to external systems, and they should correspond to the PK of a table in the system being migrated from, or integrated with.

If you are using an External Id field for a data migration or integration, I recommend you always set it as unique. In fact, I can't think of a single reason why you wouldn't enforce uniqueness on an External Id used for migrations and/or integrations. You may configure a field as an External Id because you want it to be indexed, but in this case you are not really using it as an External Id field, so it's okay if you don't enforce uniqueness.

Upserts also allow you to set related data based on an External Id. For example, if you are upserting contacts, you can specify AccountID (the Id of the parent account record) by sending in an External Id of the Account object. This feature is only available to Upsert. If you are using Insert or Update, you *must* send the Salesforce AccountId if you want to set that field value on the Contact object.

Upserts are a somewhat slower operation than inserts and updates separately, because with upserts, Salesforce must first determine whether the record exists, then perform either an insert or an update.

Delete

Delete does exactly what you expect; it deletes records based on the passed in Salesforce Ids. Deleting data en masse tends to be a lot more difficult (prone to error/failure) and more time-consuming then mass insertions or updates. This is because Delete is a lock-heavy operation.

Hard Delete

Hard Delete is similar to Delete, except the targeted records do not go to the recycling bin. This operation works as if the records were placed in the recycling bin and then were cleared from it. They can still cause locking issues up until the Salesforce process runs to delete them physically.

Undelete

Undelete restores records from the recycle bin based on the passed-in Salesforce Ids. You perform the operation against the object you are restoring from. For example, if you want to undelete Accounts, you pass in Salesforce Ids of deleted account records. After the records are deleted physically, they can no longer be restored. If a deletion caused a cascading delete, then restoring the record causes a cascading restore. To get a list of deleted records by object, use the Export All operation, where "isDeleted=1". It's rare to find middleware or an ETL tool that supports Undelete; even the Apex Data Loader does not support it.

Merge

Merge allows you to merge records that you consider to be duplicates (for example, you may have two records for the same company in the Account object). It's only supported for accounts, contacts, and leads. You can specify up to three Ids belonging to the same object to be merged, and specify one of the records as the survivor record; the other one or two records are "victims." Salesforce first updates all child object records of the victim records, "reparenting" them to the survivor record, and then deletes the victim records. In our account Merge example, if we have contacts, opportunities, and tasks related to the victim accounts, they are updated to point to the survivor account, and then the victim accounts are deleted.

A merge is processed as a single transaction. If a child record can't be reparented for whatever reason, the entire merge fails and an error is thrown.

The API does allow you to specify whether some data should be retained from the victim records. But, because we are more focused on integrations,[13] in our case we would perform the merge and then update the survivor record to look exactly as we want it to.

Like Undelete, most middleware/ETL tools don't support the Merge API call. If you know you will need this functionality, be sure to include it as a requirement when evaluating the middleware/ETL tool you choose.

Let's Give It a Try!

I know you've had a lot to absorb thus far in this chapter, but I assure you, after you perform a few simple API operations, you will see just how easy it really is to work with Salesforce data. So, that is what we are going to do for the remainder of this chapter. I'm going to walk you through performing a few basic operations using the Apex Data Loader, and will discuss Salesforce environments and connectivity. If you are already familiar with the Apex Data Loader, feel free to scan the following sections rather than study them intently.

Developer Accounts and Sandboxes

Before we begin, you need access to a Salesforce environment. If you already own Salesforce licenses, you can spin up a sandbox and use that. A sandbox is a replication of your production org with various amounts of data storage and replicated production data. Salesforce gives you various amounts of storage space and production data included with it at the time of creation or refresh[14] (see Figure 3-2).

---

[13]You never perform a merge as part of a data migration. You clean up your data in the source or in a staging area prior to migration. We review a method for detecting duplicate data in Appendix A.

[14]For more information, please see https://help.salesforce.com/articleView?id=data_sandbox_environments.htm&type=5.

Sandbox Type	Refresh Interval	Storage Limit		What's Copied
		Data	File	
Developer Sandbox	1 day	200 MB	200 MB	Metadata only
Developer Pro Sandbox	1 day	1 GB	1 GB	Metadata only
Partial Copy Sandbox	5 days	5 GB	5 GB	Metadata and sample data
Full Sandbox	29 days	Same as your production org		Metadata and all data

Figure 3-2. *Sandbox types*

To create a new sandbox (or refresh an existing one), log in to your Salesforce org, go to Setup, then type "Sandboxes" in the Quick Find box and click Sandboxes. From there, you can create a new sandbox or refresh an existing one..

If you don't have any Salesforce licenses or simply don't want to use one of your sandboxes, you can create a free developer org by visiting `https://developer. salesforce.com/signup`.

Note   I will be using a new developer account, so if you want everything you see to match what you see here, create a new developer account.

Log in Salesforce

If you are using a production org or a free developer org, go to `https://login. salesforce.com`; if you are using a sandbox, go to `https://test.salesforce.com`. Then, type in (or select) your user name and password.

If you are unfamiliar with the Salesforce UI, take some time now and familiarize yourself with it.[15] If you are using a new developer org, you will notice there are 12 test accounts and 20 test contacts in your org.

---

[15]The Salesforce Trailheads are a great way get started. See `https://trailhead.salesforce.com/ en/home`.

Generate a Token

When connecting to the Salesforce API, you need to authenticate using either oAuth or Basic Authentication. If you are using the REST API, you must use oAuth; for the SOAP and Bulk APIs you can use either oAuth or Basic Authentication. To use Basic Authentication, you need to generate a security token. So, let's do that now by following these steps[16] (see Figure 3-3):

1. Click your user icon in the top right-hand corner.

2. Click Settings.

3. Then, on the left-hand menu, click Reset My Security Token.

4. In the Reset Security Token screen click the Reset Security Token button.

You will get an email with your new security token almost immediately. It will look something like this: s8E4qYIecwL8Pg5OrMkAMpgT. Make note of it, because you'll need it later.

Figure 3-3. *Generating a new security token*

---

[16]These steps assume you are using Lightning. If you are using Salesforce Classic, click your user name and select Switch to Lightning Experience.

Download and Install Apex Data Loader

Next, we need to download and install Apex Data Loader (see Figure 3-4):

1. Click the gear icon in the top right-hand corner.

2. Click Setup.

3. Then, on the left-hand menu, expand Data, then click Data Loader.

4. Click "Download Data Loader XXX" (either for Mac or for Windows).

5. Once downloaded, run the installer and follow the installation wizard to complete the process.

   a. Make note of the installation directory because you'll need it later.

   b. Be sure to install the samples because you'll use them later.

   c. Also note that the installer may prompt you to download and install Java as a prerequisite, and the system will take you to the proper download page. Be sure to install the version of Java as the installer instructs you—either 32 bit or 64 bit.

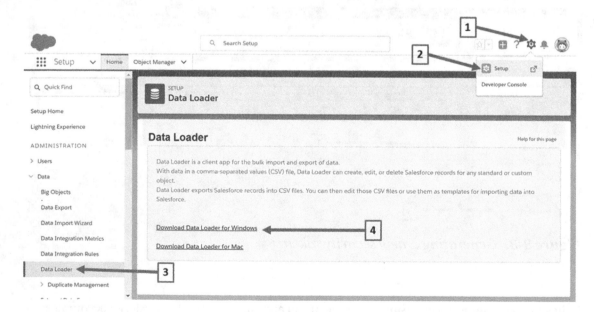

Figure 3-4. *Downloading the Apex Data Loader*

Apex Data Loader Settings/API Options

Figure 3-5 shows the Apex Data Loader settings screen (you can find it under the Settings menu). Most of these settings are pretty self-explanatory, but I cover each of them briefly. You can refer to the Apex Data Loader user manual (`https://resources.docs.salesforce.com/216/latest/en-us/sfdc/pdf/salesforce_data_loader.pdf`) for more information. It covers the settings in detail as well as provides a wealth of other good information, including how to use the command line for automating the Apex Data Loader.

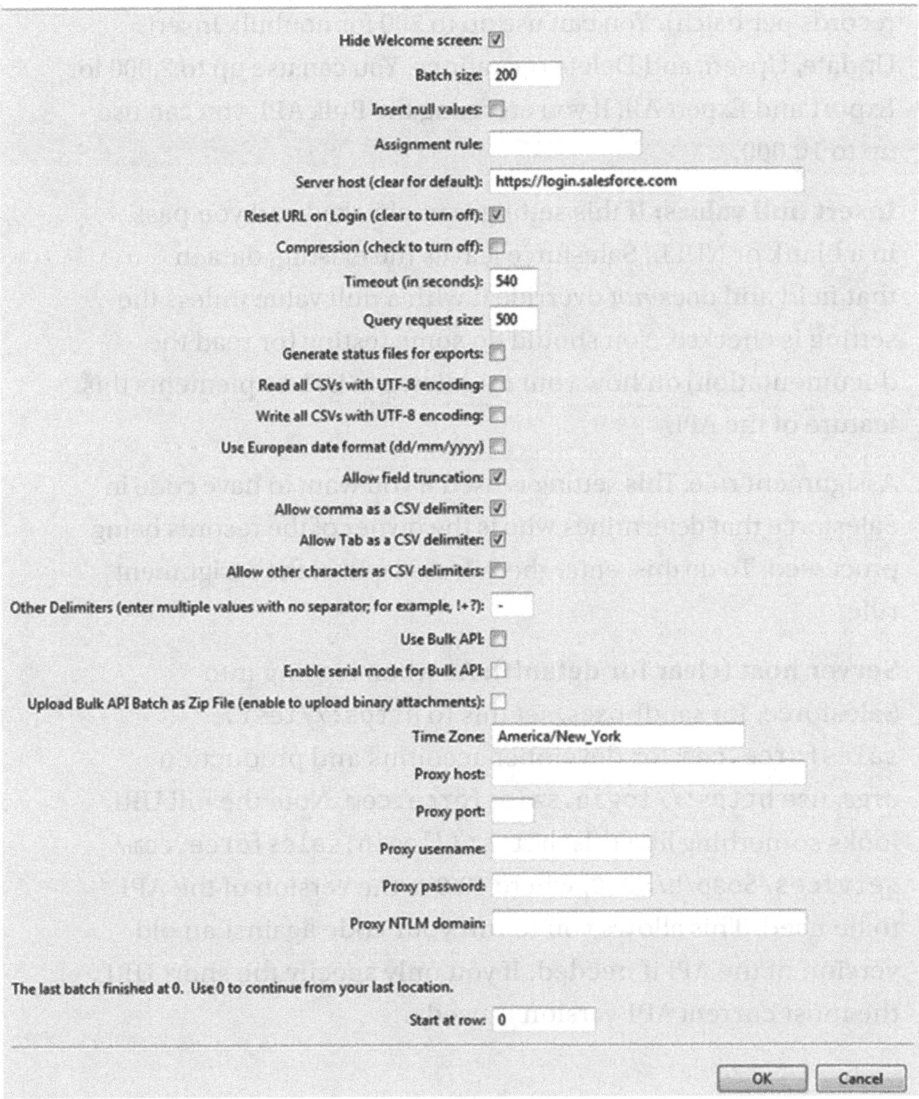

Figure 3-5. The Apex Data Loader settings screen

The following list presents the settings on the settings screen. Most of these settings are equivalent to whichever middleware/ETL tool you are using. It's important that you understand them. I have placed the most important settings in bold type.

1. Hide Welcome screen: This setting defaults to checked. I have never unchecked it. I have no idea what the Welcome screen looks like. Feel free to check it out, if you care.

2. **Batch size**: This is where you set the batch size (number of records per batch). You can use up to 200 for nonbulk Insert, Update, Upsert, and Delete operations. You can use up to 2,000 for Export and Export All. If you are using the Bulk API, you can use up to 10,000.

3. **Insert null values:** If this setting is unchecked and you pass in a blank or NULL, Salesforce leaves the existing data in that field and does *not* override it with a null value unless the setting is checked. You should do some testing (or read the documentation) on how your middleware/ETL implements this feature of the API.

4. Assignment rule: This setting is used if you want to have code in Salesforce that determines who is the owner of the records being processed. To do this, enter the Salesforce Id of the assignment rule.

   Server host (clear for default): As when logging into Salesforce, for sandboxes, set this to `https://test.salesforce.com`; for developer accounts and production orgs, use `https://login.salesforce.com`. Note the full URL looks something like this: `https://login.salesforce.com/services/Soap/u/40.0`, where 40.0 is the version of the API to be used. This allows you to run your code against an old version of the API if needed. If you only specify the short URL, the most current API version is used.

5. Reset URL on Login (clear to turn off): If checked, this setting automatically resets the server host setting after using the Apex Data Loader. So, uncheck this if you want the Apex Data Loader to remember your server host settings.

6. Compression (check to turn off): This setting implements some fancy "schmancy"[17] method of reducing the size of the XML sent over the network, reducing the overall communication time.

7. Timeout (in seconds): This setting allows you to determine how long the data loader should wait for a response from Salesforce before giving up.

8. Query request size: When exporting data, this setting allows you to specify how many records should be returned at once. The maximum is 2,000.

9. Generate status files for exports: When exporting data from, Salesforce you only get a single .csv file exported with the data exported; all the other operations give you a success and error file. If, for some reason (and I can't think of a single one), you want success and error files for exports, check this box.

10. Read all CSVs with UTF-8 encoding: Check this box if you need UTF-8 (in other words, if you need foreign languages with non-Latin characters supported).

11. Write all CSVs with UTF-8 encoding: Check this box if you need (in other words, if you need foreign languages with non-Latin characters supported).

12. Use European date format (dd/mm/yyyy): This setting allows you to use the European date format as opposed to the UTC date format.

---

[17]For more information, see https://developer.salesforce.com/page/SOAP_Compression.

13. Allow field truncation: If you load too much (long) data into a field, Salesforce will reject it and throw an error. If you check this box, rather than throw and error Salesforce will cut the data short, so it fits in the target field, and then load it in.

14. Allow comma as a CSV delimiter: Just like it says, check this box if you want to use commas as a delimiter.

15. Allow Tab as a CSV delimiter: Just like it says, check this box if you want to use Tab as a delimiter.[18]

16. Allow other characters as CSV delimiters: Just like it says, check this box if you want to use other characters as delimiters.

17. Other Delimiters (enter multiple values with no separator; for example, !+?): If you checked a delimiter box, you now specify the characters to use as the delimiters.

18. **Use Bulk API:** Use the Bulk API. If this box is unchecked, the Apex Data Loader will use the SOAP API.

19. **Enable serial mode for Bulk API**: By default, the Bulk API submits all the batches at once and Salesforce process them in parallel. This feature increases the chance of locking issues resulting from update conflicts. This option tells Salesforce to use the Bulk API but not to process the batches in parallel, but process them one at a time serially.

20. Upload Bulk API Batch as Zip File (enable to upload binary attachments): This setting has to do with using the Bulk API for loading attachments. Refer to the official documentation on how to use it.

---

[18]Obviously if you are using Tab as a delimiter it's not a comma-separated value (CSV). I don't understand why these three "use delimiter" options are check boxes instead of a radio group. But, the data loader is free and beggars can't be choosers—so, happy loading!

21. **Time Zone**: This setting indicates the time zone to be used for all data loaded. With this feature, you need to refer to your middleware/ETL tool on how the time zone is implemented and maybe do some testing on it.

22. Proxy host: If your office uses a proxy to connect to the Internet, you need to set this value. Talk to your network administrator for instructions on how to do this.

23. Proxy port: If your office uses a proxy to connect to the Internet, you need to set this value. Talk to your network administrator for instructions on how to do this.

24. Proxy username: If your office uses a proxy to connect to the Internet, you need to set this value. Talk to your network administrator for instructions on how to do this.

25. Proxy password: If your office uses a proxy to connect to the Internet, you need to set this value. Talk to your network administrator for instructions on how to do this.

26. Proxy NTLM domain: If your office uses a proxy to connect to the Internet, you need to set this value. Talk to your network administrator for instructions on how to do this.

27. The last batch finished at 0. Use 0 to continue from your last location. Start at row: You can use this setting if you want to start midway through a .csv file. I recommend you create a new .csv file that contains only the data you wish to send, rather than use this feature.

Create an External Id

We are going to Upsert account data, and then we will Upsert opportunity data related to those accounts. Next we will export some opportunity data. If you remember, to use Upsert we must first create an External Id, so let's do that now. Log in to Salesforce and then follow these steps (see Figure 3-6):[19]

1.   Click on the gear icon in the upper right-hand corner.

2.   Click Setup.

3.   Click the Object Manager tab.

4.   Click Account.

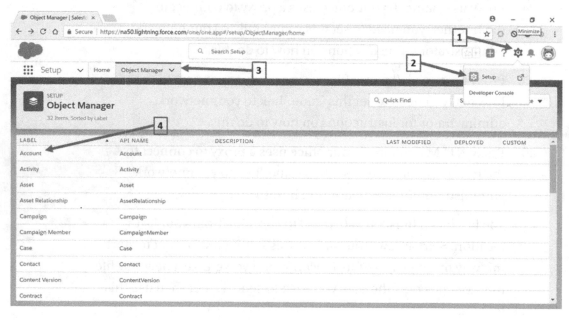

Figure 3-6. *The Salesforce Object Manager*

These actions will take you to the Account Object Manager page (see Figure 3-7). At this point, do the following:

1.   In the left-hand navigation bar, click Fields & Relationships.

2.   Click the New button.

---

[19]Although I am walking you through creating a new field now, if you don't already know how to do this, you should spend some time going through the Salesforce Trailheads (https://trailhead.salesforce.com).

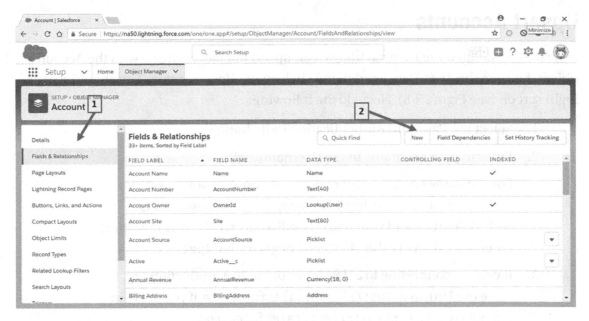

Figure 3-7. *The Account Object Manager page*

These actions take you to the New Custom Field screen.

1. Select Text and Click Next.

2. At the Field label, enter Training External Id.

3. At Length, enter 50.

4. Field Name is populated for you. It is the API name—the name used when working with the API. It must be unique on the object.

5. At Description, type External Id used for Training Exercises.

6. Type the same for the Help Text field.

7. Check the check box for Unique and leave the radio button as is for "case insensitive."

8. Check the check box for External Id.

9. Click Next for the next two screens, then click Save.

10. Next, click back on the Object Manager tab and repeat the same steps to create the External Id on the Opportunity object. (It should also be called Training External Id.)

Upsert Accounts

Now that we created the External Ids, we can upsert our data, starting with the Account object. Launch the Apex Data Loader and click on the Upsert button. You should see the login screen (see Figure 3-8). Next, do the following:

1. Select the Password Authentication radio button

2. Enter in your username in the Username field.

   For the Password field, enter your password *and* your token as a single concatenated string. For example, if your password is S@lesF0rce123! and your token is s8E4qYIecwL8Pg5OrMkAMpgT, enter S@lesF0rce123!s8E4qYIecwL8Pg5OrMkAMpgT.

3. If you are connecting to a developer org or to a production org, leave the URL as `https://login.salesforce.com` if you are using a sandbox set it to `https://test.salesforce.com`.

4. Click Log in.

5. After you see the "Login successful" message, click Next.

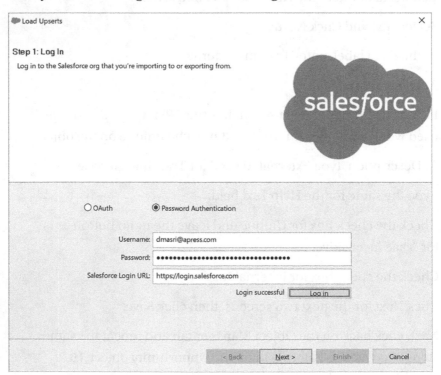

Figure 3-8. *The Apex Data Loader login screen*

Now you should see the Select data objects screen (see Figure 3-9). Select Account, then click Browse to select a .csv file to upsert. Navigate to the Apex Data Loader Installation folder,[20] then go to the Samples folder, then Data, then select the accountData.csv file. Click Open, then click Next.

Figure 3-9. *The Select data objects screen*

You will then be prompted with a message box that says, "Your operation will contain 423 records." Click OK.

Next you will see the Choose your field to use for matching screen (see Figure 3-10). From the drop-down menu, select Training_External_Id__c, then click Next.

---

[20]For a 32-bit system, the default location is `C:\Program Files (x86)\salesforce.com\Data Loader\`.

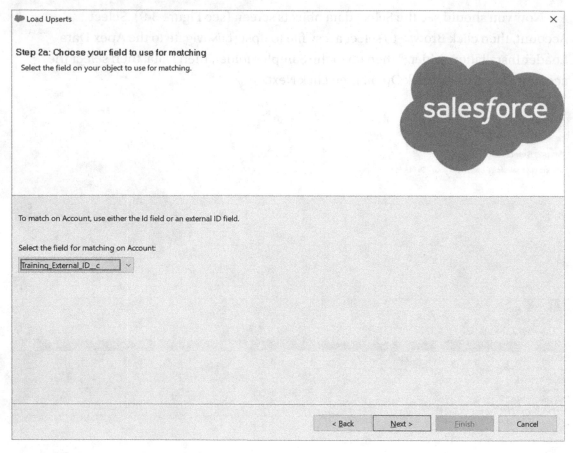

Figure 3-10. *The Choose your field to use for matching screen*

Now you will see the Choose your related objects screen. For Accounts, we don't use related objects, so click Next. Then you will see the Mapping screen (see Figure 3-11). Click Create or Edit a Map.

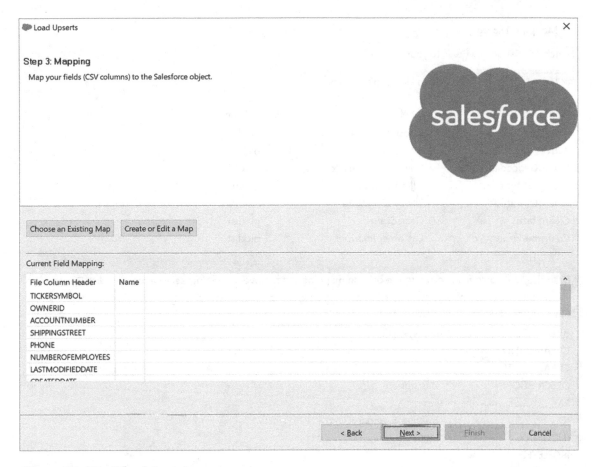

Figure 3-11. *The Mapping screen*

These actions bring up the Mapping Dialog screen (see Figure 3-12). The top grid shows all the columns in the Salesforce Account object; the bottom grid shows the columns in the .csv file. To map a field, simply drag the row from the top grid to the matching row in the bottom. Let's start with the Training_External_Id field. Select it in the top grid and drag it down to the to the Id field in the bottom grid.

Then click Auto-Match Fields to Columns to automatch a bunch of other fields. This maps the OwnerID field, but that field is *not* a valid Id field in the .csv file, so unmap it by dragging it back to the top grid.

Click OK. These actions take you back to the Mapping screen. Click Next.

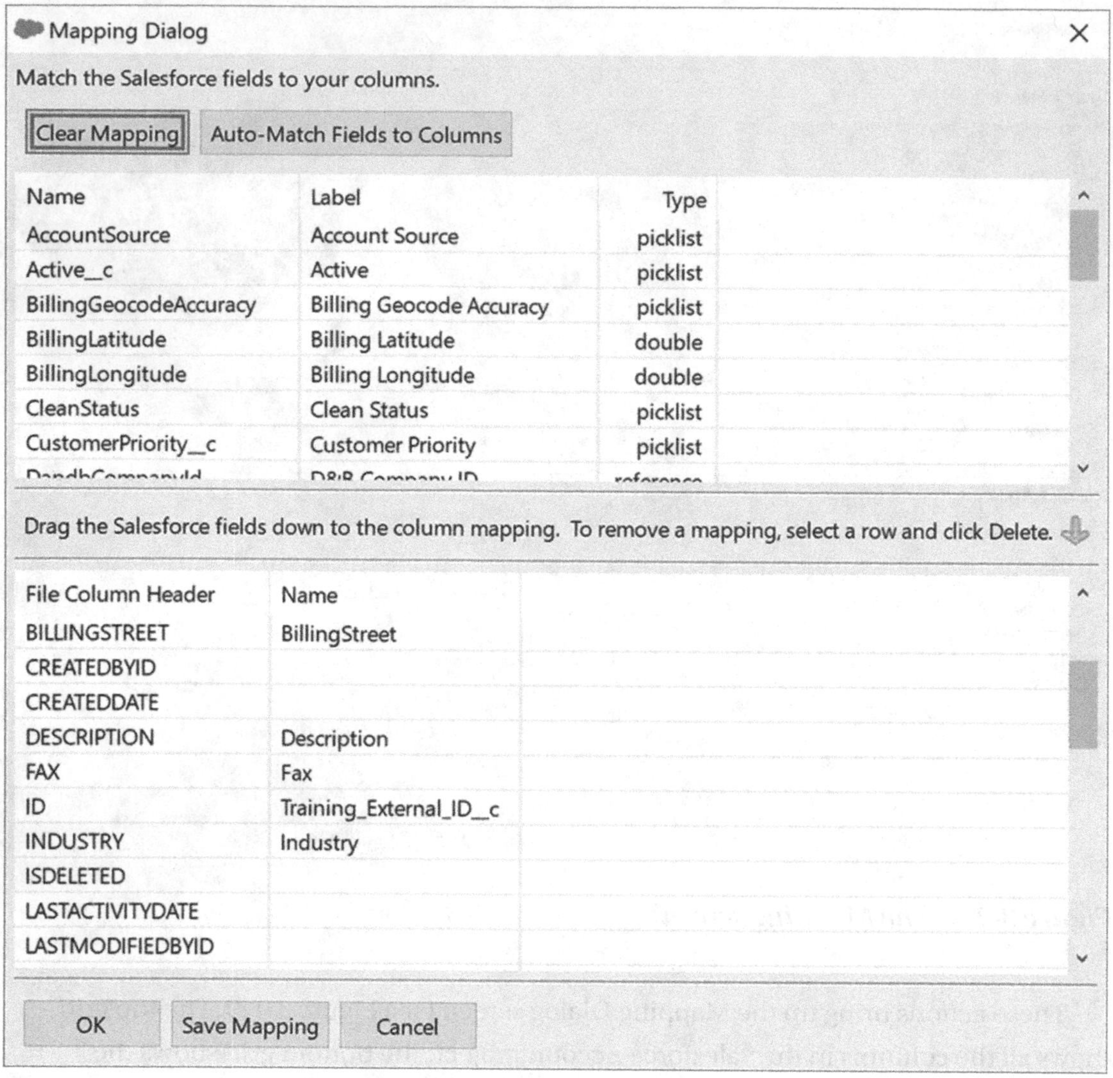

Figure 3-12. *The Mapping Dialog screen*

You are now taken to the Finish screen (see Figure 3-13). Select a directory where you want to place the success and error files. Make sure you pick a location you will remember. Next, click Finish.

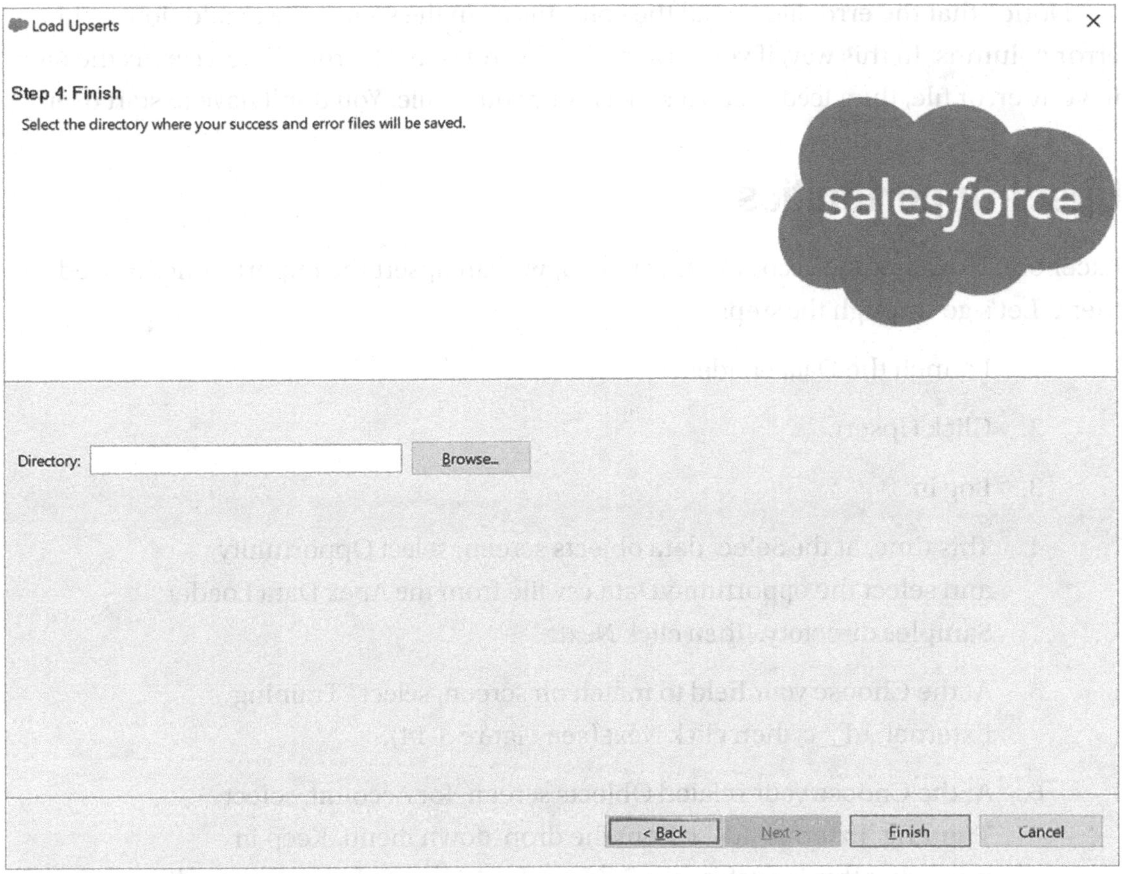

Figure 3-13. *The Finish screen*

Now you'll be asked to confirm with a warning: "You have chosen to add new records and/or update existing records. The action you are about to take cannot be undone. Are you sure you want to proceed?" Click Yes.

Great! You should get a message that says that you have 423 successful upserts and 0 errors. If you did get errors, start over and confirm you mapped properly the Id column in the .csv file to the Training External Id field, and also verify that you did not map the OwnerId field.

Take a moment to review the success and error files and familiarize yourself with them. If you want to try this again to force an error, just repeat the previous steps but "forget" to unmap the OwnerId field. You don't have to worry about creating duplicate data because you're doing an upsert. If the External Id already exists, Salesforce will update the record, not create Salesforce will create a new one!

Notice that the error file has all the columns from the source file in addition to the error columns. In this way, if you have only a few rows that "errored," you can fix the data in your error file, then feed that back in as your source file. You don't have to start over.

Upset Opportunities

Excellent. Now that the accounts are created, we can upsert the opportunities related to them. Let's go through the steps:

1. Launch the Data Loader.

2. Click Upsert.

3. Log in.

4. This time, at the Select data objects screen, select Opportunity and select the opportunityData.csv file from the Apex Data Loader Samples directory. Then click Next.

5. At the Choose your field to match on screen, select "Training_External_Id__c, then click Next (see Figure 3-14).

6. At the Choose your related Objects screen, for Account, select Training_External_Id__c from the drop-down menu. Keep in mind that this is a reference field on the Account object, so we will pass in the Account External Id and Salesforce will look up and replace it with the Salesforce Account Id. Click Next.

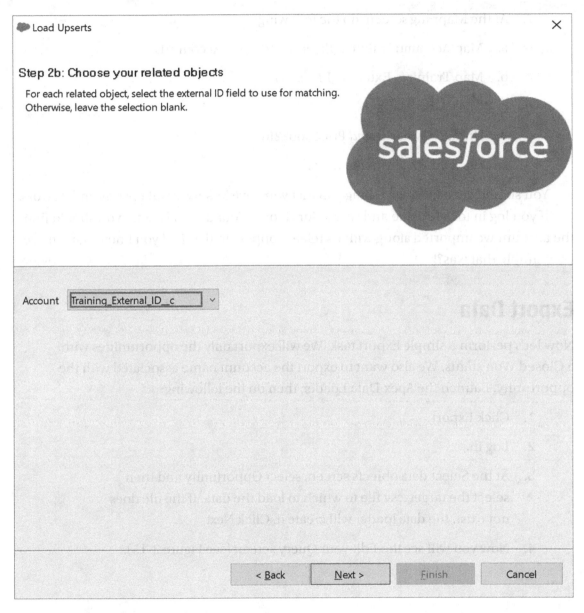

Figure 3-14. *The Choose your related objects screen*

7. At the Mapping screen, do the following:

   a. Map Account:Training_External_Id__c to AccountID.

   b. Map Training_External_Id__c to Id.

   c. Click Auto-Match.

   d. Unmap OwnerId *and* PriceBook2Id.

   e. Click Finish to run the upsert.

You should get a message telling you that you have 38 successful upserts and 0 errors.

If you log in to Salesforce and search for George Foundation Health, you should find the account we imported along with its related opportunities. Did you find it? Great! See how simple that was?!

Export Data

Now let's perform a simple Export task. We will export only the opportunities with a Closed Won status. We also want to export the account name associated with the opportunity. Launch the Apex Data Loader, then do the following:

1. Click Export.

2. Log in.

3. At the Select data objects screen, select Opportunity and then select the target .csv file to which to load the data. If the file does not exist, the data loader will create it. Click Next.

4. Now you will see the Edit your Query screen (see Figure 3-15).

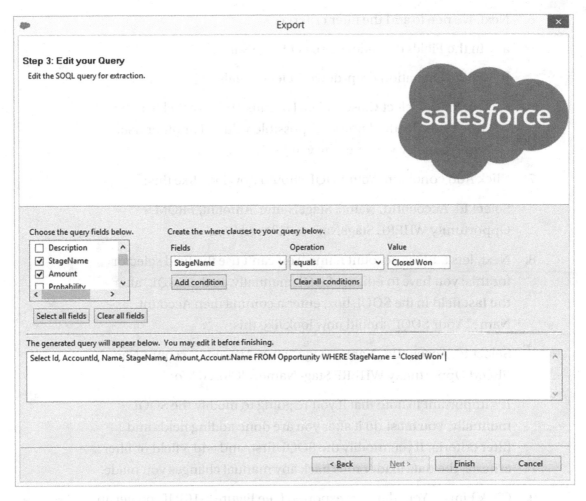

Figure 3-15. *The Edit your Query screen*

5. We need to select the fields we want to export. In the query fields list, check each of the following. As you check them, you can see the Apex Data Loader building the SOQL for you.

    a. Id

    b. AccountID

    c. Name

    d. StageName

    e. Amount

6. Next, we nee to add the filter criteria.

    a. In the Fields drop-down, select StageName.

    b. In the Operation drop-down, select equals.

    c. For Value, select Closed Won. (Because this is a picklist, the Apex Data loader knows the possible values. For other data types you have to enter the values.[21])

7. Click Add condition. Your SOQL should now look like this:

    Select Id, AccountId, Name, StageName, Amount, FROM Opportunity WHERE StageName = 'Closed Won'

8. Next, lets add the account name. You can't use the field selector for this; you have to edit the SOQL manually. In the SOQL, after the last field in the SOQL box, enter a comma then Account. Name". Your SOQL should now look like this:

    Select Id, AccountId, Name, StageName, Amount, Account.Name FROM Opportunity WHERE StageName = 'Closed Won'

    It's important to note that if you're going to modify the SOQL manually, you must do it after you are done adding fields and filter criteria. If you modify the SOQL first, and add a field or filter criteria, the data loader rolls back any manual changes you made.

9. Click Finish. Your data are exported (see Figure 3-16)! If you get an error, go back and check your SOQL. It's easy to make a mistake when editing it manually. Unfortunately, there is no Test button.

---

[21]Yes, I know I said that Salesforce doesn't have combo boxes and this is a combo box (allowing for both selection and free text), but this is not part of Salesforce; it's a separate app. Stop being a smartass. No one likes a smartass.

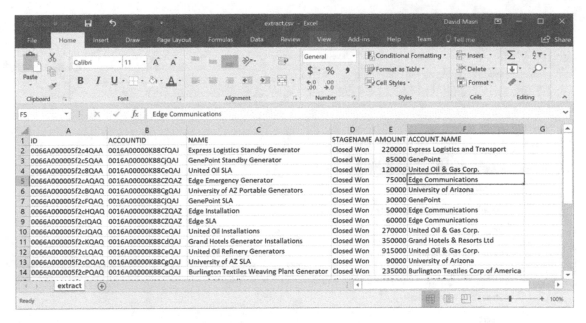

Figure 3-16. *Your exported opportunity data*

Browse through Your data with Workbench and SOQL

Before closing out this chapter, I want to bring another useful utility to your attention. Although it doesn't relate to data migration or integration directly, Developer Workbench is a nice utility for running simple SOQL queries quickly or for browsing Salesforce metadata. To use Developer Workbench, log in to Salesforce, then navigate to `https://workbench.developerforce.com/login.php`.

You will be prompted to select an environment and an API version. If you are using a sandbox, select Sandbox; otherwise, select Production. Leave the API version as is (it's the most current). Check the box to agree to the terms of service and then click Login with Salesforce.

You will then be prompted to select an action (see Figure 3-17). The Jump to drop-down lists all the features of Workbench. You can run a SOQL query, perform some of the same actions available via the Apex Data loader, or do a few other things. These are the same options available in the menu bar at the top. For now, select SOQL Query in the Jump to drop-down; for Object, select Account. Then, click Select.

Figure 3-17. *Developer Workbench select-an-action screen*

Now you'll see a nice little SOQL Query builder screen similar to the one we saw in the Apex Data Loader (see Figure 3-18). Give it a try!

There are some limitations on SOQL usage when using Workbench. For example, if you try the same SOQL we used to export opportunity data with the Apex Data Loader, you'll get an error message. You can find the complete Workbench documentation at https://github.com/forceworkbench/forceworkbench/wiki.

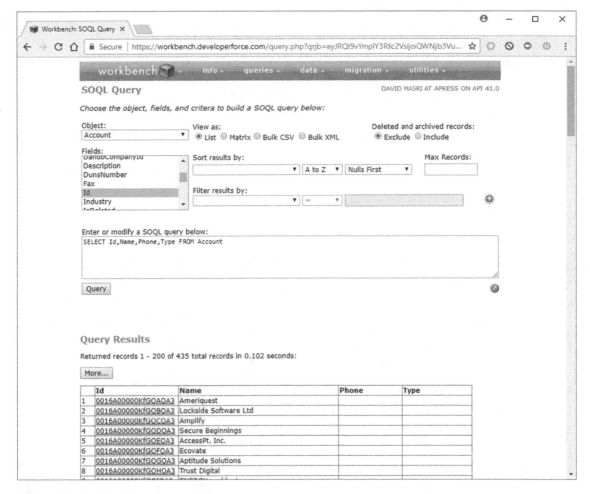

Figure 3-18. *Developer Workbench SOQL Query screen*

Summary

In this chapter we covered the Salesforce APIs and the various ETL and middleware tools that we can use to interact with them. We also spent quite a bit of time performing some simple upserts and exports using the Apex Data Loader.

Leaving this chapter, you should feel very comfortable in your knowledge of how to work with Salesforce data at a fundamental level. We are now ready to move on to best practices and, then, to common migration and integration patterns, starting with the six attributes of a good data migration!

CHAPTER 4

The Six Attributes of a Good Data Migration

If we were to Google[1] "What are best practices?" we will find an answer similar to "commercial or professional procedures that are accepted or prescribed as being correct or most effective."

But, we are left wondering *why* "are *[they]* accepted or prescribed as being correct or most effective[?]" If we then Google for specific best practices (such as Salesforce data migration best practices), we'll get (often conflicting) lists of procedures and recommendations of things to do with minimal explanation as to *why*. Often people think, *That's too much work. I'm not doing that.* And guess what? Maybe they are right. Maybe it's not worth doing. The question is: How do we know?

So, how *do* we know? If you're like me, you pick and choose based on what seems reasonable, give it a try, and then when it blows up, you say to yourself, *Hmmm. I guess I should have done X. That's good to know!* as if no one told us the best practice in the first place! At least now we know why. Lesson learned.

So, before we get into best practices, I want to discuss the *why* of best practices in terms of attributes. If your data migration meets these attributes, I can guarantee it will run smoothly. There are six simple attributes; you can almost memorize them.[2] All the best practices discussed in Chapter 5 tie back to one of more of the following six attributes:

1. Well planned

2. Automated (redoable)

---

[1]If you don't like Google, that's fine. You can Bing, Yahoo, Duck, of Duck Go. Google just works better as a verb.

[2]I did not attempt to put them into an acronym.

© David Masri 2019
D. Masri, *Developing Data Migrations and Integrations with Salesforce*,
https://doi.org/10.1007/978-1-4842-4209-4_4

3. Controlled

4. Reversible

5. Repairable

6. Testable

Think of these attributes as goals—something you should strive for. You may not be able to accomplish them 100%, but reaching some is better than none. Incremental improvements make a big difference. In other words, partially automated is better than no automation. A bad plan is better than no plan. Small increments toward goals make a big difference.

As you read through these pages, remember that we are discussing attributes here, and the goals and rationale behind them. I discuss best practices (in other words, the *how*) in Chapter 6.

Then, in Chapter 6, we examine the data migration process using the best practices to attain these attributes. Last, we complete an example data migration and bring this discussion full circle.

Attribute 1: Well Planned

Well planned is by far the most important attribute. Failure to meet any of the other five attributes can be mitigated by planning, but nothing can mitigate for a bad plan—or worse, no plan. It's so important that the first best practice of Chapter 5 is "Have a Plan."

Your data migration must be planned, and it must be planned *well*. I can't tell you how often I come across data migrations where the plan was to "get .csv files from the client and then load them in." This simply does not meet the requirements of a good plan, not even for a "small" data migration. Not even close.

Your migration plan should look like a project plan, with timelines, dependencies, and milestones. Unless you have a very technical project manager (PM) they will need your help in building this plan. It's unreasonable to expect them to understand the data migration process well enough to put together a proper plan.[3] Most likely, as the migration specialist, you will have to work with your PM to create a proper plan. Then they can take over tracking your progress.

---

[3]I say this as a certified Project Management Professional (PMP).

Your plan should answer each of the following questions or provide a deadline of when the question will be answered:

1. How and when will the data to be migrated be delivered?

2. In what format will the data be delivered?

3. Who is the source data subject matter expert (SME)?

4. Are there any data security concerns or guidelines for handling the data?

5. What middleware or ETL tool will you use to code your migration?

6. How much time is needed for data analysis?

7. When will the data mapping document[4] be completed and who is responsible for creating it?

8. When will you review the data mapping document with your client?

9. What Salesforce environment will be used for quality assurance (QA)? User acceptance test (UAT)? Production?

10. If the target Salesforce org is currently being built out, when will the various objects be available so that you can being to load data?

11. When will you perform the first complete end-to-end run of the migration?

12. Who will be performing QA? How many rounds?

13. Who will be performing UAT? How many rounds?

14. When do you go live?

15. How much time do you have to cut over? (This may be downtime for users; they may not be able to use the legacy systems or Salesforce.)

---

[4]The data mapping document records source-to-target field-level mappings and transformation rules.

The previous list is by no means comprehensive. It doesn't even touch on the technical side of planning (setting up environments, gathering transformation rules, selecting tools, and so on), but you get the point. Every migration is different, and time needs to be spent on planning and ensuring all your bases are covered. Look for the sample migration plan in Chapter 6.

Attribute 2: Automated (Redoable)

Automation enables you to redo your migration with minimal effort and with complete certainty that the results will be the same. The goal is to get your data migration as close to "one click" as possible. This means not only connecting the source data to the Salesforce APIs and automating the data loads, but also automating all the data transformations.

Automation eliminates human error and saves so much time. Our sample migration plan (see Chapter 7) will have at least three scheduled runs (and, more likely, four or five): the initial run as part of coding, at least one QA/UAT round, and the production (go-live) run.

If our migration is not automated, then all our rounds of QA/UAT are, essentially, nullified. Think about it. Suppose we spend two days running carefully through a four-and-a-half-page checklist of actions to perform a data migration. Then, our client performs UAT and finds a few defects. We patch the data and our client signs off on the patches. Now we are ready to perform the final data migration (because users have been working in the legacy system all this time, making updates). All users are then locked out of the legacy systems and we are given new data dumps to load. We spend another two days running carefully through the same checklist. How do we—and our client—know that everything is okay? Another full round of UAT.

One of the reasons the "giant checklist" approach is so common (yet no less insane) in the Salesforce world is that integration specialists usually start off in smaller shops working on smaller projects with small data migrations. They work with small datasets that can be manipulated easily in Excel and need minimal transformations. So, they can manage the migration with a short half-page checklist, and they can run through that checklist in an hour or two with minimal risk of error. Essentially, they are leveraging planning to make up for automation. Then, one day, they are assigned to a monster project with a ton of data and lots of complex data transformations. As time goes by, the checklist grows and grows until the point where it takes a week to run through it, and the entire process turns into a nightmare.

Another reason the giant checklist approach is so prevalent is that migration code is often viewed as disposable "one-time" run code, so not much effort should be put into it. This is a flawed view. It is *not* a "one-time" run. Automation saves time and produces better, more consistent results. Truth be told, even if the code really was a one-time run, automating it is not a time-consuming task. We have to code our transformations anyhow,[5] so we may as well clean up and save the code.

In addition, because it's automated, we can let the code run during off hours, 24 hours a day, as opposed to a manual process that can only be performed while someone is working. This benefit reduces the cutover time drastically and seriously reduces the stress of the go-live.

Attribute 3: Controlled

When I speak of "control" I am referring specifically to control of what data will be migrated. Data filtering control should be built into our automation scripts via set configuration parameters. The control must be centralized, so we can set one parameter that filters our dataset while maintaining referential integrity.

Please, consider the following:

- Suppose a developer asks for sample data in her development sandbox. The sandbox can store only 2GB of data. If our migration has been coded with control in mind, we simply update the connection string to point to the sandbox, set a parameter to filter the data down to a tiny dataset, and run the job.

- Suppose we have a client who wants to pilot the system with a small set of sales people. Then, after a month onboard, want to add the rest of the sales team. The ~~guinea pigs~~ pioneers don't want to lose their work when the rest of the sales team is onboard, and the sales team wants its latest data as of the day they start using the system. To meet these requirements, we put code in place to control the data to be migrated by salesperson or sales group (or geographic region or business unit or product category or call center or whatever).

---

[5]Transformations take the most effort and are the most time-intensive parts of a data migration project, except for (maybe) the data analysis, but data analysis is considered part of requirements gathering not the data migration build.

- Suppose you go live and the whole company starts to use Salesforce except for the vice president of sales. He decides it's too risky to use Salesforce and continues to use the legacy systems for six weeks before deciding to join his team on Salesforce. Now he asks us to remigrate just his data. What do we do? We update the control parameter and rerun the job! Without having that parameter in place, we would be in a pickle.

- Suppose we are coding a large-volume data migration with lots of complex transformation rules. To run the migration end to end takes six hours. We are in the middle of a QA cycle and defects are coming in at a rapid pace. How are we going to fix our transformation code and retest rapidly? Simple. We set our parameters to filter down the data to a small dataset and BOOM, we can now do rapid fix and test cycles.

In each of the previous scenarios, control was critical to success. Also note that automation is a prerequisite to control. We simply don't have fine control over the data being migrated without automation.

Even if we have no idea what criteria to use to partition our data and are sure all our user groups will be going live at the same time, control is still critical for repairability (attribute 5) as well as enabling rapid code, test, and fix cycles.

Attribute 4: Reversible

Reversibility is the ability to undo a data migration, either fully or partially in a controlled way. Our four basic reverse use cases are as follows:

1. Delete all data from the org.

2. Delete selected records from the org (and related data).

3. Reverse updates made to records (in other words, set the field values back to what they were previously).

4. A combination of 2 and 3.

The obvious case when we would need to reverse a migration is when we are migrating data to a system that is already in production and, after the data migration, it is determined the system is not ready.[6] Any organization that is mature enough to have information technology (IT) standards and procedures will require us to have a rollback plan. When dealing with traditional (noncloud) rollbacks, the procedure is simple. Backup the database prior to performing our migration. If the need to roll back arises, we simply restore from the backup.

Unfortunately, it's not that simple to do this with Salesforce. With Salesforce, we still need to backup our data,[7] but there is no full-system restore option.[8] We must overwrite every record that changed with the record's premigration values and delete the new records created by the migration.

Even if we are migrating to a greenfield[9] Salesforce org, you will need to perform several rounds of testing. Prior to each round, we must wipe out all the loaded data and run the migration from scratch; otherwise, it's not a proper test. So, even in this case, we need reversibility. And needless to say, it must be automated and controlled so, for example, we can roll back one sales division, region, call center, and so on. I once had a junior migration specialist accidentally load data from the test source system (instead of the production source) to the production Salesforce org the weekend we were going live (he forgot to update a connection string). We did have rollback procedures, but it was a very manual process and set us back nearly a full day. Our client was fuming and demanded the junior migration specialist be fired. If this was had been planned for properly, *and* was fully automated, we may not have had to admit our error to the client; we could have just rolled back with a click.

---

[6]Not necessarily because of bad data.

[7]Salesforce does have a native backup solution; it backs up all your data to .csv. If you are serious about data backups, I would not rely on this as your only backup, because working with .csv is just too cumbersome. See: `https://help.salesforce.com/articleView?id=admin_exportdata.htm&type=5`.

[8]Okay, so technically, this is not entirely true. See `https://help.salesforce.com/articleView?id=000004037&type=1`. In addition, there are several third-party products on the market that can be used to perform full org backups and restores.

[9]A brand-new system that is not currently in use. In this case, the rollback plan is usually to keep using the legacy system.

Attribute 5: Repairable

Repairability is the ability to fix data in a very targeted way after a mistake has been found. Mistakes happen. There are *always* mistakes. The key is knowing that mistakes (or even requirement changes) will happen, and then designing the migration so that it's easy to fix things after the fact.

If our code is automated and controlled, we are 90% on our way in making data migration repairable. All we need to do is make sure our data are traceable back to the original datasets. If we know where each data point came from, and where it went, it should be a breeze to fix an error in the data. We should be able to look at a record in Salesforce and know immediately exactly where it came from in the source system. Then we recalculate the correct field values and overwrite that record.

Often, defects are found weeks or months after going live, when users have made lots of changes to data. They may have even made changes to the data we are trying to fix. In such cases, we don't have the option of rolling back the migration and redoing it; we must fix the data. But if we have the original dataset and can tie it to Salesforce (so we know the current values), we can repair the data. Sure, we may have to modify our transformation rules to reflect user updates in Salesforce, but it's still repairable.

Attribute 6: Testable

Testability refers to the ease with which we or users can test the data. As with reparability, if it's easy to trace migrated data back to the original source, and if we have our transformation rules well documented, testing should be relatively simple. There are two types of testing[10] that need to be done: QA, done by trained QA professionals who test that the migration meets the exact specifications of the documentation; and UAT, done by users who test the data to confirm that (1) the data meet the specifications and (2) the data meet the spirit (intent) of the requirements as well as the actual needs of the business.

---

[10]In addition to developer unit testing. This is when developers test their own code as part of the build cycle.

QA: Testing to Specification

When performing QA, QA analysts basically open up the source data, Salesforce, and the Data Mapping Document (will be covered in Chapter 6), then—for a sample set of data, field by field—validate that the data match what is expected.

We can fully automate the data validation process, but we need to have a different developer recode all the data transformations. Doing this doubles the workload. When a mismatch is found, we must investigate which code base has the error. In most cases, this is simply not worth the effort, but I have had clients insist on it, and have done it more than once in the past. You should be aware that this is an option if your client is willing to pay for it.

UAT: Testing for Intent

For UAT, I advise my clients to open a sample set of records in the legacy system, find the same records in Salesforce, then compare them. I don't require them to use the mapping document; I want them to ask about anything that looks wrong. Users know their data and business in a very intimate way. They have insight into the minutiae of the business and data that we, as technical people, can't ever hope to have (without doing their job for a few years). Users often find issues that are coded exactly to spec, using the rules they gave us, but until they look at the data, they just don't see the issues with the rules we implemented. I call this "testing for intent" as opposed to "testing to spec." QA analysts, although great at testing to spec, simply cannot test for intent. Nobody can, except for actual users.

UAT does cause a lot of defects to be reported that are not really defects, and we have to spend time investigating them. Often, we just wind up going back to the user and saying, "The data look like this because of rule X. It works as designed." To which the user usually replies, "Oh yeah! That's right!" Spending some extra time investigating and then discussing non-defects with users is not a bad thing. This kind of dialogue strengthens the relationship between your team and the client, and builds a ton of confidence in the data work being performed.

One of the biggest mistakes I see in project planning is that not enough time is allocated to UAT. Users are busy and can often only give up a few hours a week for testing. Project managers think of UAT as similar to QA; they think we can give the same test cases to the users that we gave the QA, and then the users can run through the cases just as the QA team did. They view UAT as a formality to sign off on the data, rather than consider UAT a critical part of the process.

Here's a typical scenario. An "intent" issue will be logged and the program manager (PM) will go back to the QA group and blast them:

PM to QA: How did you not find this issue?

QA to PM: That's not in the mapping doc. It works as documented. Talk to the BA [business analyst].

PM to BA: Dude, why is this spec wrong?

BA: It's not wrong. That's a change. Issue a CR.[11]

PM to migration specialist: We need to issue a CR to fix the data. How long will it take? I need to give our client an estimate.

Migration specialist to PM: Pfft! I code with reparability in mind! Three minutes; no CR needed!

Imagine having a similar conversation four times a week. Even if we are very good at our job, so many of these little "intent" issues pop up during UAT that it's better to plan for them and bake them into our planning. Most of our time will be spent investigating nonissues, but we need to give clients enough time to ask all the questions they need until they are confident the data are good.

Summary: A Reminder

Just a reminder. For each of the six attributes, incremental improvements make a big difference. Strive to be better with each of your data migrations: better planning, more automation, increased traceability. Before you know it, the data migration track will consistently be the least risky part of your Salesforce rollouts.

Great! Now we can move on to attributes of a good data integration (Chapter 5) and then best practices (Chapter 6)!

---

[11]A change request.

CHAPTER 5

Attributes of a Good Data Integration

If you were to ask someone, "What's the difference between an integration and a migration?" you'll likely get an answer along the lines of: "Migrations are one-time runs whereas integrations are ongoing." As discussed in Chapter 4, data migrations are not really a one-time run-and-done job. Because testing is critical to success, the same code needs to be run for QA and UAT.

I'm not saying that people who answer with "one-time run" are wrong, just a bit imprecise. What they really mean is that it's a one-time run in *production*, or simply that it's not an ongoing job. Regardless of the semantics, the point I want to make is that if you look at migration code as fully automated code that moves data between two systems and that needs to run more than once, you will see it as nothing more than a specific type of integration. In fact, when we get to Chapter 9, which examines common data synchronization patterns, the first pattern is Basic Upsert-No Delete. Although I classify these patterns as integration patterns, this particular pattern is your basic data migration pattern. It upserts all data from a source system without deleting any existing data. Classifying this as an integration is okay, because it's true. If you run this pattern once (in production), it's a migration; if you run the exact same code continually, it's an integration.

That being said, it comes to reason that the six attributes we discussed in Chapter 4 also apply to data integration, with one major exception: It's not enough for an integration job to be repairable; it must also be self-repairing.

© David Masri 2019
D. Masri, *Developing Data Migrations and Integrations with Salesforce*,
https://doi.org/10.1007/978-1-4842-4209-4_5

Self-repairing

When performing a data migration, even though it's fully automated, the plan is to monitor the production run and intervene if necessary. We may even put in check points to ensure things are running smoothly, and intervene and fix things before we get too far along in the process. With data integrations, this approach is not good enough. Jobs need to run on autopilot day in and day out, without human intervention. Of course, things can and will go wrong. The trick is to design the code to make the life of the intervening human as easy as possible. So, barring any environmental changes (an OS upgrade, Salesforce code or data structure changes, source system changes, and so on), should a job fail, all that is needed to fix it is to restart it.

The integration code should not rely on the state of our staging database or data in Salesforce to run properly. For example, suppose the Internet access in the office goes down midway through the job run and the job fails as a result of a "loss of connection" error. The network operations center (NOC) gets a notification of the job failure. Then the technician on call refers to the run book for proper procedures and should find instructions along the lines of "Restart the job." That's it. The technician should not have to check on the state of Salesforce, the staging database, or anything else. The first thing the job should do upon restart is to check on and fix or reset the state (of everything it needs to) and then proceed as normal. If the job fails again, it is safe to assume there was an environmental change that caused the error, and the developer (such as you or me) should be contacted to look into it.

This is not only good practice because it makes the NOC's life easy, but also it makes authoring the run books easy and prevents you from being called at 2 AM to help the NOC technician restart the job.

Planning Differences

The other thing to consider when coding integrations, which we don't have to worry about with migrations, is code handover. With a migration, the expectation is that when the time comes to go live, we run the migration and deal with any post go-live issues that come up. With a data integration, this may or may not be the case. Regardless, the plan is to have jobs run indefinitely, so we need to consider deployment and a long-term support plan.

Deployment

In general, barring some corporate policy disallowing it, I run my data migrations from the same environment in which I coded it. I have the client deliver securely the data to be migrated. I then code the migration to Salesforce on my development server. When it's time to go live, I ask the client for a new dataset, then simply overwrite the source data with the newly delivered data, and then run the production migration directly on my development server.

For integrations, this isn't acceptable. We need to have separate environments for development, production, and, potentially, QA, UAT, and/or production support. So, our go-live plan must include standing up this new environment and deploying to it. Standing up a production environment and deploying code could mean buying new hardware,[1] acquiring software licenses, conducting software installations, configuring the environment, making user provisions, presenting to architecture review boards, conducting code reviews, and a whole host of other tasks. It's important to understand what the production code deployment procedures are, and make sure they are included in the plan.

Long-term Support

Planning for long-term support starts at product selection. When performing a migration, we are the ones who code it and run the code. With integrations, it's likely going to be our client or some other group that gets stuck with the task of providing ongoing support, so we want to pick a product (ETL tool or middleware) with which the support team is familiar and feels comfortable supporting. In addition, we need to understand the support team's scheduling tool, job monitoring processes, error-logging standards, required documentation, coding standards, and anything else they need to support our code within their existing support process. So, get the support team involved early, understand their requirements, and plan accordingly.

---

[1] I have no idea why, but for some reason, new hardware—particularly servers—never show up on time.

Summary

Now that we know that fully automated migrations are just one specific flavor of integration, we can move on to best practices. Like the attributes, the best practices are mostly the same for migrations and integrations. In Chapter 6, we examine the best practices for both, and I am careful to point out where a best practice needs to be applied differently because of the one-time nature of a migration.

CHAPTER 6

Best Practices for Migrating and Integrating Your Data with Salesforce

Now that we understand what the attributes of good data migration and integrations are, we can learn the best practices used to achieve these attributes. I'm sure you have heard the axiom "every rule is made to be broken." The software development equivalent of this is "every best practice has its use case." We don't violate (or ignore) rules or advice just because we don't feel like following them. We violate them because they don't apply to our current situation or use case. And even if they do, it's perfectly valid to decide that the benefit of doing something does not justify the effort involved. You don't want to overwork yourself for very limited gain.

This being said, I'm telling you that I follow every single one of the practices discussed in this chapter for all data migrations I perform and integrations I build. And you should too, unless it's not possible to do so for technical reasons. If this is the case, you should come up with a plan to accomplish the same goal (aspects of the attributes) the best practice aims to achieve.[1]

---

[1]Lack of budget (money or time) is not a good reason for not using best practices. If your budget does not allow you to do good work, you need to have a serious conversation with whomever put together the estimate. We have all heard of the project management triangle of scope, budget, and quality. When it comes to data migrations (or integrations), you should refuse to budge on quality. You can say you need a greater budget (for money and/or time). You can say you need to cut scope. But, never, ever, agree to cut quality—not when it comes to data.

89

© David Masri 2019

D. Masri, *Developing Data Migrations and Integrations with Salesforce*,

https://doi.org/10.1007/978-1-4842-4209-4_6

I've ordered these best practices roughly in the order in which they apply during a project life cycle, so this chapter reads somewhat like a step-by-step plan. This was intentional, but please don't think of this as a step-by-step to-do list. Your process may be very different (more cyclical and iterative), but most of these best practices will still apply.

While reading through the best practices, try not to get distracted thinking about how you would implement them. In Chapter 7, when we walk through a sample migration, you'll see just how easy it can be to implement them.

Best Practice 1: Have a Plan

Attributes: Well Planned

I'm almost embarrassed to have to list "Have a Plan" as a best practice, but it's truly astounding how many people don't plan anything in their life. Not their career, not their finances, not even their weekend.

Having a plan was discussed quite a bit in Chapter 4, so I won't regurgitate my discussion—much. So that's it. Have a plan and execute against that plan. Plan your data migration (or integration) like a project and track your progress against the plan. Track your risks and mitigate them with even more planning. Plan for failure; plan for bad requirements; plan for clients who are nonresponsive or indecisive, or who simply give you bad information (unintentionally or even intentionally). Have a plan.

Best Practice 2: Review Your Charter and Understand Your Scope

Attributes: Well Planned

The first step in having a good plan is understanding the scope of work to be done. If you are working with an external client, you should start with the statement of work (SOW) or contract. The SOW should[2] detail exactly which data are to be migrated and the source systems for that data.

---

[2]It damn well better. If not, start working with your sales team on writing proper data scope details into your SOWs.

If you are working on an internal project (internal client), you should have the same information in the project charter that you would for an external client. If you don't have a charter, work with whomever you have to, to get this information and write a mini scope document. Then, have the Powers That Be review it and confirm it's correct. If new requirements (new scope) come in later, update the document.

After you are done coding, use your mini scope document or the SOW to confirm you completed the scope of the project.

Best Practice 3: Partner with Your PM

Attributes: Well Planned

Work with your project manager, or PM, to include your plan in the master project plan. Make sure she understand your dependencies and you understand the Salesforce build plan, then work with the PM on assembling a detailed schedule that includes all your dependencies. This means that when the time comes to start coding the migration or integration of a particular object, the Salesforce build is complete for that object, has been deployed to your target environment, and you have the data from your client with enough time to analyze it and code all the transformations. For QA, UAT, and production migration runs, make sure the dates land on days that you can dedicate the time needed for the jobs to run.

Your PM is your friend and ally, if your client or the Salesforce development team is not providing you with what you need to do your job, have your PM hold them accountable. But, she can do this only if she have a solid plan that includes a detailed list of exactly what you need and when.

Best Practice 4: Start Early

Attributes: Well Planned

In the project management world, there is this thing called a *critical path*. Basically, the PM lines up all the project dependencies, along with their durations, and determines the timeline. Items are determined to be on the critical path if, in the event they start late or run long, they affect the project's go-live date.

The nature of data work (migrations and integrations) is such that it's generally not on the critical path at all, except as a dependency to start UAT. (QA of Salesforce functionality can start with no legacy data in the system.) Because of this, early in the project, data tasks are often looked at as lower priority and not set to start until midway through the project. This is a mistake, for a few reasons:

1. As your BA gathers requirements, he will have questions that, if you have the data, will be very easy to answer. These questions may include "What are the current activity types?" or "How is the sales process defined today in terms of stages and steps?" Having these answers at your fingertips helps the whole team.

2. You never know what's going to go wrong. Suppose the client is having trouble exporting the data for you, or you don't know the legacy systems data platform and have no idea how to get the data out, or there is some issue with security clearance that has to be resolved before you can be granted access, or the current system owner sees the Salesforce project as a threat to their job and is uncooperative. Discovering these things early can give you months of extra time to mitigate the risks. It doesn't take more time to do something today than it does tomorrow; it just gives you more leeway to deal with the risks and issues that arise.

3. During your end-of-sprint demonstrations, your BA can demo the system, with real data to which users can relate.

4. Data analysis is needed to confirm the information given to you and the rest of the Salesforce development team is accurate and reflects reality. Often, the information given you about the data only reflect the majority of cases and are missing at least some of the edge (or rare) cases. When these edge cases are brought to the attention of your BA, he may do some investigating that may result in major changes to the Salesforce design. It's better for the success of the project to catch these things early. This leads us to our next best practice.

Best Practice 5: Understand the Source Data, Ask Questions to Understand Intent, Analyze Data to Know the Reality

Attributes: Well Planned

After you understand what needs to be migrated, you need to understand how the data are used and how they are modeled today. Start with a conversation with business users. Maybe have them demo the current system (aka "the source system") as it is used today. Usually this work is the job of the BA, so let the BA do their job and run the meeting. Take notes and ask questions related to the data model, but in business terms. For example, you might ask, "So, there is only one head of household? Is that intentional or is that a current system limitation that you want addressed after you move to Salesforce?"

After you have a general understanding of what you are looking for, you can start your data analysis. Start by asking for (and acquiring) all the technical documentation on the current system (ERDs, data dictionaries, user guides, and so on) and access to the system's front and back ends.[3] This is a good idea even if your contract is such that the client is responsible for exporting the data and giving you a clean dataset.

The odds are that your client[4] will have no documentation. If this is the case, and your charter is such that you are responsible for extracting the data, I advise you to create your own documentation. If the client is responsible for exporting the data, then ask for

---

[3]Not production. You don't even want to encounter the possibility of affecting users negatively while doing your analysis. Use a test system or a backup of production.

[4]The larger client is, the more likely it will have a mature software development life cycle (SDLC) process and good documentation. In general, the reason an experienced client is replacing a system is because it has become too large, complex, and unmanageable, which is often a symptom (or outcome) of bad a SDLC process. So, the documents you get may be somewhat outdated. Often there is a mix, the database administration team may have good documents on the database structures and integrations, whereas the front-end team may have nothing. Treat any documentation you get as a cause to celebrate.

an initial export and treat that as the source system. Perform your data analysis on that by doing the following:

1. If it's an RDBMS, determine whether there is a built-in tool to generate an ERD.[5]

2. Query the metadata to get a list of all the objects/tables and fields.[6]

3. Create a spreadsheet with two tabs: one that lists all the objects/ tables and one that has all the fields. If you can get record counts by table, and/or population densities by field, include that data as well (see Figure 6-1). This is your *source data dictionary*.

4. Review each of the tables in the Objects/Tables tab and mark the tables that you think you may need (based on the scope defined in your charter).

5. Build an ERD that includes only the objects\tables that you need.

TABLE_NAME	COLUMN_NAME	DATA_TYPE	Length	NULLABLE	ORDINAL_POSITION	Cnt	DistinctCnt
ACCOUNT	ACCOUNTID	char	12	NO	1	19540	19540
ACCOUNT	TYPE	varchar	64	YES	2	19522	17
ACCOUNT	ACCOUNT	varchar	128	YES	3	19540	18823
ACCOUNT	DIVISION	varchar	64	YES	4	46	38
ACCOUNT	SICCODE	varchar	64	YES	5	0	0
ACCOUNT	PARENTID	char	12	YES	6	42	24
ACCOUNT	DESCRIPTION	varchar	128	YES	7	0	0
ACCOUNT	ADDRESSID	char	12	YES	8	19540	19540
ACCOUNT	SHIPPINGID	char	12	YES	9	19540	19532
ACCOUNT	REGION	varchar	64	YES	10	0	0
ACCOUNT	MAINPHONE	varchar	32	YES	11	12610	12204
ACCOUNT	ALTERNATEPHONE	varchar	32	YES	12	0	0
ACCOUNT	FAX	varchar	32	YES	13	1195	1179
ACCOUNT	TOLLFREE	varchar	32	YES	14	127	125
ACCOUNT	TOLLFREE2	varchar	32	YES	15	0	0
ACCOUNT	OTHERPHONE1	varchar	32	YES	16	0	0
ACCOUNT	OTHERPHONE2	varchar	32	YES	17	0	0
ACCOUNT	OTHERPHONE3	varchar	32	YES	18	0	0
ACCOUNT	EMAIL	varchar	128	YES	19	6906	6787

Figure 6-1. *Metadata exported from SQL Server and used to create a data dictionary*

---

[5]Both Oracle and MS SQL Server have such a feature, but it only works if you have FKs defined in the database.

[6]Every major RDBMS supports this. If the data are not in an RDBMS, it often pays to import the data into an RDBMS so you can query the metadata easily.

After you complete the data dictionary and ERD, you should have a very good understanding of the current system's data model. Use that knowledge to confirm everything that was told to you during your meetings with the business users. When you find discrepancies, gather a few specific examples, take them back to the users, and ask them about it.

Best Practice 6: Understand the Salesforce Data Model and the Hierarchy

Attributes: Well Planned

Your Salesforce development team is responsible for customizing the Salesforce system as well as documenting it. You should hold them accountable to produce good documentation. But, if they can't or won't for whatever reason, you'll have to do this yourself.[7] You want similar documentation that you have or created for the source system. You can find the Salesforce ERDs (for the native objects, obviously this won't have your customizations) here: `https://developer.salesforce.com/docs/atlas.en-us.api.meta/api/data_model.htm`.

Best Practice 7: Document Your Transformations

Attributes: Well Planned, Automated, Controlled, Repairable, Testable

Now that you understand both your source and target data models, you can start planning and documenting the data transformations needed to move the data to Salesforce. Start with your source data dictionary Objects/Tables tab, and copy the objects needed to a new spreadsheet. Add a column for the source table and target Salesforce objects, and another for notes. Then, fill these columns, including your notes that track all your open questions carefully (see Figure 6-2). This spreadsheet becomes your data mapping document.

---

[7]Often, development teams are very good at creating the initial documentation, but are bad at keeping it up to date throughout the development cycles, this is exacerbated with Salesforce being designed for rapid change.

Source Table	Salesforce Object	Comments
LEAD	Lead	15,029 records ; Now out of scope.
ACCOUNT	Relationship (Account)	20,540 records
CONTACT	Contact	151,990 Records
OPPORTUNITY	Opportunity	7568 records (5605 closed) ***Not migrating opportunities
OPPORTUNITY_CONTACT	Opportunity Contact Role	
ACTIVITY	Task, Event	Open Activities
HISTORY	Task, Event	Activity History

Figure 6-2. *A sample data mapping document with object-level mapping*

Next, move on to field-level mapping. Start a new worksheet in your data mapping document for field-level mapping. From the source data dictionary Fields tab, copy all the field data for all the objects/tables needed for your migration. Then, to the left of that, add columns for transformation notes as well as Salesforce target information (see Figure 6-3).

		Source Location								Salesforce Location				
Table Name	Field Name	Data Type	Length	Nullable?	Position	Count	Distinct Count	Transformation Notes	* Salesforce Object	Field Label Name	Included in migration	API Name	Data Type	Length
ACCOUNT	ACCOUNTID	char	12	NO	1	19540	19540	External Id, Unique in SFDC	Relationship (Account)	Legacy Account Id	11/3/2014	Legacy_Account_Id__c	Text	12
ACCOUNT	TYPE	varchar	64	YES	2	19522	17	The SLX values will be mapped to new Type values TBD. Until this is done, migrate values as-is.	Relationship (Account)	Type	11/3/2014	Type	Picklist	
ACCOUNT	ACCOUNT	varchar	128	YES	3	19540	18823	Need to determine how to handle excess characters (>80).	Relationship (Account)	Relationship Name	11/3/2014	Name	Text	80
ACCOUNT	DIVISION	varchar	64	YES	4	46	38	Will not be migrated	Relationship (Account)	*N/A				
ACCOUNT	SICCODE	varchar	64	YES	5	0	0	Will not be migrated	Relationship (Account)	*N/A				
ACCOUNT	PARENTID	char	12	YES	6	42	24	Either populate this field with update after full load, or other way to get SFID.	Relationship (Account)	Parent Relationship		Parent	Lookup	
ACCOUNT	DESCRIPTION	varchar	128	YES	7	0	0	Will not be migrated	Relationship (Account)	*N/A				
ACCOUNT	ADDRESSID	char	12	YES	8	19540	19540	This will be on Address object, with Master-Detail lookup to Relationship.	Address	*covered by Address fields				
ACCOUNT	SHIPPINGID	char	12	YES	9	19540	19532	This will be on Address object, with Master-Detail lookup to Relationship.	Address	*covered by Address fields				
ACCOUNT	REGION	varchar	64	YES	10	0	0	Will not be migrated	Relationship (Account)	*N/A				
ACCOUNT	MAINPHONE	varchar	32	YES	11	12610	12204		Relationship (Account)	Phone	11/3/2014	Phone	Phone	
ACCOUNT	ALTERNATEPHONE	varchar	32	YES	12	0	0	Will not be migrated	Relationship (Account)	*N/A				

Figure 6-3. *Sample data mapping document with field-level mapping*

If you have field mappings that are not one-to-one, feel free to add rows as needed, replicating the source details if the field maps to two targets. You must keep this document up to date with every single change that is made. If a defect is reported (during QA or UAT), update your data mapping document then fix your code.[8]

---

[8]No joke. Do it immediately. It's immensely important that your documentation remain the source of truth for all transformation rules. If your data transformations are not documented properly, how do you know whether your code is wrong? Or whether you are forgetting the agreed-to transformation rules? How can your QA team members test the data if they don't know what the data are supposed to look like?

Best Practice 8: Centralize Your Data Transformations

Attributes: Automated, Controlled, Repairable, Testable

For each object, you want to have all your transformation code in a single place, and you want to have one piece of code per Salesforce object that handles all the transformations needed for that object. I tend to use SQL views or stored procedures, but a Python script (or whatever your favorite scripting language is) can work just as well. This practice makes it very easy to compare the source data, the data after transformation, and the data as it is in Salesforce after it is loaded. It's also makes tracking down issues very easy.

Best Practice 9: Include Source-to-Target Mapping in Transformation Code, Not Just Transformation Logic

Attributes: Automated, Controlled, Testable

As part of your data transformation code, you should rename the columns to match the Salesforce object field API names. In this way, your code mirrors both the documentation as well as the mappings done in your ETL tool. Again, this just makes testing very easy. In addition, most Salesforce connectors (as part of your ETL or middleware) have an automapping feature with which, if the field names match, the tool automaps the source fields to the targets. This practice eliminates any room for human error. After the automapping is done, you can confirm there is nothing left unmapped; then you'll know nothing fell through the cracks.

If your mapping document is in a spreadsheet, you can use formulas to autogenerate the bulk of your transformation code, because most fields don't need to be transformed; they just need to be mapped. When done properly, your transformation code should be so clean that someone could reverse-generate the data mapping document from it.

Best Practice 10: Don't Hard-code Salesforce Ids; They Change with Environments

Attributes: Automated, Controlled, Repairable

Use configuration files, or reference tables, for all Ids that need to be hard-coded based off the transformation rules. For example, suppose you have a rule that says: If the contact is an employee of our firm, it must be of record type Employee, and its parent account must be the XYZ Employee Holding account. You should not hard-code the record type Id and the Id of the Employee Holding account in your code. Instead, store those Ids in configuration files or cross-referenced tables. You will likely need to use them more than once. If you have to run your code against a different environment,[9] or users change their mind and want to associate the contacts with a different account, you won't have to search through all the code to find where you hard-coded the Ids.

Best Practice 11: Store Cross-referenced Data in Salesforce

Attributes: Automated, Controlled, Repairable,

By storing External Ids on the corresponding Salesforce records, you essentially have built-in cross-reference tables that not only allow you to use Upsert functionality, but also have solid traceability back to the source system. In addition, you can download the cross-reference data easily for use anywhere else in the organization.

If you need conversion tables for your transformations, by creating an object (or a custom setting) in Salesforce for them, you get a nice UI to go along with it for maintenance. This is obviously much more important for integrations than for migrations.

---

[9]The exception to this is a full sandbox. No other sandbox maintains the production Ids when being refreshed or created. A partial sandbox does, but only for the small segment of records that got transferred to it.

Best Practice 12: Load Your Data in the Order of the Object Hierarchy

Attributes: Automated, Controlled

If you understand the Salesforce data model and have only one piece of code per object, loading your data in the order of the object hierarchy is easy and quite logical. Obviously, you need to load accounts before contacts, and both accounts and contacts before opportunities, and the three of those before you load activities. You need the parent object to exist before you can create related records.

The only exception to this is self-relations, which is when an object is related to itself, such as accounts and parent accounts. In this case, you first create all the accounts, then do a second pass to update just the self-related field.

Best Practice 13: Delete Child Records First, Then Parents, When Deleting Data

Attributes: Automated

This best practice tends to apply only to reverse code (your special code used to roll back a migration), but it could also apply if you have an integration that deletes large volumes of data from Salesforce. When deleting data, you want to start at the bottom of the hierarchy and work your way up. If you start at the top (Account), you will probably trigger so many cascading deletes that the deletions will fail, either because of locking errors or other governing limitations.[10]

---

[10]For more information, see `https://developer.salesforce.com/forums/?id=906F00000008zt IIAQ`.

Best Practice 14: Create All Necessary Holding Accounts in Code

Attributes: Automated, Controlled, Repairable

Let's go back to our example of "If the contact is an employee of our firm, its parent account must be the XYZ Employee Holding account. You want the creation of such holding accounts to be part of your code and fully automated. It's just one less manual step that needs to be done when setting up a new environment. Creating such holding accounts should be automated for both migrations and integrations. You would not believe how many times I have had users delete the holding account because it was "garbage." This practice adds to the self-repairability of your code (see Chapter 5).

Best Practice 15: Don't Forget about Owners and Record Types

Attributes: Well Planned

Because ownership and record type information are often not sourced in the source data, but derived, they are often forgotten. For example, you may be given a rule that says, "If the account is located in New York, the owner should be John Smith; if New Jersey, then Peter Doe." Always ask about the rules for defining ownership and record types early in the process.

Best Practice 16: Don't Bury the Bodies; Expose Them

Attributes: Well Planned, Testable

On occasion, after weeks of hard work, you come across some edge case in your data that was not considered and has the potential to cause upheaval to your timeline. The temptation is there to ignore the issue and pretend you never noticed it. This is particularly true when you are already behind schedule or dealing with a difficult client who is going to ask a million questions and insist on having a meeting with four other people to discuss the issue. I urge you to resist the temptation to ignore the situation and do what you know is right.

If you know what the client will decide to a high degree of certainty, but want to avoid causing the upheaval, then fix your code, update your documents, and then send an e-mail (after hours[11]) that explains what you did and that you are open to discuss it, if needed. This situation falls under the "It's easier to obtain forgiveness than permission" strategy. Needless to say, there is only so many times you can do this before people get really upset. And if you are told never to do this again, you'll have to stop (at least for this client). *Never*, ever take this approach with a production system

If you are still not convinced to do the right thing, know this: Eventually, the body will be found and the upheaval will happen. So, you may as well get it over with and get credit for finding the body, rather than getting blamed for hiding it.

If you are following the "start early" best practice, the chances of finding such an edge case so late in the game is greatly reduced.

Best Practice 17: Partner with Your BA

Attributes: Well Planned

While you are doing the data analysis of the source system, the rest of the Salesforce implementation team should be building the Salesforce data model, screen layouts, workflows, triggers, and so on. You need to strive toward building a solid working relationship with the rest of the team. It's too easy to think of the data track as a completely different project for which you only need to understand the target data model and can otherwise work independently. It's also way too easy for the Salesforce team to be so engrossed in their own work and problems, while thinking you are on top of the data track and don't need their input, nor that they need yours.

Building good working relationships with your teammates takes effort (in addition to standard things like having patience, understanding, and just being a decent person). You need to spend time working with them so that they understand fully the value you bring to the table above and beyond writing clean code to spec. This means doing things such as the following:

1. Use your data analysis and data manipulation skills to help the team better understand the source data and answer any questions team members may have.

---

[11]In this way, you can use the excuse that you didn't want to wait until the morning and lose hours of work just to get the answer you were sure you already knew.

2. Validate assumptions being made about the source data.

3. Use your data analysis and data manipulation skills to build a source system data dictionary, so the team can build out the Salesforce data model with the proper field types and lengths.

4. Explain to the team that you can offload some of the development work from Salesforce to integration code, and this may take less effort and offer more functionality. Suppose you are pushing order data into Salesforce that includes order totals and order line-item details. Because the data are owned by the external order processing system, how easy is it for you to build countless combinations of summary data and rollups? You can create weekly summaries, monthly summaries, annual summaries, product-level summaries, product category-level summaries, salesperson summaries, sales territory summaries, sales manager summaries, or any combination of these—and so much more. Not only that, but you can do it without storing the detailed data in Salesforce, or only storing the last few months of detailed data in Salesforce! It's much less effort to do this in ETL code than with Apex triggers, and the client saves a ton of money on data storage!

After you have established a good relationship with the team, the team members will take your needs into account when they make system changes—not that they were ignoring you before, but because they have been conditioned to think of data work as a critical part of the project and understand that both of you are tied at the hip. They will be much more proactive in keeping you in the loop before changing the Salesforce data model willy-nilly.

When you are validating your work, you need to work with your team to put in exceptions for migration/integration users so that validation rules and the Salesforce dupe-blocker (duplication management[12]) don't interfere with your work.

Good relationships make everything easier.

---

[12]For more information, see https://trailhead.salesforce.com/en/modules/ sales_admin_duplicate_management.

Best Practice 18: Automate When Possible

Attributes: Automated, Controlled, Reversible, Repairable, Testable

Remember, our goal is to get to a single-click migration, which means that anything that can be automated should be automated. This automation includes all data movements and transformations, including moving the original source data into a staging environment as part of preparation. If the prep work needs to be redone when new data are delivered, this task should be automated.

Best Practice 19: Limit the Number of Intermediaries (Layers of Abstraction)

Attributes: Automated, Testable

Anytime you move data from one system to another or from one format to another, you run the risk that something will be lost or modified in the translation. This situation is a classic case of leaky abstractions. If the data is delivered as .csv files and you open them in Excel, Excel drops the leading zeros or may convert text to numbers, adding decimals. Oracle may convert NULL dates to January 1, 1900. Exporting to .csv files may result in files that are not formatted properly. You may lose text formatting. Your ETL tool may limit large text fields to 4,000 characters. The risk of this happening may be low, but with each layer, the risk adds up.

Ask your client to deliver the data as close to the original format as possible. In this way, if the source system is MS SQL Server, you want an MS SQL Server backup or access to the server directly. If it's an Oracle database, then you want the data in Oracle, and so on. If your client can't do this, explain the risks involved.

If you must move the data out of the original environment, automate them as part of the overall process and run all your code with the data starting at the originating source environment. In this way, when the project undergoes QA and UAT, you are testing that these translations did not affect overall data quality negatively.

Best Practice 20: Use Proper Tools

Attributes: Well Planned, Automated, Controlled

When choosing your tool set, make sure it's meets all your needs from a feature point of view (for example, supports the Merge APIS call if needed), and can help you achieve all six attributes discussed in Chapters 4 and 5.[13]

I want to stress (again) that the Apex Data Loader is *not* the right tool for any serious migration or integration work. It has no capability for data transformations, and although you can use it to connect to Java Database Connectivity (JDBC) data sources, doing so is tedious and error prone. In addition, all the success and error data can only be output to .csv files.[14]

Using .csv files with Excel as a data transformation tool is also not a good idea. Excel does not produce clean .csv files. Excel does not support relational joins, and vertical lookups (VLookup) are slow.[15] Excel simply stops responding when dealing with large files. Most importantly, using Excel reinforces bad habits of transforming data manually rather than automating it.

I am convinced that the reason this combination of Excel and .csv files is so common for data migrations is because people tend to know of the Apex Data Loader and instinctively want to use it. (Its free! And data migrations are one-time run code!) Then, when they want to edit the .csv files, they double-click and it opens in Excel. Don't fall into this trap.

---

[13]We some of the more commonly used data tools in Chapter 3.

[14]I'm not saying you can't code a migration or integration using the Apex Data Loader that meets all the attributes I listed in Chapters 4 and 5. You absolutely can, and I have. You can use the command line to automate it fully, and some scripting language for all transformation code. I'm just saying it's not the right tool for the job.

[15]On the same note, many ETL tools have "lookup" functionality that is also very slow and, if used with Salesforce, abuses your API calls. You are much better off downloading the related data and doing a proper join in code.

Best Practice 21: Build a Library of Reusable Code

Attributes: Automated

There are some transformations you will need to perform repeatedly, not necessarily just within the same project, but for every Salesforce data migration and integration you do. Therefore, write this code so it can be used over and over again. Some examples of such transformations are

- Formatting phone numbers (Remember, you have to format your phone numbers before you load them.)

- Breaking up name fields into First Name, Middle Name, and Last Name

- Validating e-mail addresses

- Converting plain text with line breaks and special characters to HTML

In Chapter 12, I share my library of transformation code with you and review it.

Best Practice 22: Turn off Duplicate Management

Attributes: Well Planned

Salesforce's duplicate management[16] (sometime called *dupe- blocker*) feature is a great feature. Unfortunately, it has no place in data migrations or integrations. Work with your team to turn it off during the data migration and\or add an exception for the integration user, so users can get the benefits of this great feature, but your migration and integration code is not affected by it.

As a general rule, when doing a data migration, you want to make sure all the data get migrated. Using duplicate management as a filter is not a good idea. Check for duplicates *before* you push the data, not during or after. "During" is way too disruptive to the migration process; "after" implies you will go live with bad data.

---

[16]Again, see `https://trailhead.salesforce.com/en/modules/sales_admin_duplicate_management`.

With data integrations, if the source system owns the data, then it should be the system that worries about duplicates. If the source system along with your integration code decides the data are good and should be loaded to Salesforce, it's not a good idea to have Salesforce decide to reject it as a duplicate. Let the data flow in. If there is a duplicate, it should be fixed in the source system and the integration should then push the fix to Salesforce.

Best Practice 23: Have Some Way to Control/Limit Which Data Get Migrated

Attributes: Controlled, Repairable

You need a simple way to control what data get migrated for all the reasons we examined in Chapter 4. It doesn't have to be a sophisticated method, but it should be centralized and easy to modify.

I find the method that works best is to filter at the top of the object hierarchy and then let the filter cascade downward. For example, let's say you put in code to filter your Account object by region and then parameterized "region" for ease of control. Then, when it comes to contacts, you code it to filter and include all contacts related to the migrated accounts. Then, for activities, you code your filter as all activities related to a migrated account or contact, and so on.

Best Practice 24: Fix Code, Not Data

Attributes: Automated

As you code your migrations and integrations you will come across data that can be fixed via transformation code. Assuming it can be done, it's always better to alter your code(either the code within the source system or the transformation code) to fix that data rather than fix the data itself. This approach ensures that when new data are created that have the same issue, you've already dealt with it. Here are a few examples:

1. The source system has a single field for Name and it needs to be split into First Name and Last Name. You should either alter the source system to use two fields or write transformation code to split it.

2. The source system has e-mail addresses with spaces in them.

3. The source system stores address lines in separate fields
    (Salesforce wants them in one, with line breaks between the
    lines).

4. Names are all capital letters, but users want them converted to
    camel case.

5. A comments field is stored as plain text in the source system but
    is feeding a rich text field in Salesforce. (You need to convert line
    breaks to HTML <br> tags.)

For each of these cases, the biggest mistake you can do is push the data to a staging area and fix the data there manually.[17] You are going to get updated datasets and you will have to redo this work, then you will have to redo QA testing. Even if you have users fix the data directly in the source, there is no guarantee they will fix all the bad records or that new data won't be created badly (unless validation code is put into the source system to ensure all new data are created properly).

For integrations, fixing the source data and adding validation code to the source system is the best way to go, because if that system owns the data, it should also own the validation. If this can't be done for whatever reason, then do the fix in your transformation code. For migrations, it's probably not worth the effort to modify code that's being retired, so making changes in your transformation code is probably best.

Needless to say, there are some things that just can't be done in code, and a data cleanup project may be warranted. You can modify the data either in the source system before go live or in Salesforce afterward.[18]

---

[17]If you have the push-to-staging automated and the data repair automated as well, this is a perfectly good transformation layer/pattern.

[18]Based on my past experiences, any plan to clean up data after go-live, rarely comes to fruition.

Best Practice 25: Fix Errors with Parent Objects before Moving on to Children

Attributes: Automated, Controlled

Depending on how the relationships are configured in Salesforce and how your code is written, if a parent fails to load, the child records will "error-out" (either because the parent field is not valid or is not found) or the record will be created but the parent field will be NULL.

For data migrations, I recommend you put in checkpoints after each object and verify there are no errors before moving on to child objects. Even if, during your test runs, you fixed all the data issues in the source data or with transformation code, you still have the risk of coming across new issues when you get that final cut of data.

For your test runs, have your users fix the data, or put in transformation code to fix the data. For the production migration, as you come across errors, fix the data at the parent level and force the records to be created. This strategy ensures the child records are created properly. If you can't fix the data, modify it so the records get created, then take notes so you can inform your users and they can fix it manually in Salesforce after migration is complete.[19]

For integrations, simply log the errored rows, because your code is self-repairing. After the data are fixed in the source, the data will flow into Salesforce along with all related data that may have errored because of it.

Best Practice 26: Modulation Is Also a Form of Control

Attributes: Controlled, Repairable

Your code should be modularized by the target Salesforce objects so you can run the modules individually. If a small fix is needed to a single object, this approach allows for you to run only the module that effects that object while still updating the master

---

[19]If you did a good job during the build and test cycles of fixing the data in the source system and have coded bullet-proof code, this situation should be a rarity and should only impact a record or two. If it turns out you need to perform another migration, go back and have the data fixed in the source or in your transformation code.

code base. This strategy also allows for rapid code-and-test cycles and the ability to implement a very targeted fix should a defect be found after go-live.

Best Practice 27: Every Record You Insert Should Have an External Id

Attributes: Automated, Repairable, Testable

External Ids allow for the use of Upsert, but this is not the only reason for using them. External Ids make tracing Salesforce data back to the originating system incredibly easy. They are indexed automatically, so all you need to do to find the record in Salesforce is type the source system Id into the Salesforce search box. When you can pull up the same record easily in the legacy UI and in Salesforce, testing becomes a snap for you, QA personnel, and UAT testers.

I always recommend data validation be done by comparing data from the legacy UI to the Salesforce UI. In this way, you are not only validating your transformation rules, but also you are validating your data mapping document.

For reasons too obvious to state, source systems PKs are the best fields to use as External Ids. If your source system does not have a PK on one or more of the tables you are migrating to or integrating with, then make one up. By "make one up," I mean use what data you have in the source table to create a unique identifier for each row. Let's look at some examples:

1. You may have a natural key, such as driver's license Id, social security number, or phone number.

2. If you have a junction table (a many-to-many relationship), you may have a composite key that you can concatenate into a single External Id.[20]

---

[20]When concatenating Ids, always use a delimiter. Suppose you are concatenating two Id fields. On one record, the Ids are 351 and 25; on another, the Ids are 35 and 125. When you concatenate these Ids, they both result in 35125. They are no longer unique! Make it a practice to use delimiters. I usually use a colon or a hyphen. So, in this case, the Ids would be 351:25 and 35:125 or 351-25 and 35-125.

3. You can strip spaces from various text fields and concatenate them. Keep doing this until you use every field in the table if needed (FirstName+Lastname+Email+Zip+StreetNumber+Phone). Use data points that are very unlikely to change, because a data change can trigger an External Id change. Note, however, that this approach comes with that risk, which may be acceptable for a data migration, but I would advise against it for an integration.

    As an alternative, if you can have an AutoNumber added to the source system that will be maintained as new records are added, this is probably the way to go. Do not add an AutoNumber in the staging environment. If the Ids have the potential to change when updated data are delivered, the Ids will be useless as External Ids (or even as record identifiers).

Best Practice 28: Standardize External Ids and Always Enforce Uniqueness

Attributes: Automated, Repairable, Testable

Maintain consistency of formatting for all your External Ids. In this way, you can write your code and your users can search for data without constantly thinking about formatting or field names. Here are a few additional guidelines:

1. Always enforce uniqueness. This practice prevents duplicates from being created accidentally. Also, if you make a mistake and calculate nonunique External Ids, any inserts will be rejected and you will catch your error.

2. External Ids should always be text. There is no benefit to creating and External Id as a number[21]; with text, you can always add a prefix or a suffix later (with a delimiter) to make it a compound key. With Salesforce, it's very common to load multiple source objects into a single Salesforce object. Suppose the source database has tables for lawyers, accountants, and salespeople. All

---

[21]You can argue about some sorting benefits, but this is resolved easily by padding the numbers with zeroes when converting them to text.

of these tables will be loaded into the Salesforce Contact object (and maybe have different record types). They may all have a PK, but those PKs are only unique within the individual tables. In such cases where multiple tables are being loaded into a single Salesforce object, prefix the PK with some text that indicates the source table. You could have Ids such as Lawyer-001, Sales-001, and Acc-001.

I recommend always prefixing External Ids with the type, because a change may come later that creates the need to add a prefix, and you won't want to have to deal with updating all the Ids to support one. Also, a prefix can make External Id unique across your Salesforce org, which makes searching for records a bit easier.

3. Use a different External Id field for each data source and include the source name as part of the field name. For example, if you have two data sources, ABC and XYZ, create two External Id fields—one for each of them (ABC_Id and XYZ_Id)—and name them as such. Often, people just include the source system as a prefix on the data because they are only thinking about maintaining uniqueness of the Id, not about traceability. You can run into a situation when a record is sourced from both systems. If this is the case, and you have only one field, you lose the traceability back to one of the sources.

I once had a case in which we were integrating with two different systems and we only used one field for the External Id, prefixed with some code to indicate the source system. After go-live, users saw that the same contact was being created from the two systems and they wanted to merge the records. They couldn't, because whenever they did a merge, they lost one of the Ids. The next time the integration (upsert where the Id was not found) ran, the duplicate contact was recreated! We had to do a data conversion to split the External Id out into two fields. Salesforce now allows for 25 External Ids. There's no excuse to be cheap with them.

Best Practice 29: Don't Use the External Id for Anything Except the Migration or Integration

Attributes: Well Planned, Automated, Repairable

There is an endless debate in the data world on whether it's a good idea to use natural keys as the PK or whether you should always use a surrogate key. A surrogate key is an Id with the purpose of being used as a PK—"sole purpose" as in it has no other reason for existence and has no other meaning. For example, an item's SKU or UPC has purposes other than identifying the record uniquely. Yes, every record in your products table must have a SKU and a UPC, and they will both be enforced as unique (they are natural keys), but they have meanings and other uses, so some say they should not be used as a PK.[22] I'm not going to insert myself into this debate (at this time), because I prefer people not to burn this book.

That being said, when it comes to Salesforce External Ids, you want the field to be used for nothing except for use as an External Id (system linkage Id). Users can get finicky on how they want to see their data, and you don't want to have to deal with them complaining that you put prefixes or stripped out spaces from their data. So, its fine to use a natural key, but keep the External Id for your use only in your migration and/or integration, and, if needed, replicate the same data into a different field for users, where they can format it to their heart's desire.

Best Practice 30: Use Upsert When Possible

Attributes: Automated, Repairable

Upserts are a single action that encompasses a fairly complex piece of logic should you have to do it manually. It's safer and cleaner to use upserts, and because you already have proper External Ids, why not?

---

[22]This issue is debated heavily online. There are lots of great arguments for each side. So, if you have some time, read up on it and you can impress your friends and colleagues at your next social gathering!

Best Practice 31: Every Record You Insert Should Have a Job Id

Attributes: Controlled, Reversible, Repairable, Testable

It's a good idea to create a field for the job Id on every object being inserted or updated by your migration or integration, and populate it with an Id that indicates the job that performed the action. For migrations, the job Id should be a configurable value that you can set with every run. For integrations, have some mechanism of getting a job Id from the ETL tool, middleware, or scheduler you are using. If cannot come up with one, it's very easy to code this functionality yourself.

A job Id gives you a quick and easy way to identify records that were updated during the last run, which makes looking into reported defects that much easier. The alternative to doing this is to filter records by user and modify date, which is not very precise.[23]

This practice also gives you a roundabout way of performing a second migration without having to wipe out all the data first. Suppose on February 1 you received the production data to be migrated and you did so successfully, marking each record with a job Id of 2-1-2018_Migration. Then, for whatever reason, it was decided to push back the go-live date to March 1. Normally, you would have to do a full delete of all data in Salesforce, then redo the migration (because migration code generally does not perform deletions and users may have deleted records from the source system during the month of February). If you have job Ids, you can perform your migration, marking all records with a job Id of 3-1-2018_Migration, then go back and delete any remaining records with the 2-1-2018_Migration job Id. (If they were not updated, they were not in the record set).

---

[23]Other users could have updated records during or after the job run.

Best Practice 32: Real Users Must Perform UAT on the Data Migration and You Must Get Sign-off before Going Live

Attributes: Well Planned

As discussed in Chapter 4, only real system users can test for intent. You should plan for users to find quite a few "intent" issues and respect them as real issues (within reason). There is a fine line between an intent issue and a new request that warrants a CR. I like to have these tracked as nonimpact CRs, so you can at least win some points when performing them, all while not accepting blame for a high defect count (which will happen if you simply reply with, "No problem! I'll have that fixed this afternoon![24]). In addition, when you have a real CR that has an impact on your budget or timeline, you can point to the long list of "free" CRs you performed and ask your client or project sponsor to be understanding.

This is an important part of good relationship building. It's worth repeating: Good relationships make everything easier.

A sure sign that your users are not testing is if no defects are being reported. As discussed in Chapter 4, users who are testing properly will report a large number of issues that are not real issues. You will have to investigate the specific cases being reported and explain to the users why the data are the way they are. Then, you absolutely must have documented proof (in writing or in an e-mail) that the users have completed their testing and are okay with the data as is. This is especially important if users are not reporting issues (in other words, not testing). Fixing migration issues while users are in the system, making changes, is a royal PITA.[25]

---

[24]This response implies you did something wrong and have now agreed to fix your "mistake."

[25]The Apress editors complained about my use of "potty words" in previous chapters, so you will have to Google this one if you can't figure it out yourself. Sorry.

Best Practice 33: Plan for an Extended UAT Period

Attributes: Well Planned, Repairable

It can be difficult to estimate how many intent defects will be found during UAT. It's also difficult to estimate how much time users will have to work on UAT. It's more common than not that users are given the task of performing UAT in addition to their regular job duties. So, plan to give them ample time.

Best Practice 34: Build a Relationship with the Users

Attributes: Well Planned, Repairable

Be helpful and explain what you are doing to users. Explain why you are asking certain questions, and answer all their questions fully.

Per the Stereotype Content Model,[26] you want to be warm and competent. In the context of being an integration specialist, "warm" means showing concern for users' problems and demonstrating eagerness to help them. In Figure 6-4, you can see my nonscientific data specialist version of the Stereotype Content Model.

Warmth	**High**	**Well Liked But Pitied** (No one wants to work with you, but may help you)	**Well Liked and Admired** (You want to be here)
	Low	**Hated** (People are openly hostile toward you)	**Envied** (People want you to fail and won't help you succeed)
		Low	High
		Competence	

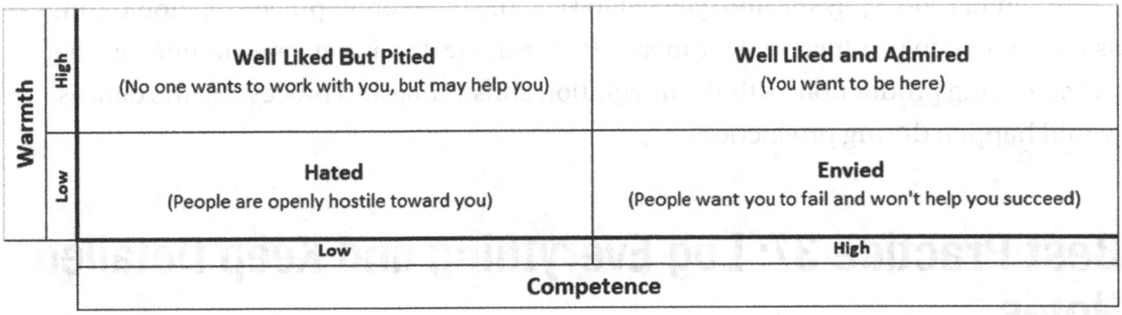

Figure 6-4. *Dave's nonscientific data specialist version of the Stereotype Content Model*

Good relationships make everything easier.

---

[26]For more information, see https://www.cos.gatech.edu/facultyres/Diversity_Studies/ Fiske_StereotypeContent.pdf.

Best Practice 35: QA and UAT is for Testing Processes Too (Not Just Code)

Attributes: Well Planned, Testable

For each round of QA and UAT, perform all tasks as they are performed during production deployment. With each round, update your deployment procedures with any changes needed and add automation when possible, removing manual steps. By your final round of UAT, deployment should be flawless, with no changes needed.

Best Practice 36: Start Fresh for Each Round of QA and UAT

Attributes: Well Planned, Automated, Reversible

For each round of QA and UAT, reset your target Salesforce org back to its originating state—that is, the state it will be in at the time of go-live. For migrations, this is the only way you can perform any testing properly. For integrations, this practice allows you not only to test your integration code, but also to test your deployment procedures (as per the last best practice #35).

For integrations, by the time you get to UAT, the integration processes should run as they would in production. This means that realistic data is delivered as often as they would during production, with the integration consuming and processing the data as would happen during production.

Best Practice 37: Log Everything and Keep Detailed Notes

Attributes: Reversible, Testable, Repairable

When something is not working right with integration code, you generally debug it the same way you would traditional code. You start by replicating the issues, making a fix, then running the code again under the same conditions you used to replicate the error, and then confirm the code is now working as desired.

Unfortunately, with data migrations, this approach simply won't work—for two reasons:

1. Your code may not be designed to be self-repairing. (You planned for manual repairability, which is okay for data migrations.)

2. Months can pass after the migration has been completed before an issue is reported and you may not remember what was done.

For data migrations, make sure your code logs everything it does: when each process starts and completes, and how many records were processed. Keep detailed notes of every manual step you take and keep a copy of every record's success or error output (success and error files, but they can be stored in database tables). Of course, if there are manual steps, they were unplanned, because you planned to have a fully automated data migration.

When a migration issue is found months after go-live, most clients will ask you to perform an investigation into what went wrong and why. Having proper notes can save you days of work.

Best Practice 38: Get a New Cut of Data for Each Round of QA and UAT

Attributes: Well Planned

For migrations, get a new cut of data from your client for each round of QA and UAT. Remember, you want to test the process completely from start to finish. This means you need to not only test your deployment procedures and code, but also the client's ability to export data in a consistent and accurate manner.

Too often, client responsibilities are thought of as nonrisks when, in actuality, client responsibilities are often the riskiest part of a project. This situation may result from the fact that your client, especially if it is a smaller shop, is less likely to be in the software delivery business, with a good set of procedures. In addition, no one may holding the client accountable to high, or even consistent procedural standards.

You cannot imagine[27] how often the second set of data exported by the same client is completely different in structure than the first. This is another reason you should insist on getting the data delivered as close to the original format as possible. Whoever is exporting that data should be following the best practice of limiting the number of intermediaries.

Best Practice 39: Record Runtimes

Attributes: Well Planned

At the start of each QA/UAT cycle, as you run through the deployment procedures and run the jobs (migration and/or integration), record the run/deployment times for each of your steps. For integrations, after the code is running smoothly without error), record the runtime for the initial run as well as for the first few scheduled runs.

Review your notes with the actual go-live plan and ensure the plan is feasible and fits into the allotted deployment or migration timeline. If it is not, adjust the plan and test it with the next round of QA and/or UAT.

Best Practice 40: When Defects Are Found, Patch the Code Then Rerun It

Attributes: Automated

When defects are found, even small ones, fix your code and rerun it. (This is another reason why you should keep your code modular.) Often, when a minor defect is found, the temptation is to patch the data quickly, tell whoever logged the issue to retest it so they can close out the issue, then go back and fix your code. This is the wrong approach because these small things add up and something can slip through the cracks quite easily.

Here is a very real example that happened to me: The legacy system had the contact names in all caps and the client asked me if I could convert them so only the first letter of the name is capitalized and the rest are lower case (camel case). I used the data loader to export the contact Ids and names, fixed the data in the .csv file, and updated Salesforce. I then went back to my master contact transformation code, added code to convert the

---

[27]This happens to me repeatedly and I still have trouble imagining it!

names to camel case, but didn't test it because the data was already fixed and it was just a simple change. What could possibly go wrong? At the beginning of the next round of UAT, I started the migration and let it run overnight so that users could start testing first thing in the morning. Well, something did go wrong. I had a typo in that "simple change" and the job failed. I didn't find out until I checked on it at 2 o'clock in the morning. *Not* a fun time to be patching code.

Summary

So there you have it. Forty best practices to make your life easier. Remember, good habits breed success, and success breeds even more success.

In Chapter 7, we walk through a sample data migration from start to finish. As you read through the chapter keep an eye out for how all the little things we are doing are intertwined to make an overall good process. You should notice two things:

1. Just how easy it is to build migration code that follows each of the best practices described in this chapter.

2. How the entire process ties together so well, you almost can't imagine there is such complexity in the rationale behind such simple actions.

Okay, let's get started!

CHAPTER 7

Putting It All Together: A Sample Data Migration

Great! Let's do it! In this chapter I put you in my shoes and walk you step-by-step through the data migration component of a typical project. We will follow the Basic Upsert-No Delete pattern (discussed briefly in Chapter 5), which is the standard migration pattern and can be used for just about any Salesforce data migration.

As we go through each of the following steps, note how consistently we follow the best practices described in Chapter 6. More important, however, note how following these best practices reduces your workload and coding time. Last, note how good habits promote even better ones. Once you start on the right path, it almost takes effort to push yourself onto a wrong one.

Project Initiation

The project "onboarding" process varies quite a bit among organizations and is very different when working on the client side (on an internal project) vs. working on the Salesforce implementation partner side (for a client). Regardless of which side you are on, at this time you will (or at least you should be) told who your teammates are, and you should be given access to whatever project documentation exists and given some background info on the project. In some cases, you may have been involved in the project conception phase, so you'll have a good knowledge base going in.

During the project initiation phase, review all the existing project information. After you understand the scope of work, devise a set of tasks or user stories, then work with your PM to integrate your tasks into the overall project plan or backlog.

© David Masri 2019
D. Masri, *Developing Data Migrations and Integrations with Salesforce*,
https://doi.org/10.1007/978-1-4842-4209-4_7

In the following scenario, we are a Salesforce implementation partner (with A-OK Consulting) and have been awarded a contract from a midsize manufacturer of specialty storage containers (Specialty Container, Inc.[1]) to replace their existing CRM system with Salesforce. Their existing CRM system is a Web-based home-grown system called SC-CRM. The company wants to go live with Salesforce and retire the current CRM system early during the fourth quarter of the current year. The SOW defines the data migration scope as follows:

A-OK Consulting will migrate the following data from SC-CRM to Salesforce:

- *Companies*

- *Contacts*

- *Activities*

The PM is planning a kickoff meeting with the client and has asked us whether we have any agenda items to add to that meeting. We tell her that, as part of the "next steps" discussion, we want to set up a call with the technology team currently responsible for SC-CRM.

We contact the author of the SOW to ask for clarifications on scope because the SOW is a bit vague. He explains that when the SOW refers to "Companies" and "Contacts," it is referring to categories of information as opposed to specific objects. The client does track more complex relationships than employees of companies, and we will need to migrate that relationship data. However, do not have to migrate things like opportunities, cases, or campaigns. The legacy system is severely lacking in these areas and they are not heavily used. When they were used, they were used wrong. The client wants a fresh start with Salesforce.

Next, we ask the SOW author about activities.

"Does migrating activities mean we have to migrate the system users who performed the activities?"

He says yes, but explains the system has been around for 15 years and many of the users tied to activities have since left the company. We need to figure out how best to handle this situation. He also notes that some employees of Specialty Container, Inc., will not be granted user licenses, but Salesforce needs some way of relating those people to activities as meeting attendees.

---

[1]They are not affiliated with Universal Containers. Their containers are way too specialized to be used universally.

Last, we ask the SOW author if the legacy system has file attachments and if these need to be migrated.

He replies, "I have no idea. I never asked. But, if they do, the SOW only covers the migration of attachments related to companies, contacts, and activities."

The kickoff meeting goes great and our call with the SC-CRM technology team is scheduled for next week. We put together a short agenda/list of questions to help us get an understanding of basic stuff. It includes the following:

- An understanding of SC-CRM's architecture

- Where is SC-CRM housed? Locally? In the cloud? Somewhere else?

- What is the database engine behind SC-CRM and how can we access the data?

- Can we get a backup of the database or is the data only accessible over web services? What other ways are there for exporting data? (Remember, we want the data as close to the original format as possible.)

- Are there any security concerns/data-handling policies we should be aware of?

- Can we do the development on our (A-OK's) servers or must all data reside on the client's infrastructure at all times?

- What documentation exists for the current system? Can we have access to it?

If this was an integration, we would also ask a bunch of questions regarding tool selection (as discussed in Chapter 3). But, because our job is a migration and the client will not need to support our code, we are free to choose what works best for us.

Coming out of the meeting we learn that the existing system is Web based, built on Classic ASP with a SQL Server back end, and is hosted locally in their data center (see Figure 7-1). It's behind a firewall and is only accessible from their internal network, although some users "VPN in." The customer is okay with giving us a backup of the back-end SQL Server database, but not the ASP code, as long as we sign a nondisclosure agreement (NDA) and agree to provide proof of data destruction at the end of the project. We can develop and run the migration from our own hardware, but the customer wants it "firewalled" off from the wider A-OK network. They have no documentation.

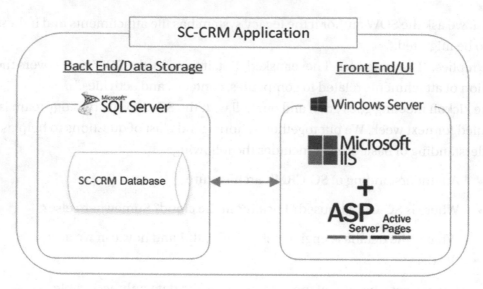

Figure 7-1. *SC-CRM's architecture*

Design and Analysis

While we are waiting for the paperwork (the NDA) to be processed, so that Specialty Container, Inc., is comfortable giving us a backup of the SC-CRM database, we can proceed with the high-level migration design. SC-CRM has a SQL Server back end, so we will need a SQL Server instance to which to restore it. We decide that SSIS is the best tool for the job for a few reasons:

1. The legacy CRM data are in SQL Server.

2. Because we need a SQL Server license anyhow, we can use SSIS at no additional cost.

3. We (I) have a very good working knowledge of SSIS.

4. Most important, the visual nature of SSIS makes it a great choice for showing data-flow screenshots.

SSIS does not have a native Salesforce connector, so we decide to use KingswaySoft's because that's our personal preference.[2]

---

[2]Tool selection and various options were described in Chapter 3. Just because I am using SSIS and KingswaySoft does not in any way mean that these are the right tools for your project. This is a sample scenario only.

IMPORTANT NOTE

You do not need to know anything about SSIS to follow along for the rest of this chapter. Nor do you need to know anything about SQL Server. I explain exactly what I am doing, and SSIS's visual nature makes it very easy to follow. There is quite a bit of T-SQL code, but if you are familiar with any dialect of SQL, you should have no issues understanding it. I explain everything that has any level of complexity. I want to stress how unimportant the choice of technology is. You can swap out every technology shown in Figure 7-2 and the pattern will remain the same. *Everything* else remains the same. You, of course, would have different code, but it will do the exact same things we are doing here. Because of this, I'm not going to walk you through the nuances of SSIS. It's just not important.

A SECOND IMPORTANT NOTE

Although you don't need to know SSIS to understand this chapter, it is heavily reliant on SQL code (T-SQL, specifically). I explain this code in detail, so you should be okay if you are at least a novice with it.[3] If SQL is new to you, I strongly recommend you get acquainted with it. In my opinion, coding in SQL is the single most useful technical skill to anyone working with data.

By performing all our transformations in SQL, we lessen our reliance on ETL/middleware to perform them for us. This strategy enables us to develop a skill that can be used regardless of the ETL or middleware our client decides to use. It also makes it very easy for us to build a library of reusable code that is ETL and middleware agnostic.

---

[3]If you don't know anything about SQL, you can still follow along, but you will have to be more focused on the text that explains what the code does.

ANOTHER IMPORTANT NOTE

I intentionally picked what I felt was a moderately complex project. I want this to feel like a real-world project with real-world problems, as opposed to an easy, straightforward one. You will have a lot to absorb in a single chapter (I get that), but don't be discouraged if you have to reread this chapter a few times. I could have given you the example we studied in Chapter 3 and left it at that. Technically, it's a full migration, but it's not a realistic scenario. It's overly simplified. So again, if you do not "get" this chapter on your first read, that's okay. I'd rather you understand 65% of a real-world example than 100% of an overly simplified one.

YET ANOTHER IMPORTANT NOTE!

Don't get caught up on the technology stack. It's the thought process that's important. Focus on the six attributes and the best practices.

ONE MORE IMPORTANT NOTE!

If you want to try out some of the concepts shown in this chapter using the same tool set, you can download all the tools used for free![4]

No more Important Notes! Back to our heroes in progress: you and me!

To meet Specialty Container's security needs, we decide to spin up an AWS EC2 Windows server with SQL Server preinstalled. This approach gives us a development environment in which we can host Specialty Container's data completely disconnected from A-Ok's infrastructure.

---

[4]Amazon EC2 for Microsoft Windows: https://aws.amazon.com/windows/products/ec2/.
SQL Server Developer Edition: https://www.microsoft.com/en-us/sql-server/sql-server-downloads.
SQL Server Management Studio: https://docs.microsoft.com/en-us/sql/ssms/download-sql-server-management-studio-ssms.
SQL Server Data Tools, the SSIS interactive development environment (IDE): https://docs.microsoft.com/en-us/sql/ssdt/download-sql-server-data-tools-ssdt.
KingswaySoft's SSIS Integration toolkit (free for developer use): http://www.kingswaysoft.com/products/ssis-integration-toolkit-for-salesforce.

We will restore the SC-CRM database to that SQL Server and then create a second database use to stage data (cross-reference data and error-log data) and to house all our transformation code (T-SQL code). Because the two databases are on the same SQL Server instance, we can create views in the staging database that query directly against the SC-CRM database (cross-database queries[5]). In this way, we can write all our code and then, when we are ready to go live, Specialty Container can give us a new SC-CRM database backup. We restore that over our current copy and all our code will work with the updated data (see Figure 7-2).

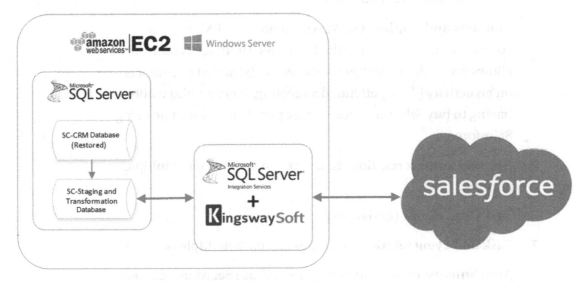

Figure 7-2. *Data migration physical architecture*

Meanwhile our superstar BA is hard at work running requirement discovery meetings with our client's sales team and designing the Salesforce data model. As he is doing that, we stand up our infrastructure, acquire the SC-CRM database backup, and restore it.

We perform our data analysis, build our data dictionaries, and write our mapping document (as described in Chapter 6). Working with our BA and PM, we finalize the scope (in terms of Salesforce objects) and the object load order.

---

[5]For more information, see https://docs.microsoft.com/en-us/sql/relational-databases/in-memory-oltp/cross-database-queries.

Salesforce Object Load Order

We will load the data in the following order (per the object hierarchy):

1. **Users**: We will do this manually because the client wants to review each one so as not to waste licenses.

2. **Accounts and an Employee Holding account**

3. **Account parent**: SC-CRM has an account hierarchy and Specialty Container wants to maintain it.

4. **Contacts and employees**: We will create SC-CRM users as contacts and relate then to the Employee Holding account. This allows non-Salesforce user employees to be added as contacts on an activity (if they attended a meeting, for example) without having to buy Salesforce licenses for people who won't be using Salesforce.

5. **Account contact relation**: Contacts can be related to multiple accounts.

6. **Tasks and events (activities)**

7. **Task and event relation**: Activities can have multiple contacts.

8. **Attachments**: For activities only, we will use Salesforce content because the Notes and Attachments functionality will be phased out in coming years.

In addition, we learn that Specialty Container wants to onboard users onto Salesforce in waves. So, the SC-CRM user Id will act as our control. We will divide them into batches and load those users one at a time, a week a part. Every SC-CRM system user's data must be migrated, regardless of whether they are still active in the system.

Awesome! Our plan is shaping up! We now work with our PM on a detailed timeline. When we've finished, it looks something like the one shown in Figure 7-3. Note that these are calendar weeks not man-weeks. The assumption is that you are not dedicated to working solely on this project, but have other work as well. With this detailed timeline, our PM then integrates it into the master project plan and we can track our progress properly.

Task	Subtask	Data Category	Project Week(s)
Data Analysis and Mapping Doc	Build	Users	1
		Accounts & Parent	1
		Contacts	1
		Account Contact Relation	1
		Activities (Task and Events)	2
		Activity Relation	2
		Attachments	2
Build	Build (& Developer Unit Testing)	Users	3
		Accounts & Parent	3
		Contacts	3
		Account Contact Relation	3
		Activities (Task and Events)	4
		Activity Relation	4
		Attachments	4
SIT	Full End-to-End run		5
QA	Full End-to-End run		6
	Data Validation & Defect Resolution	Users	6 & 7
		Accounts & Parent	6 & 7
		Contacts	6 & 7
		Account Contact Relation	6 & 7
		Activities (Task and Events)	6 & 7
		Activity Relation	6 & 7
		Attachments	6 & 7
UAT	Support & Defect Resolution	Users	7,8,& 9
		Accounts & Parent	7,8,& 9
		Contacts	7,8,& 9
		Account Contact Relation	7,8,& 9
		Activities (Task and Events)	7,8,& 9
		Activity Relation	7,8,& 9
		Attachments	7,8,& 9
Product Migration	Product Migration & Postproduction Support		10

Figure 7-3. *Data migration high-level project plan*

Let's Get Coding! Set Up

Great! We are ready to get started! So exciting! First thing first (per our object load order), we export the list of users from the SC-CRM (including the legacy user Id) and give them to our BA to review with the client and to create the desired users with proper Salesforce profiles and security access rights. We ask the BA to add a field to the Salesforce User object called "SC CRM Id"; set it as an External Id that is case insensitive, with uniqueness enforced (see Figure 7-4); and to populate the field with the legacy user Id as he creates the users. (In the Salesforce world, often a BA will be tasked with this kind of work, other times they will hand it off to a Salesforce System Architect (SA) or developer. To keep things simple, we will assume the BA is doing all the work.)

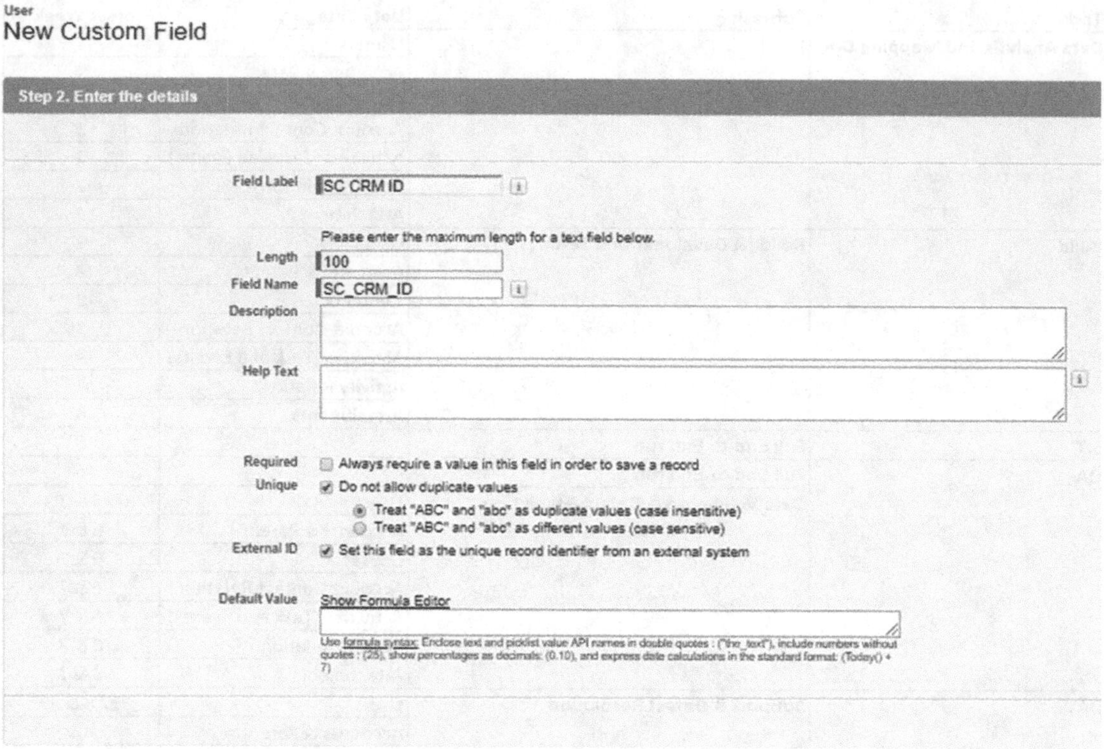

Figure 7-4. *Adding the External Id to the User object*

Next, we create two tables in our staging database[6]: a data control table and a configuration table.

The Data Control Table looks like this (Listing 7-1):

Listing 7-1. The Data Control Table

```
1.   CREATE TABLE [dbo].[Data_Control]
2.   (
3.       [SC_CRM_USERID] [char](12) NOT NULL,
4.       [SC_CRM_USERNAME] [varchar](64) NULL,
5.       [Include] [char](1) NOT NULL
6.   ) ON [PRIMARY]
```

---

[6]Remember, we don't want to modify the SC-CRM database in any way. Each week we will get a new copy with updated data from the client and will restore them over our local copy. Any changes we make to it will be lost.

We also add a PK index on SC_CRM_USERID to prevent errors and maintain performance. We populate it with the same user data we gave to our BA and mark the Include column with a "Y" for a few records that we will use for testing/coding. We want to be enabled for rapid code and test cycles without having to wait for large volumes of data to load. When we are ready to load our first batch of users, we will flag all users in that batch for migration. But for now, a few records will suffice. We don't want to restrict our data too much because we want to catch the vast majority of row-level data issues up front.

The configuration table is a basic name/value table and looks like this (Listing 7-2):

Listing 7-2. The Migration Configuration Table

```
1.    CREATE TABLE [dbo].[Migration_Configuration]
2.    (
3.         [Name] [char](12) NOT NULL,
4.         [Value] [varchar](64) NOT NULL
5.    ) ON [PRIMARY]
```

We set Name as the PK. For now, we only need to add a single row to the table for our job Id. This is the JobID that we will add to every record we load (for traceability). (Going forward, I'm not going to call out every index you need to create. As a general rule, index any column you use on the right side of a left join.)

We set the Name to JobId and the value to Dev/Test Migration. If we need more configuration values, we may add them later.[7]

Download Cross-reference Data

Our superstar BA has finished creating all the users in Salesforce, setting up record types, and adding the needed custom fields to the Salesforce objects. But, before we can start loading data, we need the cross-reference data. The users are all in Salesforce with the corresponding SC-CRM Ids; we need to download that. We also need to download the Record Type object because we have requirements to set it based on the SC-CRM data.

---

[7]If you prefer to use configuration files for this kind of stuff, that's fine. I like to use tables because I can include them in SQL code, as we will see shortly.

First, we create a new SSIS project and add a package for our data migration. We then create two connections: one to our SQL Server staging database and one to our target Salesforce org. Note that the Salesforce connection options are very similar to what we saw with the Apex Data Loader in Chapter 3. All you need is user name, password, and token (see Figure 7-5).

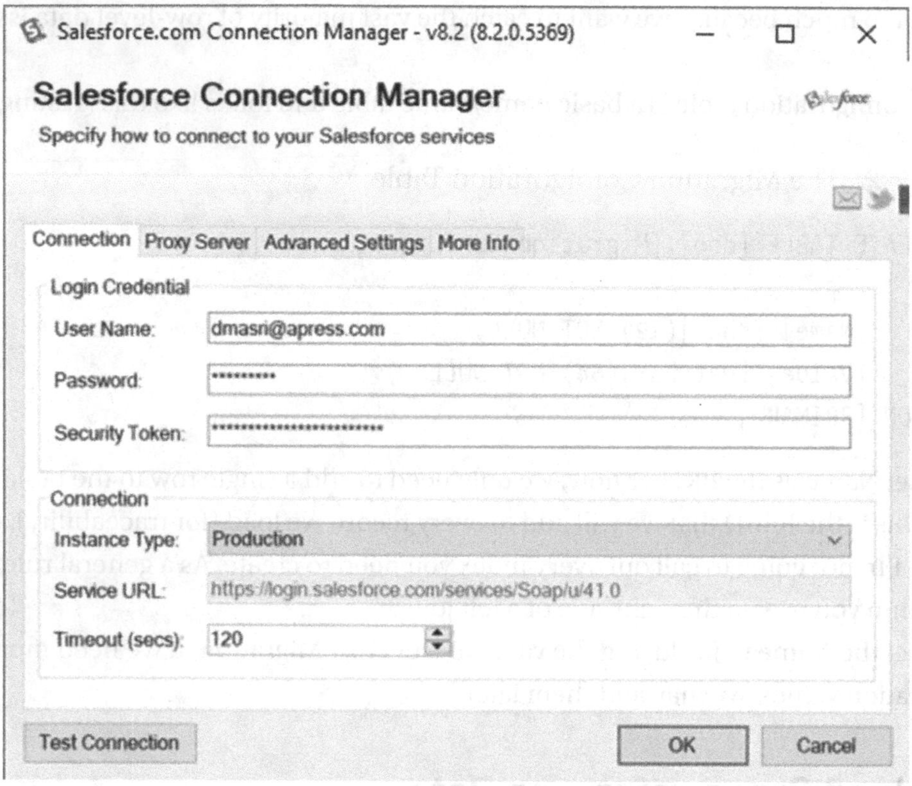

Figure 7-5. KingswaySoft's Salesforce Connection Manager screen

When you open an SSIS package, you first see the control flow, which you use to control the flow of your code. You can then add tasks to it and control the order in which they run. You can then drill into the task to configure or write code (depending on the task type). Take a look at Figure 7-6. I added a Sequence Container that contains two tasks: an Execute SQL task (Truncate Tables) and a Data Flow task (Download Xref Data).

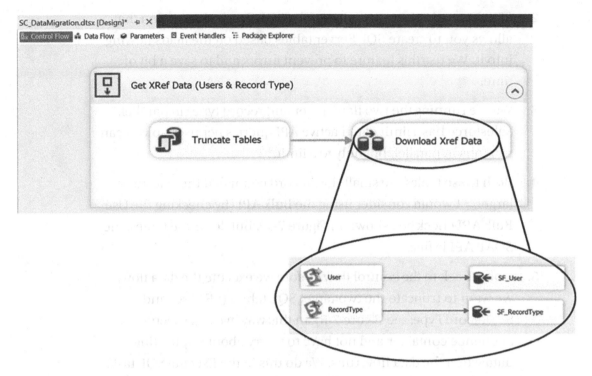

Figure 7-6. *The SSIS control flow, with two tasks in a Sequence container*

All the Sequence container does is group tasks for us logically and allow us to execute the whole container by right-clicking and selecting Execute Container. This is how we will keep our code modular.

Next let's look at the Data Flow task. If we drill into it, we see it contains two flows (see Figure 7-6): one to download users from a Salesforce source and into a SQL Server target[8] and one to do the same for record types.

A few things to note:

1. Figure 7-7 shows the Salesforce source object screens. When selecting fields from the object, we don't want to overselect fields because it can slow the download process (we are downloading more data).

---

[8]I'm actually using an OLE DB target, for irrelevant reasons. For more information, see https://social.msdn.microsoft.com/Forums/sqlserver/en-US/9f9208ad-6371-4cdf-aed4-778b8b7eea4c/sql-server-destination-vs-ole-db-destination.

2. SSIS has a nice feature as part of the SQL Server destination that
    allows you to create SQL Server tables based on the fields flowing
    into it. We use this feature to prevent errors and to save a bit of
    time.

3. We are running the two flows (user and record type) in parallel.
    Salesforce has a limit of ten active API queries per user, so you can
    run jobs in parallel, but only to a limit.[9]

4. Both these tables are small (low record counts). If there were
    larger,[10] I would consider using the Bulk API (by checking the Use
    Bulk API check box shown in Figure 7-7). But, for these tables, the
    SOAP API is fine.

5. Going back to the control flow, before we execute the data flow,
    we want to truncate the two target SQL tables (SF_User and
    SF_RecordType; see Figure 7-6). In this way, we can execute the
    Sequence container and not have to worry about duplicating
    data when the data flow runs. We do this in the Execute SQL task,
    which runs just before the Data Flow task.

6. Last, we index the SF_User table on the SC_CRM__c field, and the
    SF_RecordType table on the SobjectType and DeveloperName
    fields, because these are the fields we will use when joining to the
    tables.[11]

---

[9]If you really have to exceed ten0, you can use two connections with different users to run 20 flows
in parallel, or 3 and 30!

[10]Here you can define larger as "big enough to warrant the use of the Bulk API." I know this is
somewhat vague, but determining when to use the Bull API is not an exact science. Refer back to
Chapter 3.

[11]I know I said I wouldn't mention indexing again. This is the last time. I promise.

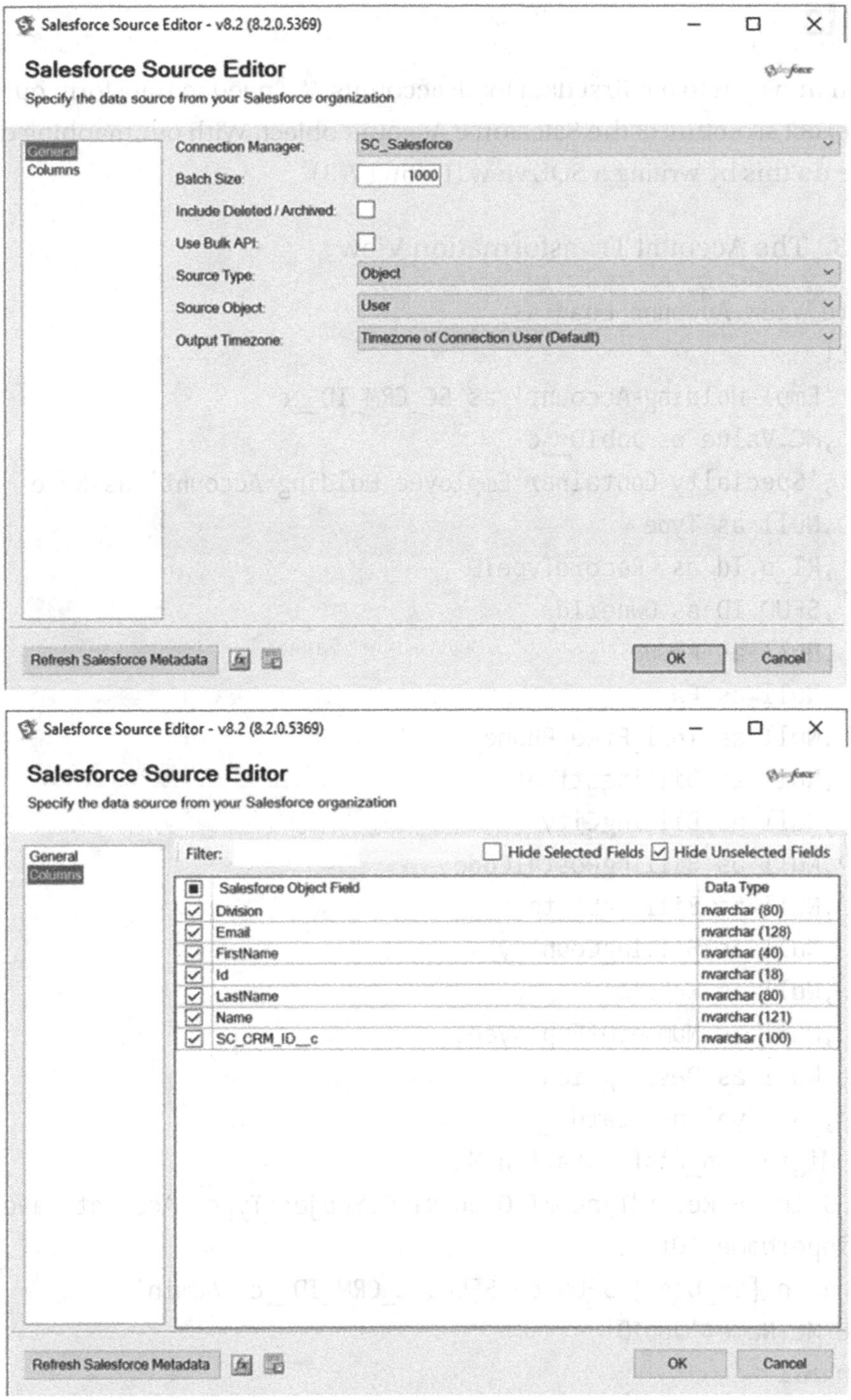

Figure 7-7. *The KingswaySoft Salesforce Source object screens*

Accounts

Now we can move on to our first data load: accounts. We need to transform our data to match the exact structure of the Salesforce Account object. With our mapping document in hand, we do this by writing a SQL view (Listing 7-3):

Listing 7-3. The Account Transformation View

```
1.   Create View Account_Load as
2.   Select
3.        'Empl-Holding-Account' as SC_CRM_ID__c
4.        ,MC.Value as JobID__c
5.        ,'Specialty Container Employee Holding Account' as Name
6.        ,Null as Type
7.        ,RT_o.Id as   RecordTypeID
8.        ,SFUD.ID as OwnerId
9.        ,Null as Phone
10.       ,Null as Fax
11.       ,Null as Toll_Free_Phone__c
12.       ,Null as BillingStreet
13.       ,Null as BillingCity
14.       ,Null as BillingPostalCode
15.       ,Null as BillingState
16.       ,Null as BillingCountry
17.       ,Null as Website
18.       ,Null as NumberOfEmployees
19.       ,Null as Description
20.       ,'Active' as Status__c
21.  from Migration_Configuration MC
22.  Left Join SF_RecordType RT_O on RT_O.SobjectType='Account' and RT_O.
     DeveloperName='Other'
23.  left join [Sf_User] SFUD on SFUD.SC_CRM_ID__c='Admin'
24.  where MC.Name='JobID'
25.  Union all
26.  Select
27.       'Company-'+a.ACCOUNTID as SC_CRM_ID__c
```

```
28.         ,MC.Value as JobID__c
29.         ,A.ACCOUNT as Name
30.         ,a.SubType as Type
31.         ,Case
32.              when a.TYPE ='Client' then RT_C.Id
33.              when a.TYPE ='Vendor' then RT_V.Id
34.              Else RT_o.Id
35.         end as RecordTypeID
36.         ,coalesce(SFU.id,SFUD.ID) as OwnerId
37.         ,dbo.fn_FormatPhone(a.MAINPHONE) as Phone
38.         ,dbo.fn_FormatPhone(a.FAX) as Fax
39.         ,dbo.fn_FormatPhone(a.TOLLFREE) as Toll_Free_Phone__c
40.         ,ad.Address1 +Coalesce(char(10)+ad.Address2,")+coalesce(char(10)+
            ad.Address3,") as BillingStreet
41.         ,ad.City as BillingCity
42.         ,ad.Postalcode as BillingPostal
43.         ,ad.STATE as BillingState
44.         ,Coalesce(Ad.COUNTRY,'United States') as BillingCountry
45.         ,coalesce(a.WEBADDRESS,A.WEBADDRESS2) as Website
46.         ,a.EMPLOYEES as NumberOfEmployees
47.         ,a.BUSINESSDESCRIPTION as Description
48.         ,a.STATUS as Status__c
49. from [SC_CRM].[dbo].[Account] a
50. join Data_Control DC on DC.SC_CRM_USERID=a.ACCOUNTMANAGERID and
    dc.Include='Y'
51. Join Migration_Configuration MC on MC.Name='JobID'
52. Left Join SF_RecordType RT_C on ='Account' and RT_C.
    DeveloperName='Client'
53. Left Join SF_RecordType RT_V on RT_V.SobjectType='Account' and RT_V.
    DeveloperName='Vendor'
54. Left Join SF_RecordType RT_O on RT_O.SobjectType='Account' and RT_O.
    DeveloperName='Other'
55. left join [Sf_User] SFU on SFU.SC_CRM_ID__c=a.ACCOUNTMANAGERID
56. left join [Sf_User] SFUD on SFUD.SC_CRM_ID__c='Admin'
57. left join [SC_CRM].[dbo].ADDRESS ad on ad.ADDRESSID=a.ADDRESSID
```

Okay. Let's Examine the code in Listing 7-3. The most important thing you should notice is that all the transformation code is centralized. This is literally one piece of code that has all the transformations needed to populate the Account object (save ParentID, which we will get to next). If I lost my mapping document, I could rewrite it just by looking at this one piece of code. Take a closer look and notice the following:

1.   The query is divided into two sections. The first half (lines 2–24) is used to create a single record for the Employee Holding account. The second half (lines 26–57) has the rest of our account data. These two record sets are stacked on top of each other using the Union command in line 25.

2.   We are joining data from our source database to data in our staging database using cross-database queries. You can discern this because some of the tables are prefixed with the database name (lines 49 and 57). This view is created in the staging database, so tables that are also part of that database don't need to be prefixed with the database name.[12]

3.   We renamed all the columns to match the Salesforce API names.

4.   We bring in our job name from our configuration table (lines 28 and 51).

5.   We use an inner join to bring in only those data for users marked for inclusion in our Data Control table (line 50.)

6.   We join back to our SF_User table to convert the SC-CRM Account Manager Id to the Salesforce user Id for the Owner field. If no match is found, we use the Admin user (lines 36, 55, and 56).

---

[12]If you run into performance issues, you may need to add an index to the source database to resolve it. (This is common because performance is one of the reasons people decide to move off their current CRM.) Of course, adding an index to the source database violates our rule of not touching the source database. We lose that change on the next restore! If you have this need, I recommend you keep a single SQL file that adds all the needed indexes to the source database, and include running the script as part of the restore process. If you are a purist and refuse to have that additional manual step, you can add a data flow to your SSIS package to move that table over to your staging database as is, and index it there.

7. We use a Case statement to build the logic used to determine the record type (lines 31–35 and 52–53).

8. If we don't have a country name, we set it to United States (line 44).

9. We merge all the address lines into a single field using the trick we learned in Chapter 2 (line 40).

10. We use a user-defined function (UDF) to format our phone numbers (lines 37–39). This is code from our reusable code library. (This function is included in the common transformations code library we review in Chapter 12)

11. We prefix our External Id (SC_CRM_Id__C) with the word *Company* per our best practice. We do this out of habit, although it is not really needed in this case (line 27).

12. For the Employee Holding account, we hard-coded a custom External Id (line 3). We will use this Id when we load users as contacts.

13. We have a few custom fields (lines 39 and 48).

Now that we have our data exactly as we want it to appear in Salesforce, all that's left to do is load it. We add a data flow to our SSIS package that selects all the fields from our view, then upsert it to the Salesforce Account object. The data flow looks like that shown in Figure 7-8.

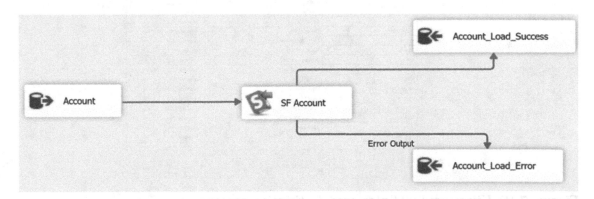

***Figure 7-8.** Our upsert account data flow*

All the way on the left, we have our SQL Server source (Account) that is just a
Select statement from our view.[13] We route the data to a Salesforce Destination object
(SF Account); then, from there, route the Success and Error rows to different tables:
Account_Load_Success and Account_Load_Error. Let's take a look at the Salesforce
Destination object (see Figure 7-9).

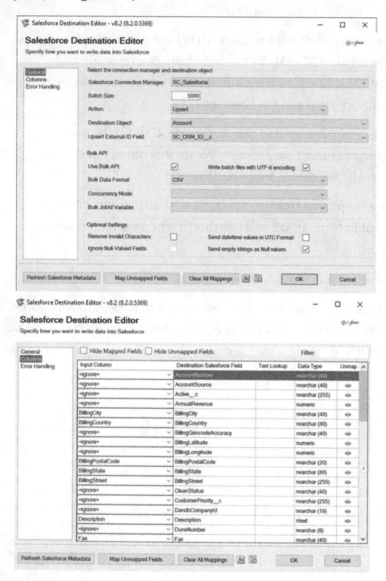

Figure 7-9. *KingswaySoft Salesforce destination screens*

---

[13]We don't do Select *. We list all our fields. This has nothing to do with Salesforce or SSIS;
  it's just good database code practice. For more information, see https://www.google.com/
  search?q=is+select+*+bad.

Look how easy that is! Just like the Apex Data Loader! You simply select your object, then select Upsert. Here we chose to use the Bulk API, so we checked that box. Then we did our mapping on the Columns page. Note that, just like the Apex Data Loader, Kingsway has an automap button (Map Unmapped Fields) that maps the fields based on matching names. So, all we have to do is confirm that all the fields in the view mapped, and we know nothing was missed![14]

But we are not done yet. We still want to modularize the Account load process, so we add an Execute SQL task that truncates the Success and Error tables and wraps it in a Sequence container (see Figure 7-10). That's it. We are ready to move on!

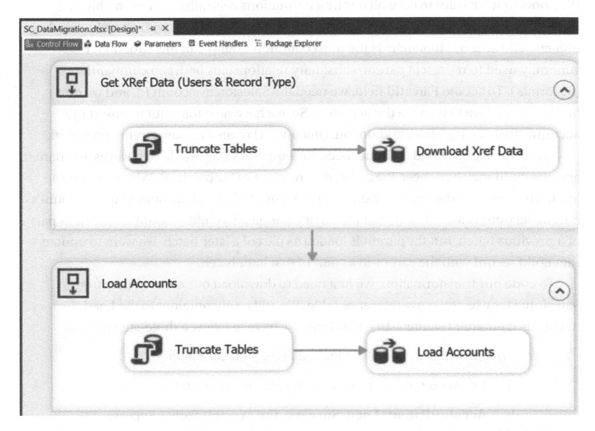

Figure 7-10. *Our control flow with the accounts Sequence container added. If we double-click the Load Accounts task, we see Figure 7-8.*

---

[14]With Kingsway, once you map a field, it drops out of the Input column drop-down, so all we have to do is click that and confirm it's empty!

But, before we actually move on, I want to remind you that in the real world, this type of project won't be such a linear process. What will actually happen is that, on your first run, you'll get a bunch of errors logged to your Load Error table. Then, you'll have to go back and fix your view. It takes a few run/fix/rerun cycles before there are no errors and you can move on. This is another reason you want your code modular and controlled to a small dataset: so you can do those cycles in rapid succession.

Account Parent

We know that we want to have all our transformations centralized for each object, but unfortunately sometimes this is not possible. Such is the case with all self-related objects. The account hierarchy is the most common example of this situation. It's generally used to represent parent/subsidiary relationships between companies (accounts). To set the ParentId field, we need the Salesforce account Id, and we don't have that until we first create the accounts. So, we have no choice but to upsert our accounts first, then go back and update (*not* upsert) them with the parent account Id.

We also have a secondary issue. Because we are loading our data in waves, the parent and the child may have been loaded in different waves (or batches). When running a load, we want to update any account with the parent Id, if that account *or* that account's parent account is included in the batch. For example, if a child account is loaded as part of a previous batch, but the parent is loaded as part of a later batch, we want to update that child record with the parent Id as part of that later batch.

To code our transformation, we first need to download our account data from Salesforce for use as a cross-reference table. We add a subcontainer to the Load Accounts container (Figure 7-10). This time, we have to follow a three-step process:

1. Truncate tables that will be loaded in the new container.

    a. **SF_Account:** The new account cross-reference table

    b. **AccountParent_Load_Success:** The Account Parent Success Log table

    c. **AccountParent_Load_Error_Success:** The Account Parent Error Log table

2. Download the account cross-reference data (into SF_Account).

3. Update every account's parent Id if the account was created in this batch or if it's parent was created in this batch (and, of course, only if it has a parent).

When done, our Account container will look like the one shown in Figure 7-11. With the subcontainer in place, we have the ability to run the entire account load module, or just the account parent module, with a single click.

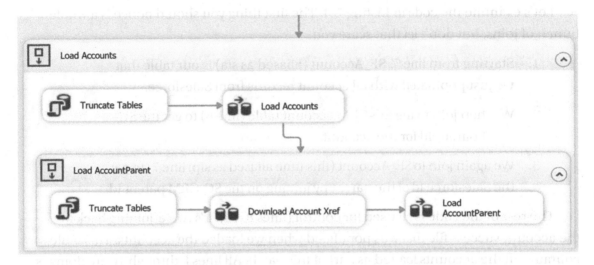

Figure 7-11. *The Load AccountParent container embedded in the Load Accounts container*

Just like with accounts, we create a SQL view with all the transformations needed to load account parents. Here is the code (Listing 7-4):

Listing 7-4. The Account Parent Update Transformation View

```
1.   Create View [dbo].[AccountParent_Load] as
2.   Select
3.        sfa.SalesforceRecordId as ID
4.        ,sfp.SalesforceRecordId as PARENTID
5.   from SF_Account sfa
6.   join [SC_CRM].[dbo].[Account] sca on 'Company-'+sca.ACCOUNTID=sfa.
     SC_CRM_ID__c
```

```
7.   Left join SF_Account sfp on sfp.SC_CRM_ID__c='Company-'+sca.PARENTID
8.   Left join [dbo].[Account_Load_Success] ALS on  ALS.SC_CRM_ID__
     c='Company-'+sca.ACCOUNTID
9.   Left join [dbo].[Account_Load_Success] ALSP on  ALSP.SC_CRM_ID__
     c='Company-'+sca.PARENTID
10.  Where (ALS.SalesforceRecordId is not null or ALSP.SalesforceRecordId
     is not null) --- Either the Parent or Child Account was included in
     this load
```

Let's examine the code in Listing 7-4. The first thing you should notice is a whole bunch of joins, but don't let that scare you.

1. Starting from line 5, SF_Account (aliased as sfa) is our table that we just populated with all account records from Salesforce.

2. We then join to the SC-CRM account table (line 6) to get the SC-CRM parent Id for the account.

3. We again join to SF_Account (this time aliased as sfp; line 7) to get the Salesforce Id of the parent by joining on the SC-CRM parent Id.

The rest of the code is all used for control (lines 8–10); it's twice-joining back to the account success file that was populated when we loaded the accounts. This table contains all the accounts loaded as part of this batch. All lines 8 through 10 are doing is checking whether the account or its parent was included in this batch.

You may be asking why we don't have a "where" clause in the code that says "Where sca.PARENTID is not null." If we added this, then only accounts with parents would be included in the query. We want our code also to remove invalid parents. In case, a parent Id was put on an account when it shouldn't have (repairability), so we intentionally left it off. Our code updates every account in the batch even if an account doesn't have a parent at all.

We don't include a job Id because, if we had to roll back this batch, we would use the same logic that we used earlier to determine what was updated in the batch, as opposed to setting a JobId field. If we set the field, our code would think we created this account record as part of this batch when, in reality, we may have only created its parent account.

Contacts

Okay, next up: contacts. Loading contacts is almost the exact same process used for accounts. First, we create a view to transform our data, then we add a data flow to our SSIS package to load in the data. Here is the view code (Listing 7-5):

Listing 7-5. The Contact Transformation View

```
1.   Create view Contact_Load as
2.   SELECT
3.       'User-'+u.userid as SC_CRM_ID__c
4.       ,MC.Value as JobID__c
5.       ,sfa.SalesforceRecordId as AccountID
6.       ,sfu.Id as Employee_User__C
7.       ,[dbo].[fn_GetNamePart](u.username,'F') as FirstName
8.       ,[dbo].[fn_GetNamePart](u.username,'L') as LastName
9.       ,[dbo].[fn_GetNamePart](u.username,'M')AS MiddleName
10.      ,Null AS Salutation
11.      ,Null AS Suffix
12.      ,'Employee' as Contact_Types__c
13.      ,dbo.fn_FormatPhone(u.HOME) AS Phone
14.      ,Null AS Fax
15.      ,Null AS Mobile
16.      ,dbo.fn_GoodEmailorBlank(u.EMAIL) as Email
17.      ,Case when dbo.fn_GoodEmailorBlank(u.EMAIL)<>u.EMAIL then u.EMAIL
            else null end as Invalid_Email__c
18.      ,Null AS Website__c
19.      ,Null AS Description
20.      ,u.TITLE AS Title
21.      ,Null AS Birthdate
22.      ,'Other' Status__c
23.      ,1 AS  HasOptedOutOfEmail
24.      ,1 AS  DoNotCall
25.      ,1 AS HasOptedOutOfFax
26.      ,Null as MailingStreet
27.      ,Null as MailingCity
```

```
28.        ,Null as MailingPostalCode
29.        ,Null as MailingState
30.        ,Null as MailingCountryCode
31.   FROM   SC_CRM.dbo.[USER] u
32.   join Account_Load_Success sfa on sfa.SC_CRM_ID__c='Empl-Holding-Account'
33.   Join Migration_Configuration MC on MC.Name='JobID'
34.   left join [dbo].[SF_User] sfu on sfu.SC_CRM_ID__c=u.USERID
35.   UNION All
36.   SELECT
37.        'Contact-'+c.CONTACTID as SC_CRM_ID__c
38.        ,MC.Value as JobID__c
39.        ,sfa.SalesforceRecordId as AccountID
40.        ,Null as Employee_User__C
41.        ,c.FIRSTNAME as FirstName
42.        ,c.LASTNAME as LastName
43.        ,c.MIDDLENAME AS MiddleName
44.        ,c.PREFIX AS Salutation
45.        ,c.SUFFIX AS Suffix
46.        ,dbo.[fn_GetContactTypes](c.CONTACTID) as Contact_Types__c
47.        ,dbo.fn_FormatPhone(c.WORKPHONE) AS Phone
48.        ,dbo.fn_FormatPhone(c.FAX) AS Fax
49.        ,dbo.fn_FormatPhone(c.MOBILE) AS Mobile
50.        ,dbo.fn_GoodEmailorBlank(c.EMAIL) as Email
51.        ,Case when dbo.fn_GoodEmailorBlank(c.EMAIL)<>c.EMAIL then c.EMAIL
           else null end as Invalid_Email__c
52.        ,c.WEBADDRESS AS Website__c
53.        ,c.DESCRIPTION AS Description
54.        ,c.TITLE AS Title
55.        ,c.BIRTHDAY AS Birthdate
56.        ,Case
57.            when c.TYPE='Vendor' then 'Vendor'
58.            when c.TYPE='Client' then 'Client'
59.        else 'Other' end as Status__c
60.        ,case when c.DONOTEMAIL='F' then 0 else 1 end AS
           HasOptedOutOfEmail
```

146

```
61.        ,case when c.DONOTPHONE='F' then 0 else 1 end AS DoNotCall
62.        ,case when c.DONOTFAX ='F' then 0 else 1 end AS HasOptedOutOfFax
63.        ,ad.Address1 +Coalesce(char(10)+ad.Address2,")+coalesce(char(10)+
           ad.Address3,") as MailingStreet
64.        ,ad.City as MailingCity
65.        ,ad.Postalcode as MailingPostalCode
66.        ,ad.STATE as MailingState
67.        ,Coalesce(ad.COUNTRY,'United States') as MailingCountryCode
68.    from SC_CRM.DBO.CONTACT c
69.    join Account_Load_Success sfa on sfa.SC_CRM_ID__c='Company-'+c.
       ACCOUNTID
70.    Join Migration_Configuration MC on MC.Name='JobID'
71.    left join [SC_CRM].[dbo].ADDRESS ad on ad.ADDRESSID=c.ADDRESSID
```

If you recall, we have a requirement to create all legacy users as contacts associated with an Employee Holding account. This is what the first half of this query does(lines 2–34) (see Listing 7-5). The second half of the code (lines 36–71) is for the actual legacy contacts, and we join the two data-sets with Union (line 35). Take a closer look and notice the following:

1. The employee code is a Select off the SC-CRM user table (line 31), the contact code is a Select off the SC-CRM contact table (line 68). We use the respective table Ids to create the Salesforce External Id (SC_CRM_Id__c; lines 3 and 37), but we added a prefix (comprised of the source table name). In this way, we don't have to worry about both tables having overlapping Ids. We can still use Upsert and enforce uniqueness on our External Ids.

2. We do an inner join to the account success file (line 69), which limits our data to only those contacts that are children of the accounts loaded successfully as part of this batch (this is our control). Note that we don't have any control for the employee section. This will migrate all employee records with every run. Of course, we are doing an upsert so we don't have to worry about duplicates, so this is okay. If it bothers you, we can always add another configuration to control when the Employee Holding account is upserted. If that account is not upserted with a run,

then the employees won't be either (because of the inner join on line 32). I included it in every run because I am concerned that new employees may have been onboarded during the weeks between runs, and I want to make sure nothing slips through the cracks.

3.   We want to include a lookup to the corresponding Salesforce User record on the Employee Contact record. We do this by joining to our SF_User cross-reference table (lines 6 and 34).

4.   We use a UDF to format our phone number (lines 13 and 47–50). This is code from our reusable code library. (This function is included in the common transformations code library, which we review in Chapter 12.)

5.   We also have a UDF to validate the e-mail address. If the e-mail is invalid, we leave it blank and put the invalid value into a custom text field (lines 50 and 51). This action ensures we can migrate all our contacts without any data loss and we can build a Salesforce report (or list) to find all records that have "Invalid_Email__c" populated, then give that to our users for data cleanup. (This UDF is also included in Chapter 12.)

6.   SC-CRM has proper FirstName, MiddleName, and LastName fields in its contact table, but the SC-CRM user table only has a single column called UserName. We use a UDF to split the name into three columns for first, middle, and last name (lines 7–8). (Also included in Chapter 12.)

7.   SC-CRM has one-to-many relationships for Contact type. We want to convert that to a multiselect picklist, so we include a UDF that accepts a contact Id and returns a semicolon-delimited list of contact types (line 46). (This UDF is also included in Chapter 12!) For employees, we simply hard-coded Contact type as Employee (line 12).

8.   We use Case statements to convert Ts and Fs to proper check box values: zeroes and ones (lines 60–62).

9. Like with the account view (Listing 7-3), we are joining data from our source database to data in our staging database using cross-database queries.

10. We included our job Id (lines 4 and 38).

11. Contacts are inheriting security from accounts, so there is no need to set the OwnerId.

12. We are not using record types. This is okay, but we always like to confirm that is correct with our Salesforce BA.

13. We renamed all the columns to match the Salesforce API names.

14. We use a Case statement to build the logic for status (lines 56–59). We question the "odd" status values and are given some business reason for it. So, alrighty then.

15. If we don't have a country name, we set it to United States (line 67).

16. We merge all the address lines into a single field using the trick we learned in Chapter 2 (line 63)

17. We have a few custom fields. You can tell because they end with "__c".

18. We had to configure Salesforce to expose some native fields that are not visible by default (MiddleName, Suffix, and the Optout check boxes).

    Next, we add a task to download all contacts in the system (to a new table: SF_Contact) because we will need it later.

That's it! All that's left is to plug this into our control flow. We add a Sequence container, with an Execute SQL task to truncate SF_Contact, our Success and Error tables. Then a data flow to upsert the data, just like we did for accounts (see Figure 7-12).

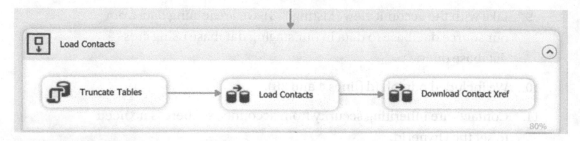

Figure 7-12. *The Load Contact container*

We can double-click the Load Contacts data flow (see Figure 7-13). It's exactly like the account and account parent data flows! Are you noticing the pattern here?!

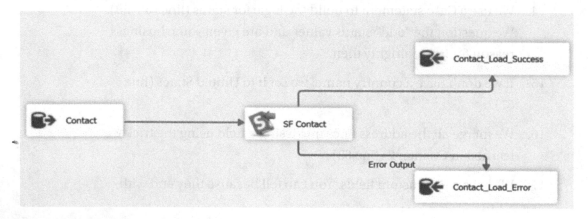

Figure 7-13. *The load contacts data flow*

Account Contact Relation

Salesforces' Account Contact Relation object enables you to associate contacts with multiple accounts.[15] When you create a new contact, and set its account Id, Salesforce creates a record automatically in the Account Contact Relation object for that relationship, and sets the IsDirect check box for the record to True. This record cannot be deleted. If you want to insert additional records, you can, but both the account Id and the contact Id are required. And, after the record's creation, they become read-only.

---

[15]It's not enabled by default and should not be enabled unless you plan on using it, because it introduces overhead. To enable it, see https://help.salesforce.com/ articleView?id=shared_contacts_overview.htm&type=5.

There is no option that allows for reparenting, as you would have on a custom master-detail field (even though they are lookups). Moreover, even if you try to update the AccountId or ContactId fields with the same values that are already in the field, you still get an error.

If you look at the Salesforce documentation for this object,[16] you will see that it supports Upsert. Although this is technically true, in truth Upsert can't be used. If it finds a match on your External Id, it tries to update the record, but it will only work if you don't send a contact or account Id. But, if it's not found, the upsert wants to do an insert, and that will only work if you *do* send a contact and account Id! So, if you use Upsert, one of two things will happen:

1. You don't send account and contact Ids and all your inserts fail because those fields are required.

2. You do send account and contact Ids and all your updates fail because those fields are read-only (when updating).

You only option is to abandon the use of Upsert and push inserts and updates separately, sending only the account and contact Ids when doing inserts. To perform an update, you need the Ids of the existing records.

So, our first step is to download the existing data (into a table called SF_ACR). Remember that Salesforce created these records automatically when we created the contacts. We don't have a Success table with the Ids.

Let's look at the insert view (transformation) code first (Listing 7-6):

Listing 7-6. The Account Contact Relation Transformation View for Insert

```
1.   ALTER View [dbo].[ACR_Insert_Load] as
2.   SELECT
3.        'AC-'+ac.[ACCOUNT_CONTACT_ID] as SC_CRM_ID__c
4.        ,sfa.SalesforceRecordId as AccountID
5.        ,sfc.SalesforceRecordId as ContactId
6.        ,ac.[ASSOCIATION_TYPE] as Roles
```

---

[16]For more information, see https://developer.salesforce.com/docs/atlas.en-us.api.meta/
api/sforce_api_objects_accountcontactrelation.htm.

```
7.            ,ac.[DESCRIPTION] as Notes__c
8.    FROM [SC_CRM].[dbo].[Account_Contact] ac
9.    join [dbo].[SF_Contact] sfc on sfc.SC_CRM_ID__c='Contact-'+ac.
      [CONTACTID]
10.   join [dbo].[SF_Account] sfa on sfa.SC_CRM_ID__c='Company-'+ac.
      ACCOUNTID
11.   Left join Contact_Load_Success cs on cs.SC_CRM_ID__c='Contact-'+ac.
      [CONTACTID]
12.   Left join Account_Load_Success [as] on [as].SC_CRM_ID__c='Company-
      '+ac.ACCOUNTID
13.   Left join SF_ACR sfacr on sfacr.AccountId= sfa.SalesforceRecordID and
      sfacr.ContactId=cs.SalesforceRecordId
14.   where sfacr.SalesforceRecordId is Null
15.   and
16.   (
17.        cs.SalesforceRecordId is not null
18.        or
19.        [as].SalesforceRecordId is not null
20.   )
```

This code is fairly simple, but let's examine it anyhow:

1. Similar to account parent, there is no need for a job Id.

2. We do an inner join to our Contact Success and the Account Success tables as our control, because we want relationships for all accounts and contacts that were created with this batch (lines 8, 9, and 16–20).

3. We do a left join to SF_ACR. If no record is found with a matching account and contact Id, we know we need to create the record (lines 13 and 14).

4. We are setting three fields in addition to the account and contact Ids—SC_CRM Id, Roles, and Notes__c—(lines 3, 6, and 7).

Easy as pie.[17] let's look at the update code (Listing 7-7):

Listing 7-7. The Account Contact Relation Transformation View for Update

```
1.    ALTER View [dbo].[ACR_Update_Load] as
2.    SELECT
3.        sfacr.SalesforceRecordId as ID
4.        ,'AC-'+ac.[ACCOUNT_CONTACT_ID] as SC_CRM_ID__c
5.        ,ac.[ASSOCIATION_TYPE] as Roles
6.        ,ac.[DESCRIPTION] as Notes__c
7.    FROM [SC_CRM].[dbo].[Account_Contact] ac
8.    join [dbo].[SF_Contact] SFC on SFC.SC_CRM_ID__c='Contact-'+ac.
      [CONTACTID]
9.    join [dbo].[SF_Account] SFA on SFA.SC_CRM_ID__c='Company-'+ac.
      ACCOUNTID
10.   join sf_ACR sfacr on sfacr.AccountId= sfa.SalesforceRecordID and
      sfacr.ContactId=SFC.SalesforceRecordId
11.   Left join Contact_Load_Success cs on cs.SC_CRM_ID__c='Contact-'+ac.
      [CONTACTID]
12.   Left join Account_Load_Success [as] on [as].SC_CRM_ID__c='Company-
      '+ac.ACCOUNTID
13.   where
14.   (
15.       cs.SalesforceRecordId is not null
16.       or
17.        [as].SalesforceRecordId is not null
18.   )
```

---

[17]My technical editor (Jarett) took issue with me saying this stuff is easy, and he's right. It's not easy. This is me trying to be encouraging, so I will take this opportunity to repeat what I said at the beginning on this chapter:

"I intentionally picked what I felt was a moderately complex project. I want this to feel like a real-world project with real-world problems, as opposed to an easy, straightforward one. You will have a lot to absorb in a single chapter (I get that), but don't be discouraged if you have to reread this chapter a few times. I could have given you the example we studied in Chapter 3 and left it at that. Technically, it's a full migration, but it's not a realistic scenario. It's overly simplified. So again, if you do not "get" this chapter on your first read, that's okay. I'd rather you understand 65% of a real-world example than 100% of an overly simplified one."

Even simpler, but let's examine it anyhow:

1. We are doing an update, not an upsert, so we need the Salesforce Id as opposed to the SC-CRM Id (lines 3 and 10).

2. Still no need for a job Id.

3. We do an inner join to our Contact Success and Account Success tables as our control, because we want relationships for all accounts and contacts that were created with this batch (lines 11, 12, and 14–18).

4. We do an inner join to SF_ACR. Only records with a matching account and contact Id are returned, plus we have the record Id to use for our update (lines 3 and 10).

5. We don't include the account or contact Id because they are read-only.

Last, we add code to our SSIS package (following the same pattern of Truncate tables, download Xref data then Insert and Update) in a Sequence container (see Figure 7-14).

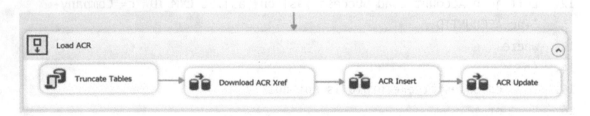

Figure 7-14. *The Account Contact Relation Load Sequence container*

All done! Activities are next!

Tasks and Events (Activities)

Salesforce has two objects for activities: tasks and events. The primary difference between the two are that tasks have things you need to do by, with a due date; whereas events are things you need to do at a specified time, with a start date and an end date.

They both have that same autoarchiving mechanism discussed in Chapter 3,[18] but they are so similar we are only going to walk through tasks; you can infer that we do the exact same thing for events.

Let's get started with the same basic pattern: We create a view for our transformations then upsert the data into the Task object. The code is presented in Listing 7-8:

Listing 7-8. The Task Transformation View

```
1.   Create View [dbo].[Task_Load] as
2.   Select
3.        'Task-'+a.ACTIVITYID  as SC_CRM_ID__c
4.        ,MC.Value as JobID__c
5.        ,Case
6.             when a.Activity_Type ='Email' or a.Activity_Type
                 ='E-Blast'  then 'Email'
7.             when a.Activity_Type ='Meet up' then 'Meeting'
8.             when a.Activity_Type ='Conf. Call' then 'Call'
9.             else 'Other'
10.       end as Type
11.       ,sfc.AccountID as Whatid
12.       ,sfc.SalesforceRecordId as WhoId
13.       ,a.STARTDATE as ActivityDate
14.       ,Replace(a.CATEGORY,',',';') as Category__c
15.       ,'Normal' as Priority
16.       ,a.DURATION*60 as CallDurationInSeconds
17.       ,a.DESCRIPTION as Subject
18.       ,a.NOTES as Description
19.       ,case when a.STARTDATE <GETDATE() then 'Completed' else Null end
            as Status
20.       ,coalesce(sfu.id,sfud.id) as OwnerId
21. from SC_CRM.dbo.ACTIVITY a
```

---

[18]Salesforce archives events automatically that are more than a year old, and does the same for tasks that are more than a year old and are closed.

```
22.  Join Migration_Configuration MC on MC.Name='JobID'
23.  join dbo.[Contact_Load_Success] sfc on sfc.SC_CRM_ID__c='Contact-'+a.
     CONTACTID
24.  left join [Sf_User] sfu on sfu.SC_CRM_ID__c=a.Userid
25.  left join [Sf_User] SFUD on SFUD.SC_CRM_ID__c='Admin'
26.  where a.Activity_Type <>'Conferance'   --- If Activity_Type =
     'Conferance' Then this is an event
```

This stuff is too easy, but let's examine the code anyhow.

1. We are back to doing upserts, so we included an External Id (line 3).

2. We included the job Id (lines 4 and 22).

3. As always, we renamed our columns to match the Salesforce API names.

4. We have a few basic transformations (lines 5-9 and 16).

5. SC-CRM had a multiselect-type category, but it used a comma as a delimiter. We need semicolons, so we replaced them (line 14).

6. We are populating the what Id based off the activity's primary contact. To do this, we simply took that contact's account Id (lines 11 and 23).

7. SC-CRM didn't have a status field, so we calculated one based off the activity date (line 19).

8. We are using the contact success file as our control. We loaded only those activities that are related to contacts that were loaded with this batch (line 23).

9. SC-CRM had a single table for activities. We used the Type field to determine whether the activity is a task or an event and we filtered the data to include tasks only (line 26).

As always, we add the data load code to our SSIS package in a Sequence container, as shown in Figure 7-15. Rinse and repeat for events.

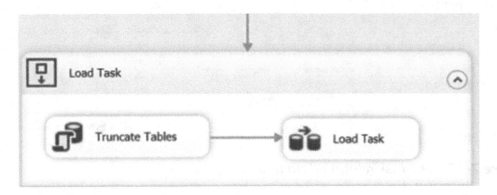

Figure 7-15. *The Task Load Sequence container*

Task and Event Relation

SC-CRM allows for activities to include more than one contact. Salesforce has the TaskRelation and EventRelation objects for this purpose.[19] Remember when we created SC-CRM users as contacts in Salesforce? Because we did that, using task and event relation, Specialty Container can add non-Salesforce user employees to activities (at least as a record that they were included).

Unfortunately, these objects cannot be customized or edited. (You can't edit the record after you create it, but you can delete it and insert a new one.) In addition, when we add the contacts as the who Id on the task or event record, Salesforce creates a relation record automatically. To code this properly, the right thing to do is to download all the relations (task or event), then build our transformation view to include missing records only. But because we are (I am) lazy (and I want to teach you another technique), we are simply going to do an insert and let Salesforce reject the duplicate rows. Our task relation data flow is shown in Figure 7-16.

---

[19]Like AccountContactRelation, the TaskRelation and EventRelation objects are not enabled by default and should not be enabled unless you plan on using them, because their use introduces overhead. To enable them, see https://help.salesforce.com/articleView?id=activities_enable_shared_activities.htm&type=5.

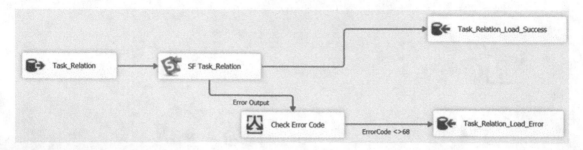

Figure 7-16. *The task relation data flow*

As you can see, it's just like our other data flows, but we added a check on the rows that error-out to determine whether the error code is 68 (duplicate value found). We route all non "68" errors to the error log; the rows that were duplicates simply go nowhere. Sure, they are not in our Success table either; but, meh, we don't need them there because we won't be using the Success table anyhow.

For the sake of comprehensiveness, let's take a look at the transformation view (Listing 7-9):

Listing 7-9. The Task Relation Transformation View

```
1.    Create View [dbo].[Task_Relation] as
2.    SELECT
3.          TS.SalesforceRecordId as TaskID
4.          ,sfc.SalesforceRecordId as RelationID
5.          ,0 as IsWhat
6.    FROM SC_CRM.[dbo].[Activity_Contact] AC
7.    join [dbo].[Task_Load_Success] TS on 'Task-'+ac.ACTIVITYID=ts.SC_CRM_
      ID__c
8.    Join SF_Contact sfc on sfc.SC_CRM_ID__c='Contact-'+ac.CONTACTID
```

All we are doing is joining to the Task Success table as our control and to get the task Id (lines 3 and 7). We are also joining to SF_Contact because we want to include all contacts related to this task, regardless of whether they have been created in this batch.

Again, we create a Sequence container in our SSIS package for modularity (see Figure 7-17).

We do the same for event relation.

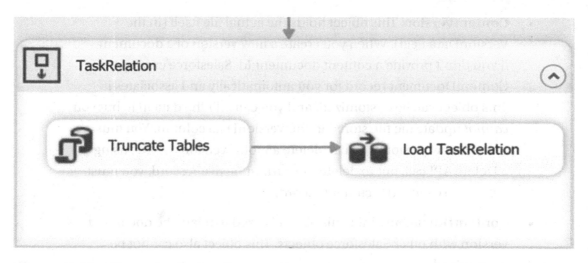

Figure 7-17. *The task relation Sequence container*

Attachments

For attachments, we use Salesforce Content because the Notes and Attachments functionality will be phased out of Salesforce in the coming years. Although Salesforce Content is clearly a step up from the (soon-to-be) legacy Notes and Attachments functionality, that functionality comes with a lot of complexity, especially when trying to work with it via the APIs.

It comes with so much complexity that I seriously considered leaving this section out of the book. But, I decided I would be doing you a disservice if I did. I did water my discussion down a bit. If you will be doing a lot of integration work with Salesforce Content, I advise you to do additional research prior to doing so. Although the approach used here works, it is not one that scales well.

Figure 7-18 shows a limited ERD of the content objects. It includes only those objects we need for our migration. The three objects are as follows:

- **ContentDocument:** This is the Master Content table. It holds data such as the file name, description, and Id of the current version. This object cannot be customized. You cannot create (or delete) records in it directly.

- **ContentVersion:** This object holds the actual file itself (in the VersionData field). When you create a new version of a document, if you don't provide a content document Id, Salesforce creates the ContentDocument record for you automatically and associates it. This object can be customized, and you can edit the data in it, but you *cannot* update the file stored in the VersionData column. You must insert a new version. You can delete all "old" version records using a Delete API call, but to delete the current "active" record, you must delete the ContentDocument record.

- **ContentDocumentLink:** This object is used to relate the document version with other Salesforce objects. This object also cannot be customized.

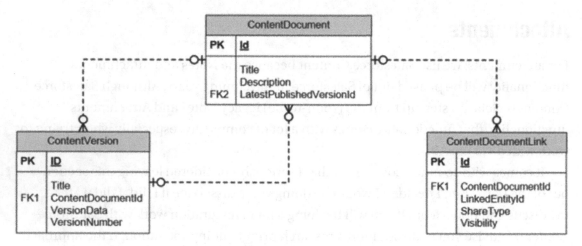

Figure 7-18. *The content-limited ERD*

For our data migration, we have a problem. We can't upsert the current records because we can't update the file data in ContentVersion. So, we do the following:

1. Download the existing ContentVersion data. (ContentVersion is the only object of the three that can be customized, so it's the only place we can store an External Id).

2. Thankfully ContentVersion has its content document Id stored in it, so we don't have to download ContentDocument Object as well.

3. For documents that already exist in Salesforce that we want
    to update we: Insert a second version of the document
    into ContentVersion with the updated document (into
    the VersionData field). But, we can't use the same External
    Id; it's enforced as unique! So, we have to pre- or postfix the
    External Id with something. The new upload is automatically set
    as the LatestPublishedVersion on ContentDocument. For
    documents that don't exist in Salesforce we simply insert them
    into ContentVersion.

4. We then delete the old ContentVersion records if we don't
    need them and want to clear up space, or change the External
    Ids so we can use them on the new ContentVersion records we
    created in step 3. Now that we no longer have a uniqness issue
    with the External Ids we can go back and update the External Ids
    for the ContentVersion records we uploaded in step 3.

5. Lastly, we upload new ContentDocumentLinks. We can't use
    an upsert, because this object cannot be customized (we can't
    add an External Id). So, we do the same cheat we did with the
    TaskRelation object and insert all records while discarding
    duplicate errors.

If this was an integration, we would have no choice but to code a process
similar to what I just described. But, because this is a migration, we are just going to
perform the much simpler process of wipeing out all files that were part of this batch and
then reload them (following the Wipe and Load pattern we will discuss in Chapter 9).
Our process is reflected in our Sequence container (see Figure 7-19).

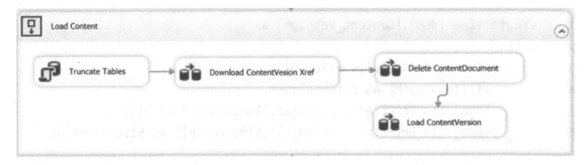

Figure 7-19. *The load content Sequence container*

As always, we start with truncating the temporary storage tables so that we can run the container as a module. Next, we download the existing content version data.[20] It contains the job Id, the SC-CRM Id, and the content document Id, so it's perfect to be used to drive our deletes. Because we can't delete "active" content versions directly, we delete ContentDocuments, and that delete cascades down to both ContentVersion and ContentDocumentLink. After the delete is done, we can reload all the ContentVersion records from this batch, and the ContentDocument records are created automatically.

Let's first look at the SQL used for the deletion (see Listing 7-10):

Listing 7-10. The Content Document Deletion View

```
1.    Create  View [dbo].[Content_Document_Delete] as
2.    SELECT distinct
3.        sfcv.ContentDocumentId as ID
4.    FROM [SC_CRM].[dbo].[Activity_Files] af
5.    join [dbo].[SF_Content_Version] sfcv on sfcv.[SC_CRM_ID__c]='File-
      '+af.[Activity_FilesID]
6.    Join Migration_Configuration MC on MC.Name='JobID' and mc.Value=sfcv.
      JobID__c
```

As you can see (Listing 7-10), we are selecting ContentDocumentID from the ContentVersion staging table because we are deleting ContentDocument records. The Id is the only field needed to push a delete to Salesforce. We keep our control in place, so we only delete records that were created with this batch (line 6). This is especially important because we are onboarding people in waves. If we miss including the control, we will accidentally delete the production data from previous waves!

Let's take a look at the ContentVersion transformation code (Listing 7-11):

Listing 7-11. The ContentVersion Transformation View

```
1.    Create View [dbo].[Content_Version] as
2.    SELECT
3.        'File-'+af.[Activity_FilesID] as SC_CRM_ID__c
4.        ,af.[Imagepath] AS PathOnClient
5.        ,[dbo].[fn_GetFileFromPath](af.[Imagepath]) AS Title
6.        ,[dbo].[fn_GetFileExtention](af.[Imagepath]) as FileExtension
```

---

[20]Of course, if this is the first time we are running the code, no data are returned.

```
7.        ,af.[FileData] as VersionData
8.        --,[dbo].[Fn_Base64Encode]([VersionData]) as [VersionData64]
9.    FROM [SC_CRM].[dbo].[Activity_Files] af
10.   join [dbo].[Task_Load_Success] sfts on sfts.[SC_CRM_ID__c]='Task-'+af.
      ACTIVITYID
```

As you can see (Listing 7-11), SC-CRM stores files as a blob in the database
(line 7), but also stores a file path (line 4) (Why? Who knows? I didn't write the thing! But
Salesforce does the same thing.) Let's examine the code further. Notice the following:

1. To load file data to Salesforce, you need to base64 encode[21] the
   binary data of the file. We are not base64 encoding the file binary
   data (line 7), because the Kingsway adaptor does it for you. I didn't
   realize this at first and used my own UDF to encode it (line 8), but
   then commented-out that line. (This UDF is included in Chapter 12,
   in case you are using a tool that does not have this feature.)

2. We are only loading file attachments related to activities that were
   loaded with this batch, so we use the Task Success table as our
   control (line 10).

3. We have UDFs to get the file name and extension from the full
   path (lines 5 and 6). (These UDFs are included in Chapter 12.)

We still need to load ContentDocumentLink. As said previously, we are going to
use the same trick that we did with TaskRelation, and let the "duplicate" rows error-out
without being logged (except this time we check for error code 98 as opposed to 68).

Figure 7-20 shows the Sequence container; Figure 7-21 shows the data flow.

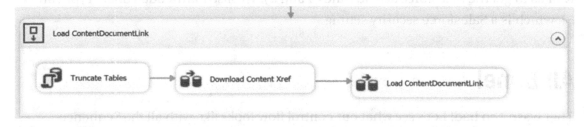

Figure 7-20. *The load ContentDocumentLink Sequence container*

---

[21]For more information on base64 encoding, see `https://stackoverflow.com/`
`questions/201479/what-is-base-64-encoding-used-for`.

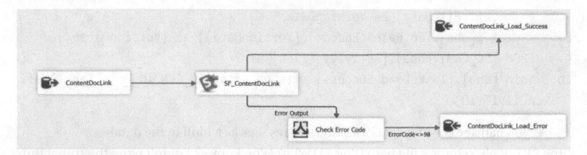

Figure 7-21. *The load ContentDocumentLink data flow*

Let's examine the ContentDocumentLink transformation code in Listing 7-12:

Listing 7-12. The ContentDocumentLink Transformation View

```
1.    ALTER view [dbo].[ContentDocumentLink] as
2.    Select
3.          sfcv.ContentDocumentId
4.          ,tls.SalesforceRecordId as linkedEntityID
5.          ,'I' as ShareType -- I=Inferred permission
6.    from  [dbo].[SF_Content_Version] sfcv
7.    Join  [SC_CRM].[dbo].[Activity_Files] af on 'File-'+af.[Activity_
      FilesID]=sfcv.SC_CRM_ID__c
8.    Join  [dbo].[Task_Load_Success] tls on tls.SC_CRM_ID__c='Task-'+af.
      ACTIVITYID
```

We had to download ContentVersion to get the content document Id (see our Sequence container in Figure 7-21), and we use our Task Success tables as our control as well as to get the Salesforce task Id (lines 4 and 8). We also hard-coded ShareType (line 5), which is a Salesforce security setting.

All Done!

That wasn't so bad! Let's see what our control flow looks like with all the Sequence containers wired together. (I collapsed them for ease of viewing) See Figure 7-22.

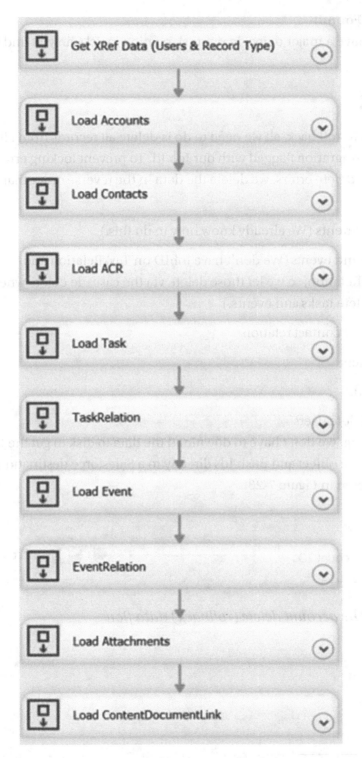

Figure 7-22. *All our Sequence containers wired together in our control flow*

A Defect Is Found!

Oh no! We have a major defect in our task relation logic! Can you find it?[22]

Roll Back

In case we want to roll back, all we need to do is delete all records from all objects included in our migration flagged with our Job Id. To prevent locking errors and too many cascading delete errors, we delete the data in the reverse order that we created them:

1. Attachments (We already know how to do this.)

2. Tasks and events (We don't have JobID on TaskRelation and EventRelation, so we let those delete via the cascade delete when we delete tasks and events.)

3. Account contact relation

4. Contacts

5. Accounts

We do not delete users.

When deleting, we don't have to download the data to disk to get the Ids. We can use a Salesforce source object and push Ids directly to a Salesforce destination object in our data flow, as shown in Figure 7-23.

Figure 7-23. *The account delete (rollback) data flow*

---

[22]No? See the third footnote of Chapter 8.

We want to delete only those records flagged with our job Id. We do this by pulling only those records in our "Get" step that meet this criterion. We do this by adding a "where" clause to the SOQL that pulls the data (see Figure 7-24).

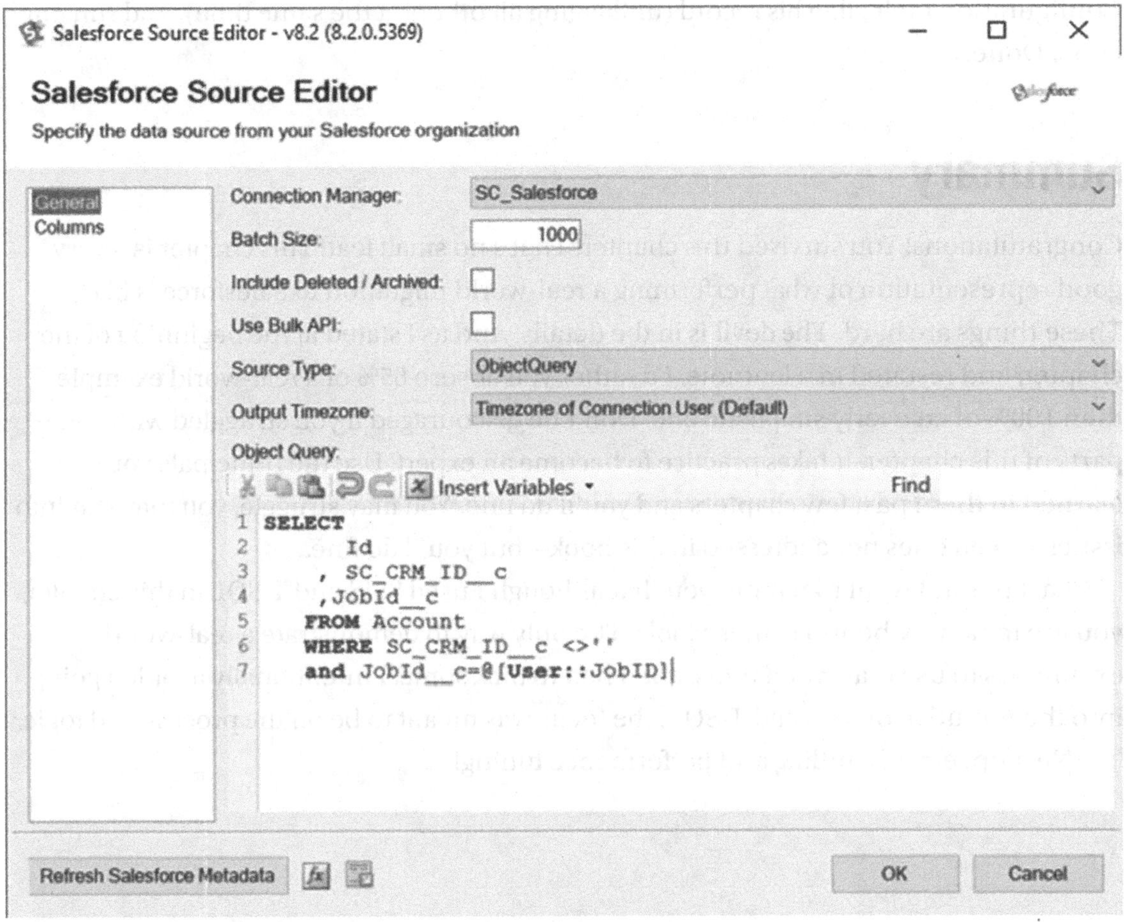

Figure 7-24. *Kingsway Salesforce source using SOQL with a "where" clause*

Note that for added protection, we also only delete those records that have an SC-CRM Id—in other words, only those records that originated from SC-CRM. Also note that we are using a configuration value for the job Id, building our SOQL dynamically.

One Month Later . . .

The VP of Sales tells us he continued to use SC-CRM after we migrated his data and asks us to redo it. Everyone else is using Salesforce. We don't get angry. We simply go to our Configuration table, flag his record (unflagging all others at the same time), and run our code. Done.

Summary

Congratulations! You survived this chapter! That's no small feat! This chapter is a very good representation of what performing a real-world migration to Salesforce is like. These things are hard. The devil is in the details. And as I stated at the beginning of the chapter, and restated in a footnote, I'd rather you absorb 65% of a real-world example then 100% of an overly simplistic one. Don't be discouraged if you struggled with some parts of this chapter. It takes practice to become an expert. Use the principals you learned in these past few chapters and you'll do fine. You may struggle, you may run into issues—even ones not addressed in this book—but you'll do fine.

Last point: I want to remind you that although I used SSIS and T-SQL in this chapter, you are in no way bound to these tools. The only way to demonstrate a real-world example is to use real-world tools, and I had to pick some. I intentionally avoided going into the minutiae of SSIS and T-SQL; the focus was meant to be on the process and logic.

Next up: error handling and performance tuning!

CHAPTER 8

Error Handling and Performance Tuning

Wow! How much fun was that last chapter?! I'm sure you have a ton of questions, but unfortunately you will have to wait until Chapter 13 (which deals with frequently asked questions) to have them answered. I tried to think of every question you could possibly ask, but there is no way that I could possibly anticipate even half of them (sorry). The good news is that if your questions are about error handling or performance tuning, then this is the chapter you are looking for! A lot of the content in this chapter has been covered in pieces throughout out the previous seven chapters, but I thought it was important to centralize this information so you can read through it with a focus specifically on error handling and performance. So, this chapter is a bit of a review. Let's get started.

Two Categories of Errors

There are two basic categories (or levels) of errors: job-level errors and row-level errors. Job-level errors are when the entire job fails for some reason. Row-level errors are errors returned from the Salesforce API stating that an action has failed for a particular row.

Job-level errors

Job level errors occur because of some environmental change, such as a network outage, Internet connectivity issues, or database or Salesforce schema changes. The job fails and stops executing the moment the error occurs. The error message for job-level errors should be self-explanatory and is likely thrown from your middleware or ETL tool rather than from Salesforce.

169

© David Masri 2019
D. Masri, *Developing Data Migrations and Integrations with Salesforce*,
https://doi.org/10.1007/978-1-4842-4209-4_8

For data migrations, we monitor the job in real time and we are generally not concerned with handing off support to someone else, so we can get away with not coding anything special to handle job-level errors. We just intervene if one occurs. Keep in mind that we will perform the production data migration almost immediately after we wrap up the UAT phase, and we will probably be running it from our development environment, so we should not have any issues when performing the production run. If we see environment stability issues during our testing rounds and are concerned that the production run won't run smoothly, we should either fix the environment or move to a more stable one.

For data integrations, we want to ensure that our code is configured to log all job-level errors properly and send out an alert.[1] The logs must contain enough information for you or the support technician to diagnose the issue. Our integrations should run for months without a job-level failure, and because our code is self-repairing, all that should need to be done in the case of failure is to restart the job after we resolve the underlying environment issue.

There are three primary causes of job-level failures:

1. **Connectivity issues:** The job can't connect to the source database, the Internet is down, or the job can't connect to Salesforce because the user password expired (or something like that).[2] Most cloud-based ETL/middleware tools have some sort of agent that needs to be installed inside a local network to facilitate connectivity to local resources (local database or file share, for example). Connectivity issues between the agent and the local resource or the cloud-based middleware is very common, particularly during the initial setup.

---

[1]You should log all job runs with proper diagnostic information regardless of whether the job fails. This information will come in handy later. For example, suppose that one day you notice the job is taking longer than normal to finish. You can go through the logs and look at the historical runtime data. When did the slowdown start? Was it on a particular day? Or has there been a slow degradation of performance?

[2]For Salesforce integrations, I like to use a dedicated Salesforce service user account with its password set to never expire. Check your client's IT security policies.

2. **Source database schema change:** A table or field (or stored procedure or UDF or any database object) in the source database no longer exists, so the database throws an error when the job tries to use (or reference) that table or field.[3]

3. **A Salesforce schema change:** A field or object was dropped from Salesforce (or the service user lost access rights to it), so the job fails when the job tries to use (or reference) that object or field.

Note that most of these errors are caused by lack of planning and could be prevented, although you can't really plan for connectivity issues/network outages. Also note that for schema changes, the right thing to do is to analyze and understand why those changes were made, then determine whether the code should be updated to reflect the new reality, as opposed to rolling back the changes and rerunning the jobs.

Row-level Errors

As we did in Chapter 7, all row-level errors should be logged to individual object error Log tables so that we can have all supporting data alongside the error messages.

With data migrations, we truncate the error log tables at the start of every module because we are using them primarily to debug and improve our code. In addition, for a production run, we should fix all errors before moving on to the next module.

For data integrations, we should still be truncating our error logs at the start of each module, because a properly coded integration detects which updates are needed and pushes only those updates.[4] So, anything that errored-out during a job run is retried automatically during on the next run. In this way, the error logs always have a distinct list of all current errors, and nothing else. If, for whatever reason, we can't truncate the error log tables with each run, we should include columns for record creation date and job Id, so at least we know when (the data and with which job run) the errors were logged.

---

[3]This is the third footnote in Chapter 7. When we loaded TaskRelation records we used the Task Success table rather than download all tasks from Salesforce. So, we won't add contacts that were loaded with this batch to tasks that where created from previous batches. What's crazy is that we examined this exact issue several times, but with regard to adding contacts that were created with previous batches. It goes to show just how easily something like this can slip through the cracks. We really need to be diligent with our code.

[4]We look at how to do this in Chapters 9 and 10, which covers data integration patterns.

Someone (I hope) is responsible for reviewing the error logs and taking appropriate action when errors are found. It's not very efficient to have this individual review ten different error log tables. So, to make their life easier, we can create a single view that "unions" the error log tables together. Of course, we can only include columns that are common to all tables (or derived columns, such as the object name based on the table in which the error was logged). So, our error log view will contain things like Salesforce object name, Salesforce Id or External Id, error code, and error message. The person reviewing the logs can always reference the originating tables if needed.

The primary causes (or most common) types of row-level errors we will encounter include the following:

- Salesforce validation errors

- Salesforce code errors

- Governor limit errors

- Record locking errors

Salesforce Validation Errors

Salesforce validation errors include errors caused by violating custom field validation rules, not populating required fields, pushing invalid data types, or trying to set invalid values for restricted picklists.

For these types of errors, we should put in transformation code whenever possible so that they don't occur in the future. Of course, when doing our initial data analysis and during QA testing, these types of errors should surface, but when we are dealing with integrations, it's always possible that new values get added to the source system or new validation rules get added to Salesforce. When coming across such an error, the individual who is monitoring the error logs has two options: either fix the data in the source (this is the best option if it's really a bad data issue, such as an invalid e-mail address) or work with us to implement new transformation rules. After go-live, we will have to deal with these types of errors on a case-by-case basis.

Salesforce Code Errors

Salesforce code errors are errors thrown by workflows, Process Builder, triggers, and other Salesforce code that runs automatically when we push updates.

When we insert or update data into Salesforce, it can trigger a wide range of things (Validation Rules, Workflows, Process Builders, Triggers etc.). If you are a Salesforce developer, you are expected to know what these things are and the order in which they run.[5] Each of these "things" can potentially throw an error. When I refer to Salesforce "code" throwing an error, I am referring to any one of these things, even though Salesforce would take offense at me calling it code, because they are technically built with clicks ("Clicks not code!"). I'm lumping all of these things into the a single category of "code" for brevity purposes, so hopefully they will forgive me.

It's relatively rare that we come across these types of issues in production. If we do, it means that someone made a Salesforce code change and did not regression test the new code with an integration run (and maybe we should push for a review of the company's or our client's code release policies[6]).

When Salesforce throws an error from code (again, anything in Salesforce, not just Apex code) that ran because of an action (a data API call), we should work with the developer to understand what that code is doing and why. Then we can determine whether we need to adjust the data we are sending with our API call or whether the Salesforce code needs to be modified to handle our use case. If the Salesforce code does not need to be run at all for our data load, but does because that's how it was coded, we should consider having the Salesforce developer modify the Salesforce code so that the code is run only when necessary, by performing some preliminary check.

For data migrations, we always have the option of turning off the offending Salesforce code (for the duration of the migration) and adding code to our migration to perform whatever the Salesforce code would have done.

For integrations, if our integration code is the only thing that modifies data in such a way that triggers the Salesforce code, then we may want to consider moving this logic into the integration code permanently.

---

[5]For more information, see https://developer.salesforce.com/docs/atlas.en-us.apexcode.meta/apexcode/apex_triggers_order_of_execution.htm.

[6]Many companies, even ones with mature change release policies and procedures, have not yet caught up to the cloud revolution and have no policies on how to release code to cloud-based systems. In all fairness, it's a tough issue. How can you hire a new Salesforce administrator then tie their hands and tell them, "No 'coding.' Oh! And you can't so much as create a new page layout without running it through IT, an architecture review board, and a regression test of the entire system, followed by the creation of a release document. Don't even think about it!" This kind of release process is simply not in the "Salesforce spirit", I get it. But a line has to be drawn somewhere, and many organizations are struggling with this.

Governor Limit Errors

Governor limit errors occur when we exceed some Salesforce limit—for example, we run out of storage space,[7] we upload a file larger than 25MB, or we trigger too many cascading deletes.

If we are exceeding execution[8] or API call[9] limits, we should refactor our code to use less calls (if possible). For data storage limit issues, we either need to buy more space or reengineer our data model to use less[10] (see Chapter 2).

Record Locking Errors

We discussed record locking errors quite a bit in Chapters 2 and 3.[11] They occur when Salesforce can't obtain a lock on a record because it's in use, so it can't update it. Ninety-five percent of the time, our own integration code will cause self-contention as opposed to some other user locking the record on us (because we are plowing too many conflicting updates at once, in an effort to improve performance). Keep in mind that it could also be Salesforce code that is triggered by our updates that require the locks, and then, not getting them, ultimately fail. Then, that error bubbles up and our updates fail.

Suppose we want to update 10,000 contacts in Salesforce. We configure our ETL to push the updates in batches of 200, serially, using the SOAP API. Per batch, Salesforce will do the following:

1. Lock the 200 contacts (in the batch).

2. Lock the parent accounts of those contacts.

---

[7]Remember, this only happens in sandboxes. Salesforce won't "break" a production org because of disk space.

[8]For more information, see https://developer.salesforce.com/docs/atlas.en-us.apexcode. meta/apexcode/apex_gov_limits.htm.

[9]For more information, see https://developer.salesforce.com/docs/atlas.en-us. salesforce_app_limits_cheatsheet.meta/salesforce_app_limits_cheatsheet/salesforce_ app_limits_platform_api.htm.

[10]For more information, see https://help.salesforce.com/articleView?id=admin_ monitorresources.htm&type=5.

[11]Salesforce also has a nifty Record Locking Cheat Sheet. See https://developer.salesforce. com/blogs/engineering/2014/07/record-locking-cheat-sheet.html.

3. Build a set of transactions to process, limiting the number of times it needs to lock the same record. So, in our case, it would group the contacts by those that share the same parent account and then process them as a single transaction.

4. If it can't obtain a lock on the parent account record, the whole transaction fails and an error is issued for each contact in the transaction.

5. If it can lock the parent account, but not one of the contacts in the transaction, it fails for that one contact only.

Continuing with the same example, let's suppose we want to send 10,000 contact records for update and our ETL tool will break our 10,000-row dataset into batches of 200 records each, based on the order of the records in the dataset. If we don't order our data, we increase the number of locks taken, and with it the potential for record locking issues. The next example demonstrates why.

Consider what would happen if we decide to send our 10,000-record dataset using the Bulk API and set it to process batches in parallel. Salesforce takes those 10,000 records, breaks them up into batches of 200 (server side), and processes them five batches at a time (in parallel).[12]

We sent the data unordered. We have four contacts that belong to the same parent account in the dataset. Because they are unordered, the four contacts each land in a different batch, and because we are running things in parallel, Salesforce tries to lock the parent account four times at once, by four different processes. None can get the lock, and all four fail.

What can we do about this? The easiest thing to do is to switch to serial processing, so only one batch is processed at a time, but that affects performance negatively and we don't want that. Our other option is to sort the contacts by parent account. In this way, all the contacts that belong to the same account have a high likelihood of being in the same batch, reducing the lock potential.

To be clear, I'm not saying that if we don't sort our data we will always get a locking issue. (Remember, Salesforce tries and gets the lock up to ten times.) I'm just saying it increases the likelihood of it happening. I'm also saying that locking is a time-intensive

---

[12]Although you can submit 10,000 records with a single API call, and Salesforce reports on those 10,000 records as a single job on the Monitor Bulk Jobs page, under the covers it's processing records in batches of 200.

process, and the retries are time intensive; so, even if we get no errors, a sorted load will perform better than an unsorted one. Even if we get no locking conflicts and Salesforce can lock the account record every time it needs to, in our example the unsorted list will lock the account record four times,[13] but our sorted load will most likely take only one lock—two, at a maximum. (Most likely, all four contacts will be in the same batch, but if they happen to be right at the end of the batch, some can spill over into the next.)

If we have a junction object, it has two parents, and we can only sort by one! So, what do we do? There's not much we can do, except to sort by the one most likely to cause locking issues based on our knowledge of what custom Salesforce code will run when pushing the updates. Barring that, as a general guideline, we can do the following:

1. Sort by Master-Detail fields before lookups.

2. For lookups, sort required lookups before nonrequired ones.

3. For nonrequired lookups, sort ones set to "Don't allow deletion of the lookup record that's part of a lookup relationship" before ones set to "Clear the value of this field. You can't choose this option if you make this field required" (see Figure 8-1).

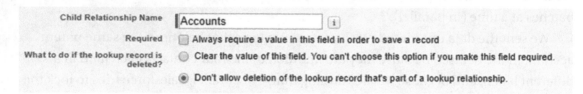

Figure 8-1. *Lookup options that affect locking and performance*

It's important to know that, when we select "Clear the value of this field. You can't choose this option if you make this field required.", updates to that record will *not* lock the parent. Unfortunately, this is not the default selection, so our Salesforce SA (or administrator or developer) may have left the default selection ("Don't allow deletion . . ") simply because they had no business rules or reason to change it. We should work with our Salesforce development team to determine whether this setting can be changed and, if so, change it to "Clear the value of this field . . . ."

---

[13]And presumably update it four times, if my inverted index theory I mentioned in Chapter 2 is correct. Regardless, Salesforce must be updating something on the account record; otherwise, why would it need to lock it?

If you go back to Chapter 7, you will see that I didn't sort any of my queries. This is because I fall into the "Only 'performance-tune' when needed" camp. First you focus on getting the business/programmatic logic right, then performance-tune only if needed, and in our case, there was no need. Also, because it's a migration as opposed to an integration, we can plan easily around minor performance issues. You can read all about the premature optimization debate online.[14]

On occasion, you will have a parent record that has thousands of child records. This situation, as you can imagine, can cause locking problems. Salesforce calls this "lookup skew." The only real way to resolve lookup skew is to work with your Salesforce team to reengineer the data model (and hence a discussion of this topic is outside the scope of this book). Salesforce has a great article on managing lookup skew on the developer site.[15]

Also note that, for performance reasons, as a best practice, Salesforce recommends not having more than 10,000 child records per master-detail relationship.[16]

"Bulkifying" Triggers

Salesforce triggers need to be coded in such a way as to be able to process batches of data. This process is referred to as "bulkifying" the trigger.[17] If a Salesforce trigger is not properly bulkified, anytime we push a batch with more than one record, it will fail. In addition, with bulkified triggers, if one record fails, the entire batch may fail with an obscure error message.

Suppose we have a trigger on the Contact object that is properly bulkified. The trigger takes all the contacts in a batch, groups them by account, does some math to calculate a data point, and then does a single update to the Account record. If one of the contact updates fails (because of an invalid e-mail address or some validation rule), the entire batch fails with some generic error.

---

[14]For more information, see https://www.google.com/search?q=premature+performance+opti mization+debate.

[15]For more information, see https://developer.salesforce.com/blogs/engineering/2013/04/ managing-lookup-skew-to-avoid-record-lock-exceptions.html.

[16]For more information, see https://help.salesforce.com/articleView?id=relationships_ considerations.htm&type=5.

[17]For more information, see https://developer.salesforce.com/page/ Best_Practice%3A_Bulkify_Your_Code.

This is a nightmare for the people who monitor the row-level error logs! They have 200 records in the error log and no idea which record is the bad one or what is wrong with it! In these cases, I recommend that you process the code twice—once normally, catch the errors, then reprocess only the errors with a batch size of one. In this way, we get the good performance of using large batch sizes, and at the same time only records with real errors are not processed and are logged with a proper error message, making it easy to identify and fix the issues.

Performance Tuning

Great news! You already know all you need to know about Salesforce performance tuning. Why is that? Because when it comes to performance tuning Salesforce data migrations and integrations, everything you do to avoid locking errors is exactly what you do to performance-tune your code! But, to make things extra simple for you, here is a checklist of things you should do/check when trying to speed up your code:

1. Don't push unnecessary updates. This strategy will, by far, give you the biggest bang for your time. Don't simply push all your data because that was the easiest to code. Also, when downloading cross-reference data from Salesforce, use a "where" clause to download only those records that you need, and download only those fields that you need.

2. Performance-tune your data transformation code using traditional performance-tuning techniques.

3. Never use "remote lookups." Some ETL tools allow you to do a remote lookup to get related data as part of a dataflow/ETL transformation. Often, these things run one record at a time, making a web service callout for each record checking for related data. You are much better off downloading the entire lookup object and doing the joins locally (just as we did in Chapter 7).

4. For integrations, if your integration code is the only thing that modifies data in such a way that it triggers a specific piece of Salesforce code, you may want to consider moving that logic out of Salesforce and into the integration code permanently, or into a Salesforce batch process that runs after your integration completes.

5. The Bulk API can only parallelize API batches to a single object. You can parallelize across different objects in your ETL code. Take advantage of this fact and always download cross-reference data in parallel.[18] When pushing updates, you can parallelize objects that don't have common parents with no risk of lock contention.

6. Sort your datasets as described earlier.

7. Start with the Bulk API and run things in parallel.

    a. If you are getting too many locking errors, use the Bulk API in serial mode.

    b. If you are still having issues, switch to using the SOAP API and a batch size of 200. Then, reduce the batch size slowly until the code runs without locking errors. If it's still not performing well enough, you'll have to work with your Salesforce developer to optimize their code (or move it out into your code).

8. If you are getting good performance but are getting some locking errors, consider leaving the code as is, catching the errors, then reprocessing just the errors at a smaller batch size. This technique often performs better than trying to get the entire dataset to process in one go without error. (It must be automated!)

9. When possible, configure your lookups to "Clear the value of this field."

---

[18]Remember that a single Salesforce user can only have ten active API queries running at once, so there are limits to how much you can run in parallel in your ETL package.

That's It!

Like most systems, performance-tuning data loads in Salesforce is somewhat of an art. There is some good information online,[19] but for the most part, if you follow the guidelines I've presented here, you are 85% of the way there and can spend most of your time performance-tuning your transformation code and working with your Salesforce development team.

---

[19]For more information, see https://developer.salesforce.com/page/The_Salesforce_Bulk_ API_-_Maximizing_Parallelism_and_Throughput_Performance_When_Integrating_or_ Loading_Large_Data_Volumes. Also see https://resources.docs.salesforce.com/sfdc/pdf/ salesforce_large_data_volumes_bp.pdf.

CHAPTER 9

Data Synchronization Patterns

Data synchronization jobs are by far the most common type of integration job,[1] during which we take data from one or more systems and move it into another (keeping the data in sync)—in our case, Salesforce. Data can flow from one system to another, and back. Sometimes this causes data conflicts that must be dealt with. Getting synchronizations working right can be tricky, particularly when there are heavy transformations and/or summarizations involved.

In this chapter, we study various data synchronization patterns and the pros and cons of each. Keep in mind that these are *object*-level patterns, not *job*-level patterns. You can mix patterns within a synchronization job. For example, you may perform an incremental update on the Contact object, but a wipe and load on the (custom) Contact Transactions object, all with in the same job. A synchronization job uses one or more of these patterns and synchronizes one or more object. Also, when I say *object* level, I don't even mean the whole object; it can be a subset of records, a subset of fields, or both.

Before we dive into the patterns, let's cover a few key concepts.

---

[1]In general, synchronization jobs are for integrations as opposed to migrations because the need for data synchronization is usually required to be ongoing. This is not to say we can't use these patterns for migrations when we want to phase out a system (as opposed to turning it off one day) and need to keep data in sync until the legacy system is fully phased out. In addition, if we are migrating large amounts of data and are concerned about the time needed for the migration, we can use one of the incremental patterns to perform the migration in parts. In this way, we only have to load a delta when we are ready to go live.

181

© David Masri 2019
D. Masri, *Developing Data Migrations and Integrations with Salesforce*,
https://doi.org/10.1007/978-1-4842-4209-4_9

Three Types of Data Synchronization

There are three basic types of synchronization:

- Unidirectional
- Bidirectional
- Two-way unidirectional

Unidirectional Synchronization

Unidirectional syncs are a one-way synchronization during which data flow from a source system to a target system. The source system is referred to as the *master* system because it "owns" the data. The goal is to bring the target system up to date with the latest data from the source system. In general, you don't allow updates to the target system on any field owned by the master system. I say "in general" because there are instances in which there is a requirement to allow users to override the data in the target system, not push back that data to the source, and not have it overwritten by the source data the next time the synchronization job runs.[2]

Bidirectional Synchronization

Bidirectional synchronizations are used when you need to keep data in sync between two systems and allow for users to update the same piece of data in both systems. For example, let's say we want to allow users to update a company's shipping address in the enterprise resource planning (ERP) system and in Salesforce, and we want the update to be reflected in the other system regardless of in which system the update was made. In this, case both systems are considered to be the source and the target.

I tend to recommend that bidirectional syncs be avoided whenever possible because of the complexities of dealing with update conflicts. You may think that a general rule of "the

---

[2]We examine how to handle this use case in Chapter 13.

last system updated wins" will work, but it's usually not that simple. We need to come up with rules on how to manage the data when it's updated in both systems simultaneously.[3]

In lieu of a bidirectional sync, I recommend you make two fields (or sets of fields) in Salesforce. Going back to our example, we would create two sets of fields: one for the ERP shipping address and one for the Salesforce shipping address, and then either have a trigger (or a workflow) that has rules to populate the native Salesforce shipping address fields or a formula that calculates it based on some set of conflict resolution rules. This practice essentially turns your bidirectional sync into a two-way unidirectional sync, eliminating the risk of data loss.

Two-way Unidirectional Synchronization

A two-way unidirectional sync is when you sync the same object in both directions, but each system syncs only some fields or records where there is no overlap. This lack of overlap means there can't be any data conflicts, so you can just sync system A to system B, then system B to system A with no risk of data loss. It really is just two unidirectional syncs. It's important to understand that this is fundamentally different than a bidirectional sync. With bidirectional syncs, you must deal with data conflicts; with two-way unidirectional syncs, you don't. The terminology is often confused. People say "bidirectional" when they mean "two-way unidirectional." What's important is always to ask for clarification. Ask specifically if there is the potential for data conflicts and, if so, be sure to put in rules to handle them. Here are the two most common two-way unidirectional use cases:

1. Prospect conversion is the first case. From the time a lead is created, up until a person (or company) places an order, Salesforce owns the Prospect record. After an order is placed, the prospect is converted into a customer and the ERP (or order processing system) takes ownership of the record. This is clearly a two-way unidirectional sync, because we have a clear line of which system owns which records at any given time, and there is never joint ownership of any record.

---

[3]In this case, "simultaneously" does not mean at the same moment; it means between job runs. Let's say your sync job runs once every four hours. If both systems are updated in that same time window, the updates are considered to have been done simultaneously. Keep in mind that the user who made the second update never saw the new data entered. His update was made while looking at "old" data, because the updates existed only in the first system at the time the second system was updated. This situation is called an *uninformed update*.

2. In the second case, Salesforce owns some key information about an object, but data from some other system need to be surfaced in Salesforce, so a designated set of fields is updated on a regular basis from that other system. For example, the ERP system owns and pushes updates for billing addresses (which is made read-only in Salesforce), but mailing addresses are owned and maintained in Salesforce and get pushed to the ERP (where they are read-only). Again, a clear line is drawn to which system owns which fields, and there is never any joint ownership of any field.

Synchronization Patterns

We are going to walk through six data synchronization patterns together. You should choose a pattern or patterns based on your use case. Again, keep in mind that the patterns are to be used at the object level. It's perfectly fine to use a different pattern for every object you are syncing. While reading the following, it may seem like they are all patterned as unidirectional. They are not. For bidirectional syncs, all the conflict resolution rules should be coded into the transformation layer. After you have that layer in place, you can reverse the direction and the sync becomes bidirectional. So, to summarize:

- The patterns look unidirectional, but that's only because to code bidirectional or two-way unidirectional, you simply swap the source and target, and run a sync in the other direction.

- For bidirectional syncs, all conflict resolution code is written into the transformation layer.

Because this is a Salesforce book, and writing to Salesforce is much more complex than reading from it (and I have no way of knowing what your source systems are), all the patterns here are assumed to be from some source to Salesforce. It should not be difficult to imagine using these patterns in the other direction or even between two non-Salesforce systems. Second, each of these patterns builds on the previous pattern, but grows a bit in complexity, so you should read/study these patterns in order. There is also a great deal of value in understanding how each pattern evolves naturally to the next, solving issues with the previous patterns.

There are six patterns in total. The first three are classified as full-load patterns; the second three are incremental or differential patterns. Full loads always synchronize every record from the source system to the target with every run, regardless of whether they changed . Incremental and differential patterns only synchronize records that have been updated since the last job run, but differ in the mechanism used to identify changed records.

Pattern 1: Basic Upsert-No Delete

The Basic Upsert-No Delete pattern is the simplest of all integration patterns. You simply transform your source data to match the Salesforce object structure you will be loading, then upsert the data into it. You never delete data from Salesforce. So, if a record gets deleted in the source system, it remains in Salesforce. This is the most common pattern used for data migrations and is the pattern we used repeatedly in Chapter 7 (see Figure 9-1).

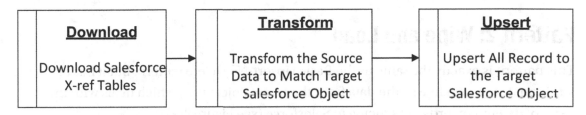

Figure 9-1. *The Basic Upsert-No Delete pattern flow*

Pros of Basic Upsert-No Delete

- This is a very simple pattern. The code is easy to maintain and understand.

- Row-level error logs can be truncated as part of the job, because every record is upserted again with the next run. So, there are no duplicates in the error logs (because of previous failures).

- This pattern is self-correcting. If we introduce changes to our transformation layer (after going live or as part of a later release), all data are updated in Salesforce to reflect the new transformation rules. We don't have to perform a onetime data conversion as part of the deployment process (except, potentially, to delete records that are now being filtered out as part of the new transformation rules).

Cons of Basic Upsert-No Delete

- If a record is deleted in the source, it will remain in Salesforce. There is not even a flag to indicate it was deleted in the source system.

- This pattern can't be used for a bidirectional sync because the transformation layer has no knowledge of the data in Salesforce to check for conflicts (or implement resolution rules).

- It's not very performant. We are pushing a lot of unnecessary updates and it can take a long time if there are a lot of records to sync. This may be okay if we are running the sync nightly, but not if we need to run it every ten minutes.

- This pattern updates records that have not changed, which results in Salesforce updating the LastModifiedDate field when nothing really changed, so it has an invalid (and almost useless) last-modified date.

Pattern 2: Wipe and Load

This pattern is exactly the same as the Basic Upsert-No Delete pattern, but it has an additional step to delete all the data from the target object first, which deals with the issue of deleted records not syncing to Salesforce (see Figure 9-2).

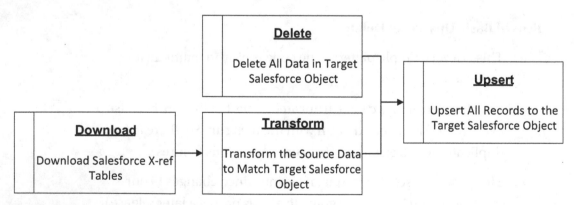

Figure 9-2. *The Wipe and Load pattern flow*

Pros of Wipe and Load

- This pattern handles deletes, so it is a true sync.

- This is a very simple pattern. The code is easy to maintain and understand.

- Error logs can be truncated as part of the job, because every record is upserted again with the next run. So, there are no duplicates in the error logs (because of previous failures).

- This pattern is self-correcting. If we introduce changes to our transformation layer (after going live or as part of a later release), all data are updated in Salesforce to reflect the new transformation rules. We don't have to perform a onetime data conversion as part of the deployment process (including for deletions).

Cons of Wipe and Load

- This pattern won't work if there are cascading deletes to objects that are not synced or if there are some fields that are owned by Salesforce (in other words, there is a two-way sync).

- This pattern can't be used for a bidirectional sync because the transformation layer has no knowledge of the data in Salesforce to check for conflicts (or implement resolution rules).

- We don't have the option to perform a soft delete in which we flag records as "Deleted in source" and hide them from the user. The pattern simply does not allow this.[4]

- Salesforce (or at least the object being synced) is offline during the job run, because the system is in a bad state (missing large chunks of data). This may be acceptable for a nightly job, but probably not for intraday ones.

---

[4]I guess you could flag all records as deleted in lieu of the deletion step, and then unflag them as part of the upsert-all step, which will only unflag the records that exist in the transformed data source.

- A job failure can result in data loss or a system outage. If the job fails, there are no data in the object! This is much worse than simply having outdated data, which would then be a result of any of the other patterns failing.

- This pattern is not performant at all (full delete then full load). It can take a long time if there are a lot of objects/records to sync. Plus, as we know, deletions (as discussed in Chapter 3) are lock-heavy operations and much more prone to failure than inserts, updates, or upserts.

- This is just a bad pattern for all but a very small set of select use cases. It may be a good option for a custom object that changes daily with no use for history. For example, let's say on a nightly basis you want to load a Daily Action Plan object with a checklist of things for each employee to do that day. Every day the list is created from scratch in some other system and you don't want the old data in Salesforce.

- This pattern updates records that have not changed, which results in Salesforce updating the LastModifiedDate field when nothing really changed, so it has an invalid (and almost useless) last-modified date.

Pattern 3: Basic Upsert-With Targeted Delete

Again, building on the previous pattern, we now introduce a targeted delete. Rather than deleting all the object's records from Salesforce, we delete only those records that no longer exist in the source (presumably because they have been deleted, but it can also be that data on the record changed in such a way that the transformation layer now filters it out). We first download the data from Salesforce, then transform the source data to match the Salesforce object's structure, then delete all records from Salesforce that do not exist in the transformed source dataset. Then, finally, we proceed with our upsert (see Figure 9-3).

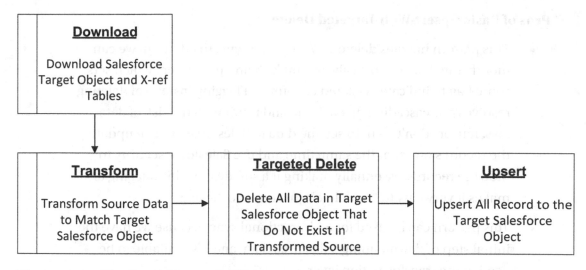

Figure 9-3. *The Basic Upsert-With Targeted Delete pattern flow*

After we have the Salesforce data loaded locally, it's very easy to identify records that exist in Salesforce but not in the transformed source. All you need to do is use a left join and include a "where is null" clause (see Listing 9-1).

Listing 9-1. Using "Where Is Null" to Identify Deletion Targets

```
1. Select
2.     sfo.Id
3. from SF_Object sfo
4. left join Transfomed_Source ts on ts.ExternalSourceId = sfo.
   ExternalSourceId
5. where sfo.SourceId is Null -- --  Record does not Exists in Salesforce
```

Of course, you don't have to do this in SQL at all, but the logic would be the same no matter how you accomplish it.

Note that we have the ExternalSourceId field indexed in the transformed source so this will perform well.[5]

---

[5]For a good discussion on the various ways to get "records where not in," see https:// sqlperformance.com/2012/12/t-sql-queries/left-anti-semi-join.

Pros of Basic Upsert-With Targeted Delete

- This pattern handles deletes, so it's a true sync. In addition, we can modify the delete step easily and make it an update step, which sets some flag to indicate "Deleted in source." Flagging instead of deleting resolves our cascading delete issue and minimizes the risk of data loss. If users don't want to see the data in Salesforce, we can update the record's owner at the same time and use Salesforce security to hide the records, essentially making it a soft delete. This flagging also makes it very easy to "undelete"; just remove the flag.

- This pattern can be used for a bidirectional sync because we have the initial step of downloading Salesforce data, and it's available to be used in the transformation layer.

- This is a relatively simple pattern. The code is easy to maintain and understand.

- Error logs can be truncated as part of the job, because all failures are retried automatically with the next run. There won't be any dupes in the error logs (because of previous failures).

- This pattern is self-correcting. If we introduce changes to our transformation layer (after going live or as part of a later release), all data are updated in Salesforce to reflect the new transformation rules. We don't have to perform a onetime data conversion as part of the deployment process (including for deletions).

Cons of Basic Upsert-With Targeted Delete

- This pattern is also not very performant. It can take a long time to sync if there are a lot of records, because we are still loading a lot of unnecessary updates.

- You need to download data at the start of the job, which also affects performance negatively.

- Again, this pattern updates records that have not changed and results in Salesforce updating the LastModifiedDate field when nothing really changed, so it has an invalid (and almost useless) last-modify date.

A Quick Recap (Full-Load Patterns)

The first pattern, Basic Upsert-No Delete, is good for data migrations but not integrations, unless we know for a fact that data will never be deleted in the source system (or filtered out in the transformation layer). This is the pattern we used in Chapter 7 for our data migration.

The second pattern, Wipe and Load, is good for data migrations as well as a very small number of integration use cases in which we know all data in an object changes every day and that data will not cause a cascading delete. If we look back at Chapter 7, and made our rollback code a prerequisite to running the data load, that would be a perfect example of the Wipe and Load pattern.

The third pattern, Basic Upsert-With Targeted Delete, brings us to a point where we have a viable integration sync job pattern for most use cases. Yes, we have some performance issues and, yes, the audit fields have invalid data in them. But, if our client doesn't care about the last-modified date or simply views it as a current as-of date, and the job runs only at night when no one is in the system, and there is plenty of time to run, this may not be of real concern either. Even if the job has to run on a regular basis midday, there is no system outage during the job run (like there is with Wipe and Load). So, as long as there is enough time between job runs (for example, the job takes a half hour to run and needs to run every two hours), our client may be okay with this approach.

These first three patterns are classified as full-load patterns because they always push all records (the full dataset) to Salesforce. From a performance perspective, they are not the optimal way of doing things and they have the additional side effect of updating the Salesforce audit fields (LastModifiedBy and LastModifiedDate) unnecessarily.

As we learned in Chapter 8, the first rule of performance tuning is "Don't push unnecessary updates." Doing just this is the focus of the next three patterns. The next pattern is an incremental-load pattern, in which we basically let the source system tell us what changed, then load only those data.

The fifth and sixth patterns are differential load patterns, in which, rather than rely on the source system to tell us what changed, we rely on a "data compare" to identify what is different (hence the term differential).

By pushing only the updates we need, we also solve the audit field update issue.

Pattern 4: Incremental Date-Based Upsert-With Targeted Delete

We continue to build on our previous patterns. This pattern is exactly the same as Basic Upsert-With Targeted Delete, but as opposed simply to upserting all records, we only upsert records that have changed since that last run. We identify changes by recording the timestamp at the end of each run, then use that as an input to the next. If it's the first run, we use a default value (such as 01/01/1900). See Figure 9-4.

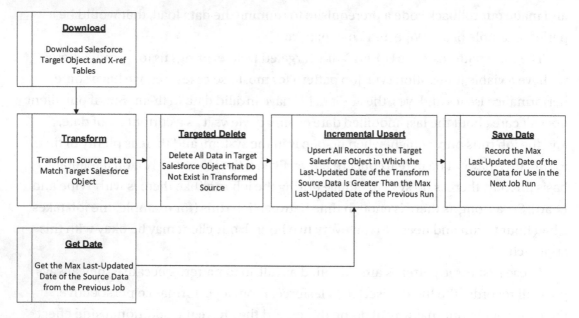

Figure 9-4. *The Incremental Date-Based Upsert-With Targeted Delete pattern flow*

It's important to note that we *do not* take the timestamp of the job run because this will introduce a whole host of clock synchronization issues between the middleware/ETL server and the source system, time zone conversion issues, daylight savings time issues, and issues caused by the time lapse from when you start pulling data to when it gets returned. Clock synchronization is an incredibly difficult problem to solve,[6] so it's best to avoid it altogether.

We do this by querying the transformation data set to get the max last-updated date directly from the source system (as opposed to the last job run date from the integration server). So, if the source system says the last time any record was updated was on 3/14/2019 at 2:34 PM EST, that is the time we pass in on the next job run, even if the current time is three weeks later and the last run was two hours ago. If nothing was updated since the last run, we continue to pass in the same date/timestamp. This solves all our clock synchronization issues (because we are only useing one lock, the one in the source system) and makes it impossible to miss a record because of one such issue.

Pros of Incremental Date-Based Upsert-With Targeted Delete

- This pattern has much better performance, but still no downtime during the job run, so it can be run intraday.

- This pattern can be used for a bidirectional sync because we have the initial step of downloading Salesforce data, and it's available to be used in the transformation layer.

- This pattern handles deletes, so this is a true sync. We can also modify the delete step easily and make it an update step that sets some flag for "Deleted in source," removing the possibility of cascading deletes. If users don't want to see the data in Salesforce, hide them using Salesforce security (soft delete). This flagging also makes it very easy to "undelete."

- I would not call this a simple pattern, but it's not too difficult to code and is relatively easy to maintain and understand.

---

[6]It is, in fact, so difficult to solve that, during the early 1900s, dozens of patents where being filed to solve the issue. For example: How do you synchronize clocks between two train stations hundreds of miles away? This is exactly the type of patent Albert Einstein was working on when he was employed as a junior patent officer in the Berne Patent Office. It's a direct result of thinking about these issues that Einstein realized that simultaneity is not absolute but relative, and his theory of special relativity was born (not to be confused with Universal general relativity, which is way too specialized to be used universally). It's also why so many of his fun thought experiments involve trains. For more information, see `https://www.telegraph.co.uk/culture/books/3601647/Space-time-and-patents.html`.

Cons of Incremental Date-Based Upsert-With Targeted Delete

- You still need to download data at the start of the job, which affects performance.

- Source data modify dates aren't always reliable and can be hard to calculate.

  - You don't really know what the source system is doing. What if a database administrator issues an Update statement against the source database and forgets to update the LastModifiedDate field?

  - The source system may not capture the last-modified date at all.

  - If we have complex transformations that involve lots of joins, it can be very difficult to determine the last-modified date of a (transformed) record. We have to check the last-modified date of every table involved in the joins! For example, let's say we have a Contact table that is joining to a Type table on the TypeId field to get the Type description. If someone changes the Type description in the Type table, the Contact records associated to that Type's last-modified dates won't be updated, so we have to check the Contact records' last-modified date as well as the joined Type records. If we have six more joins, we have to check six more tables.

  - Although many systems track the last-modified date at the record level, very few do so at the field level.[7] So, even if you can identify records that changed in the base tables, we don't really know that the resulting transformed record changed, so we will still be pushing some unneeded updates.

  - If your source data is a SQL view or a stored procedure and someone changes logic in that view, our code has no way of knowing what records changed!

- This pattern is *not* self-correcting. If we introduce changes to our transformation layer (after going live or as part of a later release), we have to perform a onetime data conversion as part of the deployment process to fix the existing data in Salesforce.

---

[7]And if they do, it will usually be in a data structure that's not easy to use, such as an audit log.

- If a Salesforce administrator (or anyone else) bypasses security and accidentally changes (or deletes) data in Salesforce that is owned by the source system, this issue will remain until someone, by coincidence, updates the source record, triggering an update.

- This pattern *not* self-reparing. Error logs *cannot* be truncated as part of the job because the errors will *not* be retried automatically with the next load. You should add columns to the row-level error logs to track when the error occurred and whether it has been fixed. Someone will have to keep track of which errors have been resolved and which have not.

Despite its popularity, and as you may be able to tell, I'm not a huge proponent of this pattern. But, it does have its use cases and it is very performant, pushing only those updates that are really needed. If you do go this route, I recommend you have a weekend (or nightly) Basic Upsert-With Targeted Delete job that fixes the data in case something goes wrong. This strategy gives the pattern the needed level of self-correction to meet our requirement (attribute) of being self-repairable (as discussed in Chapter 5). I'm still not thrilled with this idea either, because we are now using two different patterns for the same object sync, but it's better than ignoring the need for self-repairability.

Pattern 5: Differential Upsert-With Targeted Delete

The Incremental Date-Based Upsert-With Targeted Delete pattern solved our performance issues but introduced a whole new set of potential issues—the largest being that it may not even be possible to have the source system identify changed records for us. This fifth pattern—Differential Upsert-With Targeted Delete—approach to this situation is first to download the existing data from Salesforce and then do a field-by-field compare of them to the transformed source dataset to identify any records in the transformed source dataset that either don't exist in Salesforce or have at least one field different from Salesforce (again, this is a Differential Load). See Figure 9-5.

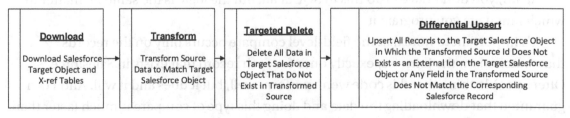

Figure 9-5. The Differential Upsert-With Targeted Delete process flow

Once you have the Salesforce object locally, finding the differences is easy. All you need to do is use a left join from the transformed data source to the local copy of the Salesforce object and include a "where is null" clause and a "where" clause (see Listing 9-2).

Listing 9-2. Using a Left Join to Compare Datasets and Detect Data Differences

```
1.   Select
2.         ts.SourceID
3.         ,ts.f1
4.         ,ts.f2
5.         ,ts.f3
6.         ,ts.f4
7.   from Transformed_Source ts
8.   left join SF_Object sfo on sfo.SourceID = ts.SourceID
9.   where sfo.id is null -- Exists in Source but not Salesforce (Need to
     insert)
10.  or -- Exists in Both Salesforce and Source but a value does not match
11.  (
12.        coalesce(sfo.f1,")<>coalesce(ts.f1,")
13.        or coalesce(sfo.f2,")<>coalesce(ts.f3,")
14.        or coalesce(sfo.f3,")<>coalesce(ts.f3,")
15.        or coalesce(sfo.f4,")<>coalesce(ts.f4,")
16.  )
```

You can see how similar this is to the deletion SQL. The biggest difference is that we are starting with the transformed data table (or view) and joining to the Salesforce data table, and then we filter for all records that need to be created in Salesforce, as opposed to the inverse, as we did with the deletion SQL. We also added a "where" clause to check if any field in the Salesforce table differs from the transformed data source.

Again, you don't have to do this in SQL at all, but the logic is the same no matter in which language you program it.

It's important to note that the field-level compare occurs only on the records that matched on the join—so, exactly once for each record that exists in Salesforce. Often, people think that this code won't perform well, but it does and it will. And I can guarantee that downloading the data and doing this type of compare is much faster than pushing unneeded updates to Salesforce. Of course, if you are in a situation in which the bulk of your data changes in the source system between job runs, you may be better off simply using one of the full-load patterns and not bothering with a data compare.

Also note that we are coalescing[8] all text fields to an empty string because, if we don't and a field is NULL in both Salesforce and the transformed data set, the row will return as a detected change because NULL does not equal NULL.[9]

One last note, before we get to the pros and cons. As we know from our data type discussion in Chapter 2, sometimes Salesforce makes small modifications to your data you we load it (trims off extra spaces, reorders multiselect picklists, and so on). When you build your compare code, you need to realize the possibility of that stuff causing false positives (detecting a change where there is none). What I like to do to test for this is to run the job twice back-to-back. The second run should not push any updates. If it does, check your compare code (the "where" clause).

Pros of Differential Upsert-With Targeted Delete

- This pattern demonstrates very good performance (but still not as good as the incremental, because we have the additional step of downloading data from Salesforce). There is still no downtime during the run, so it can be run intraday.

- This pattern can be used for a bidirectional sync, because we have the initial step of downloading Salesforce data, and it's available to be used in the transformation layer.

- This pattern handles deletes, so this is a true sync. We can modify the delete step easily to make it an update step that sets some flag for "Deleted in source," removing the possibility of cascading deletes. If users don't want to see the data in Salesforce, hide them using Salesforce security (soft delete). This flagging also makes it very easy to "undelete."

- I would also not call this a simple pattern, but it's not too difficult to code and is relatively easy to maintain and understand. Personally, I find this pattern to be simpler than an incremental sync, but I can see how some people may disagree.

---

[8]Coalesce takes in any number of parameters and returns the first one that is not null.

[9]For more information, see `https://stackoverflow.com/questions/1843451/why-does-null-null-evaluate-to-false-in-sql-server`.

- Error logs can be truncated as part of the job, because all errors are retried automatically with the next job run. No dupes are seen in the error logs (because of previous failures).

- This pattern is self-correcting. If we introduce changes to our transformation layer (after going live or as part of a later release), all data are updated in Salesforce to reflect the new transformation rules. We don't have to perform a onetime data conversion as part of the deployment process.

Cons of Differential Upsert-With Targeted Delete

- We need to download the Salesforce data at the start of the job, which introduces overhead and affects performance. This issue is a larger concern if we need the job to run frequently and the Salesforce object has a large volume of data.

Pattern 6: Differential Upsert-With Periodic Rebuild

This section brings us to our final pattern, where we try to eliminate the need to download the full dataset from Salesforce repeatedly. This is especially important if we want our jobs to run on a frequent basis.

The basic approach is to maintain a copy of the Salesforce data locally, then, after upserting the changes to Salesforce, we upsert (or insert/update) the local copy of the Salesforce data to bring them back in line with what now exists in Salesforce. We then have a current local copy of the Salesforce data ready at the start of the next job run (see Figure 9-6).

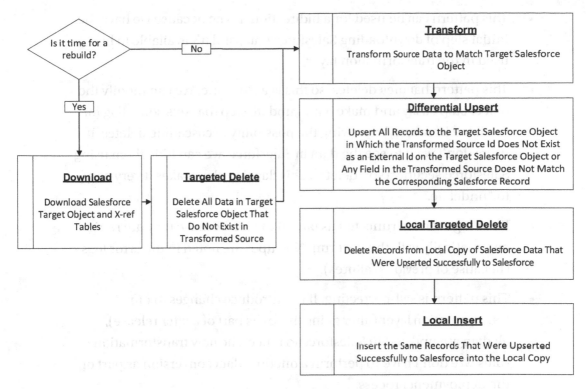

Figure 9-6. *The Differential Upsert-With Periodic Rebuild pattern flow*

As you can see, the flow is very similar to the Differential Upsert-With Targeted Delete pattern, but we have a check at the beginning to determine whether it's time for a rebuild. This can be something like "24 hours since the last rebuild" or "first Saturday run."

In addition, at the end of the flow (the last two steps in Figure 9-6), we replace all the records in the local copy of Salesforce data with the success data returned from the upsert. We don't update it from the transformed source because we want to be sure to exclude errored records, so that they are detected as changes and retried on the next run.

Pros of Differential Upsert-With Periodic Rebuild

- This pattern has much better performance. It's still not as good as an incremental, because we have the small bit of overhead introduced by the data compare, but it's very close. It's much faster than having to download large amounts of data from Salesforce with each job run.

- This pattern can be used for a bidirectional sync because we have the initial step of downloading Salesforce data, and it's available to be used in the transformation layer.

- This pattern handles deletes, so this is a true sync. We can modify the delete step easily and make it and update step that sets some flag for "Deleted in source," removing the possibility of cascading deletes. If users don't want to see the data in Salesforce, we can hide them using Salesforce security (soft delete). This flagging also makes it very easy to "undelete."

- Error logs can be truncated as part of the job because they are retried automatically with the next run. No dupes are noted in the error logs (because of previous failures).

- This pattern is self-correcting. If we introduce changes to our transformation layer (after going live or as part of a later release), all data are updated in Salesforce to reflect the new transformation rules. We don't have to perform a onetime data conversion as part of the deployment process.

Cons of Differential Upsert-With Periodic Rebuild

- This pattern includes complex code logic.

- If a Salesforce administrator (or anyone else) bypasses security and accidentally changes (or deletes) data in Salesforce that are owned by the source system, these data - SMH remain wrong, but only up until the next rebuild cycle. (This is much better than with an incremental load, in which the data get fixed only when they are updated coincidentally in the source.)

A Quick Recap (Incremental and Differential Patterns)

The biggest issue we faced with the full data load patterns is that they load the entire dataset with each run, which introduces performance issues that may or may not be acceptable, depending on the data volumes and the required run frequency.

If we have a requirement to sync deletions as well, we must either do a full wipe and load or download the Salesforce data so we can perform a targeted delete. This approach introduces even more overhead, which means, of course, longer runtimes.

We have two basic methods to avoid having to load the entire dataset: using the incremental and differential load patterns.

With an incremental approach, we allow the source system to determine what changed. This may be very easy to do when looking at a single table (or object) in the source system, but is not necessarily so after a bunch of joins and/or complex transformations. The incremental approach also has a serious self-repairability issue (as in, it doesn't self-repair and rows with the error are not automatically retried with the next run). Last, we completely bypass the clock synchronization issue, so this is not a concern.

With a differential approach, which solves the self-reparability issue, we remove the complexities involved in having the source system identify changes independently by performing a full data compare after the transformations are complete. Next, we remove the need to download Salesforce data regularly by adding a mechanism to maintain a current copy of Salesforce data locally without having to redownload it again and again. And last, we harden the pattern by adding a scheduled redownload of the Salesforce data to guard against the case in which someone does something they shouldn't in Salesforce.

Incremental Delete

You might ask, "Why didn't we take an incremental approach for the targeted delete? Why take a differential one?" These are great questions. The answer is: "To keep things simple." For differential patterns, we already need the data locally, so we may as well do a compare; for the full loads, we either always delete all records or never delete any so it's a nonissue.

This leaves us with the Incremental Load-With Targeted Delete pattern. If you feel that systems are not great at tracking data modifications,[10] they are even worse and less trustworthy when it comes to keeping track of deletions.[11] Take Salesforce, for example.

---

[10]Just to clarify this again, I do think systems are very good at tracking what records have changed, but not great at reporting the relevant changes when transformations (with lots of joins) are involved. These are often very complex queries to write.

[11]Also, as a general rule, I tend not to trust systems I don't control.

If you query an object for all records where the IsDeleted=True and the last-modified date is after some date, how confidant are you that every record that was deleted in the timeframe will be returned? You just might be more confident than you should be.

- Remember, we have no idea how long records remain in the recycle bin.

- Users can empty the recycle bin at will.

- If the recycle bin fills up, it empties the older records automatically.

- Users can do a hard delete bypassing the recycling bin altogether.

- We have no idea when the garbage collector will come by and clear out the deleted records permanently.[12]

So, even when I am syncing data out of Salesforce (from Salesforce to some other target system), I don't rely on the IsDeleted flag to identify deleted records. I do a full compare.

Summary

Coming out of this chapter, you should have a solid understanding of data synchronization patterns and how every approach has its pros and cons. You can mix and match these patterns as needed, even within the same synchronization job (assuming you are syncing more than one object in that job). This is by no means a comprehensive list of all possible synchronization patterns, but it is a solid foundation and you should be able to build on these patterns if you are facing unique challenges.

Of course, there are many other types if integrations that do not involve data synchronization We tackle some of the most common ones in the next chapter.

---

[12]See the discussion in Chapter 3 on the Salesforce recycle bin.

CHAPTER 10

Other Integration Patterns

As you can imagine, there are many other reasons to integrate systems that aren't centered around data synchronization. In this chapter we review some of the more common batch integration patterns I have come across in recent years. For the most part, these patterns are much simpler then synchronization patterns.

System Handoff (Prospect Conversion)

We often have jobs that need to handle complex use cases that switch the system of record. For example, suppose Salesforce owns an Account, Contact, or Lead record while the record is a prospect, but after we land that prospect as a client, we want those data to flow over to our ERP system. The ERP system then becomes the system of record going forward. The basic process flow is shown in Figure 10-1.

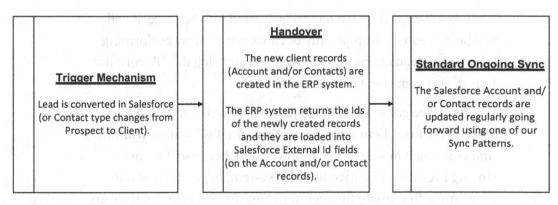

Figure 10-1. *The System Handoff (Prospect Conversion) pattern flow*

© David Masri 2019
D. Masri, *Developing Data Migrations and Integrations with Salesforce*,
https://doi.org/10.1007/978-1-4842-4209-4_10

This makes perfect sense. CRM systems are traditionally used for presales activity (prospecting, opportunity/pipeline management, sales activities, and marketing campaigns), whereas ERP systems generally deal with postsale activity (order fulfillment, billing, and so on).

This pattern has three basic steps:

1. A trigger mechanism

2. A handover (initial transfer to the handover system)

3. Ongoing sync

The trigger mechanism is just the event that "tells" (triggers) the systems that we need to switch a record's system of ownership. In our case, this event would probably either be a Lead record being converted to an account and contact, or a change of account type (or record type) from Prospect to Client.

After this event occurs, we need to perform our second step: the handover. All we need to do is create the record in the ERP system and get the Id (PK) of the newly created record, then update the corresponding Salesforce record's External Id with it. The records are now linked and we can continue to keep the data in sync (step 3) between the two systems using any of the patterns described in Chapter 9.

You could also store the Salesforce Id on the ERP record, then push updates for ERP records that contain a Salesforce Id when they change, but there are issues with this approach, such as the following:

1. It's less self-repairing. If a record is deleted in Salesforce, it will not be recreated automatically because we are now performing updates instead of upserts. We have to catch/log the "Record not found" error and deal with it somehow.

2. We may have cases when a sale just "walks in the door" and we want to create a client record directly in the ERP system without first creating it in Salesforce. But, we can't, because if we are storing the Salesforce Id in the ERP system, to get the Salesforce Id we must first create the record in Salesforce. However, if we are storing the ERP Id in Salesforce, we can still upsert it, even if the client never existed in Salesforce as a prospect.

3. We only own Salesforce and may not have the technical expertise or the security rights to modify the ERP system.

Often, this pattern is implemented manually. When a prospect becomes a client, a user creates a record manually in the ERP system, then types the ERP Id into the Salesforce ExternalId field, creating the linkage.

Record Merge

Suppose we are synchronizing data from some system that allows record merging [a master data management (MDM) system, for example] to Salesforce. A duplicate is detected in the source system and the two records are merged (after both records have been created in Salesforce). What happens to the two corresponding records in Salesforce?

If we are using any of the sync patterns discussed in Chapter 9, the surviving record gets updates and the victim record gets deleted (or tagged as "Deleted in source") because it no longer exists in the transformed dataset. This may seem like the right thing to do, but a problem exists if the victim record has child records. We need to reparent those child records to the survivor record.

For example, suppose we have two accounts in the source system, both with activities in Salesforce. If we simply delete the victim account, we lose the activities. The correct thing to do is first to reparent all the victim account's activities to the survivor account, then delete the victim account. This is exactly what Salesforce's Record Merge feature does.

So, yes, a Salesforce Record Merge (either via the UI or via an API call) handles the reparenting for you, but it does *not* correct any data issues caused by the merge—specifically, issues related to duplicate records in child objects. Suppose we have a custom Hobbies object that is a child of Contact. This object allows you to add hobbies to a contact and enter notes (free text) and a skill level (numbers 1–10) against it. Now suppose you merge two contacts, each of which had a child hobby record for Golf. The result is a single Contact record with two Golf hobby records with different skill levels and notes. Horrible.

If we merge records that result in duplicates, in an object that does not allow them (Account Contact Relation, for example), the merge fails. Terrible.

To deal with these issues, we introduce a cleanup step, during which we have logic to clean up the child data. This strategy results in a pattern with five basic steps (the pattern flow is presented in Figure 10-2):

1. Download

2. Identify

3. Clean up child records

4. Merge (and resolve any data conflicts if needed)

5. Archive

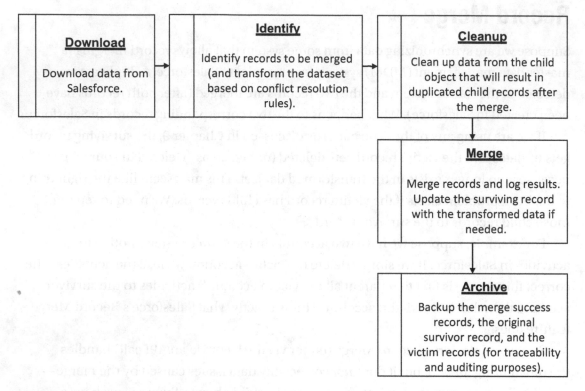

Figure 10-2. *The Record Merge pattern flow*

We download the necessary data needed to perform our analysis from Salesforce and identify which records need to be merged[1] and any data that are needed for implementing conflict resolution (either at the merged record or child record level).

We then clean up the child records (remove dupes and resolve conflicts[2]), perform the merge (and make updates to the surviving records if needed), and, last, archive

---

[1]Most systems that allow for record merging have some logging mechanism that tracks historical merges. You should be able to use that log to identify records in Salesforce that require merging.

[2]For our golf hobby example, we may decide to always take the highest, lowest, or average skill level; concatenate all the notes data into a single field; and then delete the extra record.

copies of the original data somewhere for audit purposes. "Somewhere" can be in Salesforce, a local database, flat files on a network drive, a data lake—just about anywhere will do.

As stated in Chapter 3, unfortunately, most middleware/ETL tools don't support the Merge API call.[3] If you know you will need this functionality, be sure to include it as a requirement when evaluating which middleware/ETL tool you will use. If, for whatever reason, using a tool that supports a merge is not an option, you can always code the merge manually In other words, code an update to reparent the children, and then a delete to delete the victim record. Coding the merge manually is also a good option if you are going the route of tagging records as deleted rather than deleting[4] them physically.

ETL-based Rollups and Formulas

As we know, Salesforce has native rollup and formula functionality (see Chapter 2). There will be times when we may want or need to perform these types of calculations outside of Salesforce, and then load them back in. The two primary reasons for this are as follows:

1.   There may be limitations on the native Salesforce rollup or formula functionality that prevent us from performing the needed calculations (again, see Chapter 2).

2.   Using a rollup, formula, or even a trigger will interfere with an integration because it causes locking errors or affects performance negatively.

This pattern is basically a sync pattern, with Salesforce as both the source and target. You download the data from the source (Salesforce), transform it, and then sync the transformed data backup to Salesforce. See the process flow in Figure 10-3.

---

[3]However, most support some form of custom scripting, so you can code a call to the Salesforce APIs to perform the merge using the custom scripting feature (rather than the tool's Salesforce connector).

[4]By "delete physically," I mean a Salesforce delete, which is technically a soft delete.

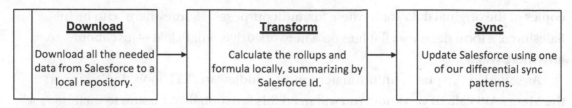

Figure 10-3. *The ETL-based Rollups and Formula pattern flow*

This pattern has the obvious disadvantage of not being real time, whereas the Salesforce rollups, formula, or triggers are. Although this is not a concern if our calculations are based on data that are populated solely by an integration, all we need to do is add the calculation as an additional step in the integration (immediately after we load the data used for the calculation).

If we are using a high-performing sync pattern (Chapter 9), we could potentially get this type of job running every few minutes, which is very close to real time.

Note   If we are using the Differential Upsert-With Periodic Rebuild pattern, because the source is Salesforce, we need to download the source data repeatedly, which could be a slow operation (compared with using local data). To get around this issue, we can do an incremental update of our source tables and then rebuild those periodically, which results in an Incremental Date-based Upsert-With Periodic Rebuild pattern. (Look how easy it is to come with new variations of the patterns we studied in chapter 9!) Rather than truncate and reload, we first download all updated or new records from Salesforce,[5] then use them to update our local copy of the source data. Next, we perform our calculations (transformations) and then, finally, upsert it.

To use our "pattern speak", we do the following:

1. Keep a local copy of the Salesforce data used for the calculations. We keep these data in sync using the Incremental Date-based Upsert pattern (but with Salesforce as the source and the local copy as the target).

---

[5]When downloading the data from Salesforce, we include a "where" clause in our SOQL: where LastModifyDate > X.

2. The local copy now acts as our source, and we update Salesforce using the Differential Upsert-With Periodic Rebuild" pattern.

3. We perform a periodic rebuild of the local copy. (In step 2, we do a periodic rebuild of the target data; here we are rebuilding the source.)

Formulas and Rollups on Encrypted Fields

Data encryption is a huge topic in and of itself and is outside the scope of this book. But, you should know that Salesforce has a native encrypted field type, and a platform encryption product (Salesforce Shield[6]), and that there are at least a few third-party options for encrypting data within Salesforce. Every one of these products introduces limitations to what Salesforce can do with encrypted data/fields. Most of these limitations stem from back-end Salesforce processes not being able to decrypt encrypted fields, and therefore you can't use them in triggers, formulas, or rollups[7] at all. Many of these products don't support encryption of numeric data types at all.[8]

When accessing encrypted data via the Salesforce APIs,[9] the encryption happens on the Salesforce side of the API call, so we can work with the data through the APIs as normal. This strategy allows us to use ETL code to get around a lot of these limitations by using the ETL-based Rollups and Formula pattern, with an added step to handle formatting (see Figure 10-4).

---

[6]I'm wrong to say that Shield is a platform encryption product. It's really a data security product with a Platform Encryption feature. For more information, see `https://www.salesforce.com/products/platform/products/shield`.

[7]Both formula or rollups are calculated on back-end processes.

[8]As of this writing, Salesforce Shield does not support encrypting of numeric fields. For more information, see `https://help.salesforce.com/articleView?id=security_pe_custom_fields.htm&type=5`.

[9]Or a third-party API gateway. Third-party encryption tools often implement an API gateway that sits between the user and the Salesforce APIs. This gateway catches the API call, encrypts the data (based on configurations), then forwards the API message with the encrypted data to Salesforce. When pulling data out of Salesforce, a web service call is made to the gateway, the gateway calls the Salesforce APIs, which returns encrypted data. The gateway then decrypts those data and forwards them back to the original caller.

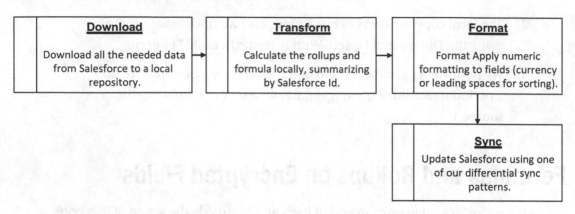

Figure 10-4. *The Rollups and Formula on Encrypted Fields pattern flow*

Suppose we have a requirement to encrypt a currency field and roll it up to the parent object. Our encryption layer does not support the Currency data type (or any number). We can create an encrypted text field and work with our Salesforce developer to build a Lightning component with front-end validation (in other words, JavaScript) to enforce that only numerics can be entered in the field. We can also use a Lighting component to format the display. We can then use the ETL-based Rollups and Formula pattern to download the data, convert the text to numbers, calculate the rollup, then convert it back to text and load it into an encrypted rollup field (also text). This strategy get around Salesforce's inability to encrypt currency and numeric fields.

Displaying numbers as text can be ugly, so we may want to do a bit of formatting——maybe add a dollar sign or whatever. See the formatting I applied in Figure 10-5.

	Accounts **Formatted Number** ▼		New	Import

3 items · Sorted by Number as text (Formatted) · Filtered by my accounts · Number as text · Updated a few seconds ago

	ACCOUNT NAME	∨	NUMBER AS TEXT	∨	NUMBER AS TEXT (FORMATT... ↑ ∨	
1	ActiveSight		$12.34		$.......12.34	▼
2	ABC Fixed Asset Inventory Inc.		$123.45		$.....123.45	▼
3	Acme		$1478.43		$...1478.43	▼

Figure 10-5. *Formatting text as currency. Disgusting.*

What I did in Figure 10-5 was, in addition to adding a dollar sign, I left-padded the numbers with dots, so that I can still sort the numbers as if they were numbers.[10] The numbers are right-aligned properly and the decimals line up properly. I wish I could pad them with spaces, but Salesforce won't display them! Figure 10-6 shows what would happen if I sorted the numbers (as text) without the padding.[11]

	ACCOUNT NAME	NUMBER AS TEXT ↑	NUMBER AS TEXT (FORMATTED)	
1	ActiveSight	$12.34	$......12.34	▼
2	Acme	$1478.43	$...1478.43	▼
3	ABC Fixed Asset Inventory Inc.	$153.45	$.....153.45	▼

Figure 10-6. Formatting text as currency, sorted alphabetically without padding

The options here are endless. We can use integration jobs like this to perform tasks that would normally be left to triggers, rollups, or workflows, but can't because the data are encrypted.

File Attachments (Salesforce Content)

We discussed file attachments extensively in Chapter 7 when we did our sample migration, so we won't rehash it here. For integrations, unless we come up with a fancy (and efficient) way of comparing file content, our only real option for file attachments is the Incremental Date-based Upsert pattern. Also as discussed in Chapter 7, we can't use upsert for Salesforce content. Instead, we need to perform deletes and inserts. I have mapped out the process flow in Figure 10-7.

---

[10]Sorting works (or may not work at all) based on what encryption tool you are using and how it's configured.

[11]Because this is a text field, Salesforce sorts the data alphabetically rather than numerically. The padding makes the alphabetical sort equivalent to the numeric sort.

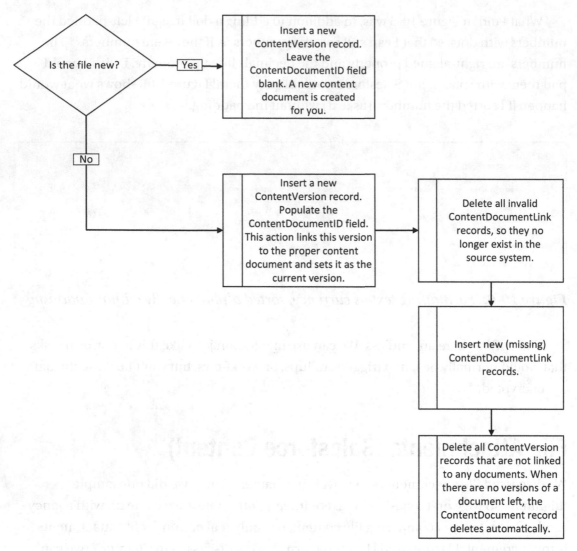

Figure 10-7. *The File Attachments (Salesforce Content) pattern flow*

Data Archive

As we know, Salesforce data storage costs can get expensive. In an attempt to limit this cost, we may be asked to archive data out of Salesforce and into some local database table (which should match the Salesforce object's structure). The Data Archive pattern does just that.

Archiving data using this pattern is a pretty straightforward process. First, we create two local tables that mimic the Salesforce object's data model: a Temp table and an Archive table. Then (as shown in Figure 10-8) we do the following:

1. Download all the object's data in to the Temp table. Truncate it first, if needed.

2. Delete all the data in the Archive table for which the Salesforce Id is in the Temp table.

3. Copy all the data from the Temp table into the Archive table.

4. Delete records from Salesforce that

   a. Meets our archive criteria (in other words, is older than x number of months)

   b. Exists in both the Archive and Temp tables

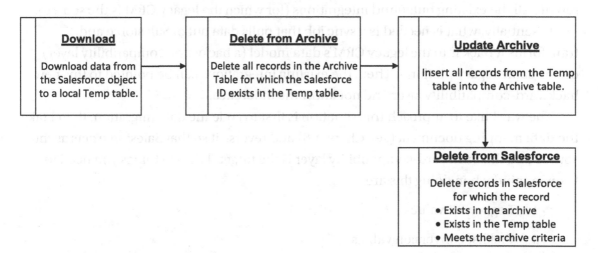

Figure 10-8. *The Data Archive pattern flow*

The key point here is that the Archive table has all the data that currently exist in Salesforce and ever existed in Salesforce. We use the Archive table as the driver in the deletion process as a safety measure. We only delete data from Salesforce if it meets our archive criteria *and* has been archived successfully.

After data are archived, we can use them as a data source for integrations. For example, let's say we want to have a rollup (or a summary report) that includes archived data. We can summarize the data in the archive, then push it back into Salesforce. This strategy allows us to have summarized data in Salesforce without incurring the cost of storing all the detail records.

Backward-Compatibility Layer

When rolling out a new Salesforce instance, we are often replacing an existing CRM system, so we have to migrate our data to Salesforce. As part of that migration, we transform our data to match our new Salesforce org data model. As you can imagine, often these legacy CRM systems are not only heavily customized, but also heavily integrated, with the CRM as a target and/or source. It's surprisingly common for clients to want to maintain backward compatibility of the data structures so they don't have to rewrite all the existing outbound integrations (for which the legacy CRM is the source).

Essentially, what is needed is a sync job that pulls data out of Salesforce and transforms it back into the legacy CRM's data model (a backward-compatibility layer) on the same legacy platform. Then, the existing integrations can be pointed to this new backward-compatibility layer and not know the difference.

The way I like to approach this situation is first to code the data migration, then I take the data mapping document (see Chapter 6) and reverse it so that Salesforce acts as the source and the backward-compatibility layer is the target. The two things you need to keep in mind when doing this are

1. Legacy PK values

2. Picklist conversion values

Legacy PKs

The legacy system tables likely have very different PKs, and may even be of a different data type then Salesforce keys. Integrated systems may be storing those keys, so we not only have to maintain the existing keys on migration, but we also have to generate new legacy keys for new records created in Salesforce.

To do this, we create three fields on every Salesforce object that needs to be in the backward-compatibility layer. The first field holds the existing legacy Id and is used as the External Id for our migration. The second field is used for new records and can be an AutoNumber[12] (for which we start based off the maximum Legacy Id at the time of migration). We then have the third field, which is a formula field that takes the legacy Id if populated. Otherwise, it takes the newly generated AutoNumber legacy Id. This formula field is the field that represents the legacy Id in the backward-compatibility layer.

Picklist Conversion Values

Relational databases usually use small reference tables in lieu of picklists, and many-to-many relationships in lieu of multiselect picklists, which means we need the following:

1. Have a legacy Id for the picklist values.

2. A way to handle new picklist values in Salesforce that never existed in the legacy system.

3. The legacy reference tables may have had additional fields in them (Name, Description, Numeric Rank, whatever). We need a place to store this additional data.

To meet these requirements, we need a conversion table to convert each picklist value into a legacy record with a legacy Id, and we need a UI so that an administrator can maintain these data going forward, adding and removing values as needed. Personally, I like to do this in a custom object within Salesforce so that the conversion table can be maintained within Salesforce (and we get the maintenance UI by default).

When adding new picklist values to Salesforce, we (well, someone will) need to ensure that new values don't cause problems with downstream systems or existing integrations. If they do, we simply have to map the new values to one of the existing legacy values until the downstream systems or integrations can be fixed. It's perfectly okay to have more than one Salesforce picklist value map to the same legacy value (legacy Id).

---

[12]If an AutoNumber won't work (because the legacy system doesn't use integers for PKs), we may have to work with a Salesforce developer to write code that builds new legacy Ids. Or, we could include that code as part of the integration.

After we have these two things in place (a mechanism to produce new legacy Ids and a picklist conversion table), we code our transformation layer to transform our data to match the structures needed for the backward-compatibility layer.

Time Series Backups (Time-based Snapshot)

Often, companies want to do time-based comparisons. They ask questions such as, "How many open orders do we have now compared to this time last year?" Or "How do our current three-month sales projections compare to this time last year?" To answer these types of questions, we need a snapshot of our data exactly as they existed for the same time the previous year.

Salesforce has a great feature called *Reporting Snapshots*[13] that helps to answer such questions. Reporting Snapshots are based off Salesforce reports, so the snapshots have all the limitations of Salesforce reporting.[14] And because snapshot data are stored using Salesforce storage, our clients will incur any costs associated with that storage. For these two reasons, we may want to write our own integration-based snapshot code.

This process is similar to the Data Archive pattern, except we never delete data from either Salesforce or the archive. We simply append the data into the Archive table with an additional timestamp field (the snapshot "as-of date"), which indicates the time the snapshot was taken. The combination of the as-of date and the Salesforce Id can identify any record uniquely. If you want a particular snapshot, simply query the table for all records in which the as-of date equals the as-of date of the desired snapshot. Easy.

Let's take this one step further. Suppose we want to take a snapshot of our data on the last day of every month, and include all current data as well. We would then perform the process shown in Figure 10-9 on a daily basis.

---

[13]For more information, see https://help.salesforce.com/articleView?id=data_about_analytic_snap.htm&type=5.

[14]For more information, see https://help.salesforce.com/articleView?id=rd_reports_limits.htm&type=5.

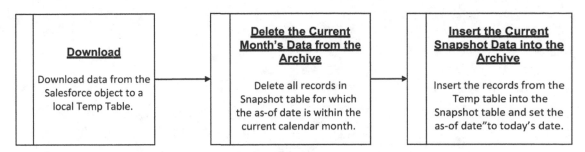

Figure 10-9. *The Monthly Snapshot process flow*

Note that on the first day of the month, nothing will be in the Snapshot table for the current month, so nothing will get deleted. The previous day's snapshot (the last day of the last month) becomes the permanent end-of-month (EOM) snapshot, because it is never deleted. So, we maintain exactly one snapshot per month at all times, even though the job runs daily.

Even if we don't want the current data and only want the EOM data, the daily process I described here is better than simply scheduling the job to run once at the end of each month, because we don't have to worry about EOM calculations (with weird leap-year rules). And if the job fails on the last day of the month, we still have the previous day's copy, which is better than nothing. However, if the job runs once a month, on the last day of the month, and it fails, we lose the record for that month.

Summary

In this chapter we covered a few of the many possible nonsync data integration patterns. If you are doing Salesforce integration work regularly, it's just a matter of time before you come across at least one or two of these patterns. More likely than not, you will come across some integration requirement that we did not study explicitly. For those cases, use the concepts from these last few chapters to design an integration pattern that meets your requirements.

I'm under no delusion that I could possibly cover every pattern you will ever need. The goal here was to give you a taste of the kind of integration patterns you are likely to come across, and a solid foundation in the thought process used when designing them.

Up next: real-time integrations!

CHAPTER 11

Real-Time Data and UI Integrations

So far, we have looked at batch integrations that run either on a schedule or are triggered to run by some event, and then process whole batches of records. These jobs all center around data movements—moving data from some source, transforming it, and then loading it into Salesforce. Depending on your business requirements, this may not be the best solution for your users. In this chapter, we examine some alternatives to batch integrations, with a focus on real-time integrations. Remember, this is a patterns and practices book, so I do not focus on the details of how to implement them; I want to make you aware of your options and point you in the right direction.

Real-time integrations are integrations triggered by a user (or some system) action, and the integration must be processed immediately (or within some time stipulated by the service-level agreement). Often, the user or system that triggered the integration must be notified of the result. There are lots of reasons for wanting data in real time. Here are a few common examples:

1. A customer service rep has a customer on the phone who wants to change their credit card as part of some transaction. The customer service rep wants a response from the credit card processing system that the charge was successful before ending the phone call.

© David Masri 2019
D. Masri, *Developing Data Migrations and Integrations with Salesforce*,
https://doi.org/10.1007/978-1-4842-4209-4_11

2. A travel agent needs to know which seats are available on a flight. The seats need to be put in a state of reservation until the customer has booked a flight. Then, that seat is booked and the rest are released.[1]

3. A sales rep needs to see customer purchase history, but it's way too much data to store in Salesforce, so it was decided it was best to pull and display the data as needed (when the sales rep views the Customer page).

4. After a customer agrees to buy an insurance policy, the sales rep needs the customer's information moved over to the new policy application system, where the sales rep needs to complete the application.

I'm going to categorize real-time integrations into two categories:

1. **Real-time data integrations:** When the integration is centered around a data interchange. Data move back and forth. Data may or may not be saved to Salesforce, but the data are displayed using the native Salesforce UI.

2. **Application UI automation integrations:** When the integration is centered around surfacing another system's UI in Salesforce, automating it, or simply making it more accessible.

Real-time Data Integrations

Let's start with real-time data integrations. Here is the list of options we will review in this section:

- Direct call to the Salesforce APIs

- Salesforce Connect

---

[1] If you don't lock down the seats being discussed, some other agent may give them away during the discussion. Then, when the passenger finally decides on a flight, the seats are no longer available. This was the collective experience of college students trying to book classes at the start of every semester in the early 1990s. Why didn't universities learn these lessons from the airline industry?! Rage inducing.

- Salesforce outbound messaging

- Salesforce Streaming API

- Salesforce platform events

- Apex callout

- Apex web services

- Web-to-Case

- Web-to-Lead

- E-mail-to-Case

- Apex e-mail service

- Salesforce outbound e-mails

- Web service triggered ETL

- Service-oriented architecture (SOA) middleware

Direct Call to the Salesforce APIs

Performing direct calls to the Salesforce APIs is such an obvious option I almost forgot to include it. Then, when I remembered, I had to think about the paper that is wasted in printing this description. But, because I decided to include this section for comprehensiveness reasons, I want to include all options.

If an external system needs to interact with Salesforce data in real time, if that systems supports it, you can code real-time calls from that system to Salesforce, pushing and pulling data as needed, using either the Salesforce Rest or SOAP APIs.

There are lots of really great examples on the Salesforces developer website of how to use these APIs by writing code using various languages:

- **A C# example:** https://developer.salesforce.com/page/ Consuming_Force.com_SOAP_and_REST_Web_Services_from_.NET_ Applications

- **A Java example:** https://developer.salesforce.com/docs/ atlas.en-us.api.meta/api/sforce_api_quickstart_steps_walk_ through_code.htm

- **A Python example:** https://developer.salesforce.com/blogs/
  developer-relations/2014/01/python-and-the-force-com-rest-
  api-simple-simple-salesforce-example.html

- **A JavaScript/jQuery example:** https://developer.salesforce.
  com/blogs/developer-relations/2015/08/creating-jquery-
  application-using-rest-api.html

Salesforce Connect

Salesforce Connect (previously called *Lightning Connect*) is a native Salesforce feature that allows us to connect Salesforce to an external oData[2] dataset without code. From within Salesforce, you configure an external data source and then map the needed oData entities to Salesforce, creating an external object. After that external object is created, it acts much like a native Salesforce custom object, except that no data for that object are stored in Salesforce. On an as-needed basis, Salesforce makes a web service call to the oData source and pulls in the data in real time, displaying them for the user. Salesforce Connect can be used to update data (via the oData web service) in addition to reading it.

If your source/target system does not have a native oData connector, Salesforce Connect does have a feature to write a custom adapter.[3] If you are using a common RDBMS, a simple Google search should return a plethora of options for implementing an oData layer on top of it.

There are some limitations on Salesforce external objects:

- Limitations on the use of SOQL[4]

- Limitations on the use of Salesforce reporting[5] and security

- No ability to track the history of field changes (the ability to do this is in beta test)

---

[2]oData is web service standard based on REST.

[3]For more information, see https://developer.salesforce.com/docs/atlas.en-us.apexcode.
meta/apexcode/apex_connector_custom_adapter.htm.

[4]For more information, see https://help.salesforce.com/articleView?id=platform_
connect_considerations_soql.htm&type=5.

[5]For more information, see https://help.salesforce.com/articleView?id=platform_
connect_considerations_reports.htm&type=0.

For more information on Salesforce Connect, see `https://trailhead.` `salesforce.com/en/modules/lightning_connect/units/lightning_connect_` `introduction`.

For more information on oData, see `http://www.odata.org/`.

If you want to try it out but don't have an oData source, you can use the oData.org full-access (read-write) sample service located here: `http://services.odata.org/V3/` `(S(nmnbydh3l5Ojxjievpy4pset))/OData/OData.svc/`.

You can find the full set of oData.org sample services here: `http://www.odata.org/` `odata-services/`.

Salesforce Outbound Messages

Salesforce outbound messaging is another really nice Salesforce feature. Basically, it allows you to, as part of a workflow, send out a web service message to an external system (a preconfigured target endpoint) for processing. For example, let's say we want to notify some other system every time an account address is changed. We can set up a workflow to fire in real time—on Create or Update of any account—and send an outbound message to the web service endpoint that receives the message (with the updated address information) and process it into the target system. Outbound messages have a few other nice features, such as automatic retries if the endpoint can't be reached.

Unfortunately, endpoints need to be made specifically for receiving Salesforce outbound messages, because outbound message formats cannot be customized. You can select the fields you want to send, but that's about it.

The Salesforce documentation walks you through setting up a custom endpoint[6] using a utility called *wsdl.exe*.[7]

For more information on Salesforce outbound messaging, see `https://` `developer.salesforce.com/docs/atlas.en-us.api.meta/api/sforce_api_om_` `outboundmessaging_understanding.htm`.

---

[6]For more information, see `https://developer.salesforce.com/docs/atlas.en-us.api.meta/` `api/sforce_api_om_outboundmessaging_listener.htm`.

[7]wsdl.exe is a utility provided by MS. You can find the documentation for it here: `https://docs.` `microsoft.com/en-us/previous-versions/dotnet/netframework-1.1/7h3ystb6(v=vs.71)`. WSDL stands for **W**eb **S**ervice **D**escription Language and it's XML based.

Salesforce Streaming API

The Salesforce Streaming API lets you push notifications of data changes in real time to active listeners while making no guarantee of delivery.[8] So, you can trigger a push notification every time an object has a record inserted, updated, or deleted.

Think of the Salesforce Streaming API as the technology behind a stock ticker. You want updates to be pushed in real time to all listeners, but only while they are listening, and you don't really care if some messages are lost.

More information is available for Salesforce Streaming API:

- **Streaming API Developer Guide:** `https://developer.salesforce.com/docs/atlas.en-us.api_streaming.meta/api_streaming/intro_stream.htm`.

- **Streaming API Trailhead:** `https://trailhead.salesforce.com/en/modules/api_basics/units/api_basics_streaming`

- **Outbound messaging vs. Streaming API:** `https://developer.salesforce.com/forums/?id=906F0000000kCeKIAU`

Salesforce Platform Events

Salesforce platform events are similar to the Streaming API, but instead of being triggered by data changes, they are triggered by process builders or Salesforce triggers, and the message is customized; it does not mirror the object. As with the Streaming API, Salesforce cannot guarantee message delivery of platform event notifications.

You can think of platform events like a custom object (it ends with __e instead of __c) with the sole purpose of use with the streaming API. So, to trigger a notification, you simply create a record in the Platform Events object (you created). This strategy has the benefit of using the standard Salesforce SOAP and REST APIs to insert records into the custom Platform Event object and it will trigger a notification.

---

[8]The listener app can make a call to Salesforce to get missed messages for 24 hours. For more information, see `https://developer.salesforce.com/docs/atlas.en-us.api_streaming.meta/api_streaming/using_streaming_api_stateless.htm`.

For more information on Salesforces platform events, see

- **Platform Events Developer Guide:** `https://developer.salesforce.com/docs/atlas.en-us.platform_events.meta/platform_events/platform_events_define_ui.htm`

- **Platform Events Trailhead:** `https://trailhead.salesforce.com/modules/platform_events_basics`

- **Real-time integrations with platform events:** `https://www.youtube.com/watch?v=wvKbNtnHPNM`

- **How to use platform events with MuleSoft's Salesforce Connector:** `https://dzone.com/articles/how-to-use-platform-events-with-mulesofts-salesfor`

Apex Callout

An Apex callout allows us to code custom outbound web service calls using Apex for just about any SOAP or REST web service and bring data back into Salesforce for display or storage. This can be from a trigger, Lightning component, Visualforce page, or an Apex batch.[9]

For more information on Apex callouts, see `https://developer.salesforce.com/page/Apex_Web_Services_and_Callouts#Apex_Callouts`.

Apex Web Services

Apex web services are the counterpart to Apex callouts. They allow us to build custom endpoints in Salesforce to receive web service calls and then process them using Apex. This is a good option if we need to receive a complex web service message and the native Salesforce APIs won't satisfy our use case.[10]

For more information on Apex web services, see `https://developer.salesforce.com/page/Apex_Web_Services_and_Callouts#Apex_Web_Services`.

---

[9]For information on an APEX process that can run on a schedule, see `https://developer.salesforce.com/docs/atlas.en-us.apexcode.meta/apexcode/apex_batch_interface.htm`.

[10]This can happen, for example, when the data sent to Salesforce do not line up well with the Salesforce object model and we can't transform it in the source system.

Web-to-Case

Web-to-Case is another nice feature of Salesforce. We can use the Salesforce UI to configure and create a web form as an HTML code snippet. We can then post that code snippet on our web site (or anywhere online). Then, when people visit the web site, they can fill out that form and click Submit. The form posts the data to Salesforce, and Salesforce creates a case based off it, all without writing a stitch of code! Of course, we can always add Salesforce workflows or triggers to fire when a case is created, which extends this functionality even further.

For more information on Salesforce Web-to-Case, see `https://trailhead.salesforce.com/en/modules/service_basics/units/service_basics_create_customer_channels#Tdxn4tBKheading3`.

Web-to-Lead

Salesforce's Web-to-Lead feature works almost exactly like the Web-to-Case feature, except we can use the generated web form to create a lead (and assign it to a campaign) instead of creating a case.

For more information on Salesforce Web-to-lead, see `https://help.salesforce.com/articleView?id=setting_up_web-to-lead.htm&type=0`.

Email-to-Case

Email-to-Case is similar to Web-to-Case, but instead of creating a web form, we configure a custom e-mail address, and any email sent to that address is used to create a Salesforce case. If we have our own e-mail servers, we can route the e-mail through that first. If not, we can set up an e-mail address that goes directly to Salesforce for processing. Again, here too we can always add Salesforce workflows or triggers to fire when a case is created, extending this functionality even further.

For more information on Salesforce Email-to-Case, see `https://trailhead.salesforce.com/en/modules/service_basics/units/service_basics_create_customer_channels#Tdxn4tBKheading4`.

Apex E-mail Service

Suppose we wanted to do something else with an incoming e-mail rather than open a case. If so, we can use Salesforce's Apex e-mail service to write custom Apex code to process the e-mail. Just like with Email-to-Case, we configure a custom e-mail address, and any e-mail sent to that address is then processed by that custom code. Our code has access to all the information in the e-mail, including the From, CC, and Subject fields; the body of the e-mail; and any attachments (up to a total size of 10MB).

If we want to have users send e-mails to trigger code, or if we need a real-time integration with a system that can't be customized to send real-time outbound web messages, but can configure it to send e-mail, then using the Apex e-mail service may be a good option.

For more information on the Apex e-mail service, see https://developer. salesforce.com/docs/atlas.en-us.apexcode.meta/apexcode/apex_classes_email_ inbound_what_is.htm.

Salesforce Outbound E-mails

Salesforce has lots of native functionality for sending e-mails, which is usually used for sending out notifications. Much like using the Apex e-mail service for integrations, there is nothing to prevent us from using an e-mail notification to send outbound messages to another system.

For more information on Salesforce outbound e-mails, see https://developer. salesforce.com/docs/atlas.en-us.apexcode.meta/apexcode/apex_forcecom_email_ outbound.htm.

For information on sending e-mails using Apex, see https://developer. salesforce.com/docs/atlas.en-us.apexcode.meta/apexcode/apex_forcecom_email_ outbound.htm.

Web Service Triggered ETL

Using Salesforce outbound messages, Apex callouts, or even an outbound e-mail, we can set up a system that catches that message and then runs an ETL job (perhaps based on one of the patterns discussed in Chapters 9 or 10). If the integrations are coded for it, we can use data from the message as the control in our ETL, limiting the job run to focus on very specific data.

With the boom in Salesforce's popularity, many third-party middleware providers have native endpoints built to receive Salesforce outbound messages, which then trigger an ETL job based off them with no code (just configurations). If our ETL tool does not support this, we may have to write a custom endpoint to process the message and trigger the job (see the previous section on outbound messages).

For more middleware-specific information, see

- **Informatica,** *Real-Time Data Synchronization through SFDC Outbound Messages:* `https://network.informatica.com/docs/DOC-15227`

- **Dell Boomi,** "Receiving Outbound Messages from Salesforce": `http://help.boomi.com/atomsphere/GUID-93B41067-BA2D-4C19-8B75-C04B9A728A6A.html`

- **Jitterbit,** *Configuring Outbound Messages with Harmony API:* `https://success.jitterbit.com/display/DOC/Configuring+Outbound+Messages+with+Harmony+API`

- **Scribe,** *Introducing Event Message Maps for Salesforce:* `https://www.scribesoft.com/blog/2014/07/s01e17-introducing_event_message_maps_for_salesforce/`

SOA Middleware

SOA middleware is a generic term that is a catch-all for middleware applications that are designed to wire together web services (APIs), and possibly add in workflow and routing logic between them. This includes traditional Enterprise Service Bus (ESB) solutions and more modern cloud-based integration paradigms, such as cloud-based Enterprise Application Integration (EAI).

An ESB is an application that facilitates messaging between systems. It often has a wide range of connectors/adapters for common applications. Think of an ESB as the hub of a hub-and-spoke-type architecture that routes messages between the service layers of different applications.

I really wish there was a proper name for cloud-based EAI, but unfortunately there is not. What I am referring to here is the use of various cloud services to build an integrated environment. Cloud services are designed to be components that can be cobbled together to build, extend, or integrate applications.

Needless to say, this is a *huge* topic and there is no way I can cover it properly here (even if I wanted to), but at the same time I don't want to ignore the topic. I would only recommend using an ESB or custom-built EAI if you already have one in place or your company has some initiative to move in that direction. With the acquisition of MuleSoft and it's Anypoint platform, Salesforce is aggressively going after this market. I suspect we will start seeing a lot more Mulesoft in the coming years.

Here are some links to information on a variety of related topics and service providers:

- **What is an ESB?:** https://www.mulesoft.com/resources/esb/what-esb

- **The difference between a service bus and a message queue:** https://stackoverflow.com/questions/7793927/message-queue-vs-message-bus-what-are-the-differences

- **Serverless Computing and EAI:** https://www.techmeet360.com/blog/serverless-computing-and-enterprise-application-integration/

- **MuleSoft**

  - **MuleSoft Anypoint:** https://www.mulesoft.com/platform/enterprise-integration

  - **MuleSoft Integration keynote at Dreamforce 2018:** https://videos.mulesoft.com/watch/Dtj9VS9eMqpfCQZRmVdVeb

- **Amazon**

  - **Amazon Web Services (AWS):** https://aws.amazon.com/

  - **Amazon Simple Queue Service:** https://aws.amazon.com/sqs/

  - **AWS Lambda:** https://aws.amazon.com/lambda/

- **Heroku (a Salesforce Company):** https://www.heroku.com/products

- **Microsoft Azure**

  - **Azure:** https://azure.microsoft.com/

  - **Microsoft Azure EAI using logic Apps:** https://msdn.microsoft.com/en-us/magazine/mt703438.aspx

  - **Azure Service Bus:** https://azure.microsoft.com/en-in/services/service-bus/

  - **Azure Functions:** https://azure.microsoft.com/en-in/services/functions/

- **Google Cloud**

  - **Google Cloud Platform:** `https://cloud.google.com/terms/services`

  - **Google Cloud Pub/Sub:** `https://cloud.google.com/pubsub/`

  - **Google Cloud Functions**: `https://cloud.google.com/functions/`

Application UI Integration through Automation

More often than not, users need to work with more than one application to do their job. Even if you can build real-time data integrations between that system and Salesforce, toggling between systems and searching for the needed records can be time-consuming and laborious. Rebuilding those UIs and functionality in Salesforce is expensive and can take years.[11]

This situation is extremely common in call centers. Call center agents are using Salesforce for case management, but they may need to log in to six or seven other apps, depending on the reason for the call. Call centers monitor closely things like total call time, first-call resolution rates, total time to resolution, and so on. Shaving even a few seconds off each call can save millions of dollars per year.

The need here is to make Salesforce and these other systems act as one, reducing time spent toggling among systems, searching for corresponding records and limiting the need for duplicate data entry.

Making two applications act as one can get pretty complex. Before deciding on any of the options described in this section, I recommend working with the systems owners (or the system vendor) to determine your best approach. Here is the list of options we will review in this section:

- Native apps

- Embedded iFrame

- Hyperlink

- Canvas

- FAT Application Automation

---

[11]And of course, Salesforce may simply not be the right tool for the job,

- Web browser automation

- Web browser extensions

- Windows automation

Native Apps

Native apps are apps that are built on the Force.com platform, which can be installed directly into a Salesforce org. Salesforce is an extendable system, and many software providers have prebuilt native Salesforce applications that tightly integrate their software with Salesforce. If a Native App is available, making use of it is a no-brainer. Even if you have no need for real-time or a UI integration, I strongly recommend you check whether the application with which you want to integrate has a native Salesforce app in the AppExchange. I would also recommend you check the application vendor's web site for any pre-built integrations they may have.

The Salesforce App exchange can be found here: `https://appexchange.` `salesforce.com/`.

Embedded iFrame

An iFrame is a standard HTML tag that allows you to embed one web page into another. It's kind of like a window into another web page, but you can't interact with the other page in anyway except for passing in a URL to which to navigate.

If the app you need to integrate with is web based, this may be a good option, particularly if the application allows you to go to specific records (or search) by URL. For example, if we want to embed an iFrame into the Account page that searches Google for the latest news about that account, we could have the iFrame navigate to `https://www.google.com/search?q=<<CompanyName>>&tbm=nws&tb` `s=sbd:1,`[12] where we would substitute <<CompanyName>> dynamically for the account name of the record we are looking at. So, if we're looking at IBM's Account page, the iFrame would go to `https://www.google.com/search?q=IBM&tbm=nws&` `tbs=sbd:1`.

---

[12]The q parameter is the "search for" query string; tbm=nws tells Google to search news, tbs=sbd:1 tells Google to sort by date, newest first.

Unfortunately, once an iFrame navigates to the URL, it's completely independent and we have no way of interacting with it. We can, of course, use one of our data integration methods (batch or real time) in conjunction with the iFrame.

For more information on the use of iFrames in Salesforce, see https://developer. salesforce.com/docs/atlas.en-us.pages.meta/pages/pages_compref_iframe.htm.

Hyperlink

A hyperlink is just your standard HTML link tag used to link to other webpages. With an iFrame we are embedding a webpage with in a Salesforce page, but with a Hyperlink it opens over the current page or in a new tab. So just as we built a dynamic URL for use in an iFrame. So too can we build a dynamic URL to be used with a Hyperlink (We can even do it with a formula field).

With the iFrame we embedded news into the page, with a Hyperlink that same URL can be used, to put a link on the Account page that when clicked will open a new we web tab to display current news for that account.

To give you another useful example, the URL below can be dynamically built (if you have the tracking number) to track UPS packages in real time. (Of course you could use this URL with an iFrame too).

```
http://wwwapps.ups.com/WebTracking/processInputRequest?HTMLVersion=5.0&loc=
en_US&Requester=UPSHome&tracknum=<<UPS_Tracking_Number>>&AgreeToTermsAnd
Conditions=yes&track.x=37&track.y=13
```

As with an iFrame, once a Hyperlink is clicked and the web browser navigates to the URL, it's completely independent from Salesforce, and we have no way of interacting with it. We can of course, use one of our data integration methods (batch or real time) in conjunction with the Hyperlink.

For more information on Hyperlinks see: https://success.salesforce.com/ answers?id=9063A000000iQ74QAE

Canvas

Canvas is a set of tools and APIs provided by Salesforce so that we can interact with a user's active Salesforce session. Where an iFrame may be a good option when we don't own the app with which we are integrating or have very limited ability to customize it. Canvas is a great option when we can customize the to be integrated application.

Think of Canvas as a way to embed an iFrame into Salesforce, but have the application be fully aware that it's embedded into Salesforce, who the active user is, and what they are doing, as well as fully interact with Salesforce's data. The only downside to Canvas is that it needs to be coded directly into the target application.

For more information on Salesforce Canvas, see `https://developer.salesforce.com/docs/atlas.en-us.platform_connect.meta/platform_connect/canvas_framework_intro.htm`.

FAT Application Automation

Back in the day, people used to buy computers to install apps on them, not just web browsers. So, your computer would have a lot of apps installed on it, and each app would have an icon. If you wanted to launch an app rather than go to some web site, you would click the icon—kind of like what people do with smartphones today. These applications are collectively called *FAT*[13] (or *thick*) applications, because they take up a lot of room on the computer's hard drive, as opposed to thin applications, which run in a web browser and don't take up any hard drive space at all.

Many of these applications have an automation library that can be used to automate them; these are class libraries that need to be included within your code to be used. These libraries require the target application to be installed on the same server (or computer) as the automation code. If you need to automate an application, and it has an automation library, that's the way to do it.

---

[13]The reason FAT is all uppercase is because it's really an acronym for file allocation table. A FAT is how some operating systems manage file locations on hard drives. Anyhow, FAT kind of lost its original meaning and now is just used to mean "installable app". As stupid as it sounds, it's perfectly okay to say, "I'm going to install a FAT application on my NTFS-based Windows server."

It's very possible that this footnote is completely wrong, and I'm the only moron who made a mental association between FAT and fat (now lowercase) applications, but I don't think so.

One of the most common FAT applications still in use today is MS Office, and of course it has an automation library. It's actually the same class library used when writing MS Office macros.

If needed, we can write a FAT (or Canvas or even a server-side process) application that connects to the Salesforce APIs, gets data, and then uses those data when automating the app to do whatever you need it to do. You can then (at least in the case of a FAT application) hand back control of the application to the user or simply shut it down.

As a security measure, most[14] of these automation libraries require the app to be launched via the library to automate it. This makes sense. Software vendors don't want some malicious piece of code taking over the app while someone is using it, or monitoring what users are doing by using their libraries.

FAT application automation may also be a good option if we to need automate a Telnet (an old green screen-type) application. Let's say we have some FAT app and have no access to its back end. We want to push data (account information) into it when a button is pressed in Salesforce. We add a button to the Salesforce Account page that, when clicked, sends the account data to a web service running on our web servers. That web service, using the app's automation API, launches the app, enters the data via the UI, and then shuts it down.

Here is a great how-to article on automating MS Excel using the C# and the MS Excel object library: `https://support.microsoft.com/en-us/help/302084/how-to-automate-microsoft-excel-from-microsoft-visual-c-net`.

Web Browser Automation

A web browser is a FAT app, it can be automated using a browser object library or a tool like Selenium HQ. When automating a web browser you have access to the web page the user is viewing and can modify or automate the page. Web pages have something called a DOM, or document object model, that is an object used to access all the "things" on a web page. The DOM can be used to manipulate those objects, filling in forms pressing buttons, etc.

For example, let say we want to automate filling out a form on some government web site by pressing a button in Salesforce. We add a button to Salesforce that, when pressed, sends the necessary data to a web service running on our web servers. That web service, using browser automation, navigates to the government web page, fills out the form, and clicks Submit.

---

[14]Maybe all. I have never heard of an automation library that did not require the app to be launched from code.

Browser automation is an option if you need to automate a web site you don't own. Be wary of doing this, because it may make some web site owners very upset. In addition, the web site owner can make small changes to the site—changes to the DOM or implement a CAPTCHA (short for completely automated public turing test to tell computers and humans apart)—that breaks your code.

For more information on browser automation, see the following:

- **Introduction to the DOM:** https://developer.mozilla.org/en-US/docs/Web/API/Document_Object_Model/Introduction

- **Selenium HQ** is a product used to automate browsers. Its most common use case is for automated testing, but it can be used to automate browsers for any reason: https://www.seleniumhq.org/.

- **How to automate a web page in the [.net] WebBrowser control:** https://code.msdn.microsoft.com/windowsdesktop/How-to-automate-a-web-page-ae9d6ca1

Web Browser Extensions

Web browser extensions, sometimes called *add-ons*, are code that becomes part of your browser. So, rather than write an external application for browser automation, you can include a button or a menu directly in the browser to facilitate the automation. In theory, you can also launch a FAT application and automate it using its object library directly from the extension. Every major web browser supports extensions, but unfortunately, mobile browsers generally don't.

Using the same government form example use earlier, let's create a browser extension and add it to our web browser (as a button on the menu bar). That button, when pressed, gets the Salesforce record Id of the current record (off the currently viewed page or URL) and then makes a call to the Salesforce API (passing in the record Id) to get the rest of the necessary data needed to populate the government web form. It then loads the government web form/page in a new tab and fills it out. The browser extension can now either submit the form or hand it over to the user to complete (or at least beat the CAPTCHA) then click Submit (manually).

We will need to install the browser extension on every user's computer.

For more information on browser extensions, see the following:

- **Google Chrome:** https://developer.chrome.com/extensions/getstarted

- **Firefox:** https://developer.mozilla.org/en-US/Add-ons

- **Safari:** https://developer.apple.com/library/archive/documentation/Tools/Conceptual/SafariExtensionGuide/Introduction/Introduction.html

- **Microsoft Edge:** https://docs.microsoft.com/en-us/microsoft-edge/extensions

- **Internet Explorer:** https://stackoverflow.com/questions/5643819/how-to-get-started-with-developing-internet-explorer-extensions

- **Opera Explorer Edge:** https://dev.opera.com/extensions/

Windows Automation

On occasion, you will run into a need to integrate with some application that was simply not designed to be integrated with, is a FAT application, has no object libraries, and uses some cryptic back-end data storage system that you can't access, but you simply *must* integrate with it. Desperate times call for desperate measures. You can use the Windows automation APIs to automate any application running on it. Doing this will be such a hellish experience I don't even want to discuss it, so read up on it yourself.

For more information on the Windows automation APIs, see https://docs.microsoft.com/en-us/windows/desktop/winauto/windows-automation-api-overview.

I will note that the one occasion I had to do this, I opted to automate by taking a screenshot of the desktop, analyzing it,[15] then automating the keyboard and the mouse to act like a user using the application. Also not recommended.

How to: simulate mouse and keyboard events in code: https://docs.microsoft.com/en-us/dotnet/framework/winforms/how-to-simulate-mouse-and-keyboard-events-in-code.

---

[15]Analyzing the bitmap to know where to move the mouse.

Summary

In this chapter we discussed a bunch of options for building real-time integrations via real-time data interchanges or via application automation. It's important to know your options so you can do a deep dive into the details and be able to prove the concept of the potential techniques when needed. It's also important to know that if you are willing to jump through enough hoops you, can integrate anything with Salesforce. Table 11-1 should help you chose the best option for you.

Table 11-1. *Real-time Data and Application Automation Integration Options Summary*

Real-time Data Integration	
Option	**A good option if**
Direct call to the Salesforce APIs	• The event that triggers the integration occurs outside of Salesforce • The integrated system supports web callouts and can be customized to make this call. • There is no need to surface the integrated application's UI
Salesforce Connect	• The integrated systems have an oData point • There is no need to store data physically in Salesforce • There is no need to surface the integrated application's UI
Salesforce outbound messaging	• The integrated systems can consume the outbound message • You only need to send simple messages • The event that triggers the integration occurs from within Salesforce • There is no need to surface the integrated application's UI
Salesforce Streaming API	• You need "ticker"-like displays or real-time changes • The integrated systems can consume the outbound message • The messages are based off insert, update, or delete of a Salesforce record • The event that triggers the integration occurs from within Salesforce • You don't need to guarantee delivery (message can be lost after 24 hours) • There is no need to surface the integrated application's UI

(continued)

Table 11-1. (*continued*)

Real-time Data Integration	
Option	**A good option if**
Salesforce platform events	• You need a "ticker"-like display or real-time changes • The integrated systems can consume the outbound message • The event that triggers the integration occurs from within Salesforce • You don't need to guarantee delivery (message can be lost after 24 hours) • There is no need to surface the integrated application's UI
Apex callout	• The integrated systems can consume the callout • There is a need to send complex messages and, potentially, to process replies • The event that triggers the integration occurs from within Salesforce • There is no need to surface the integrated application's UI
Apex web services	• The event that triggers the integration occurs outside of Salesforce • The integrated system supports web callouts and can be customized to make this call • There is no need to surface the integrated application's UI • The message to (or reply from) Salesforce is too complex to use the native Salesforce APIs
Web-to-Case	• You need web forms that can be used to create Salesforce cases
Web-to-Lead	• You need web forms that can be used to create Salesforce leads (and match to a campaign)
Email-to-Case	• You want to support creating Salesforce cases from an incoming e-mail
Apex e-mail service	• You want to support doing anything (other than creating a case) in Salesforce from an incoming e-mail

(*continued*)

Table 11-1. (*continued*)

Real-time Data Integration

Option	A good option if
Web service triggered ETL	• The event that triggers the integration occurs outside of Salesforce • The event that triggers the integration occurs from within Salesforce • There is no need to surface the integrated application's UI • The integrated application has no API to hit or is closed off to the Web (So, you need a back-end integration, but want to be real time.)
SOA middleware	• You currently have this infrastructure in place and want to be consistent with what your organization is doing elsewhere

Application Automation Integration

Option	A good option if
Native Apps	• The integrated application has a native Salesforce App
Embedded iFrame	• All you need to do is automate navigation • The integrated application is web based
Hyperlink	• All you need to do is automate navigation • The integrated application is web based
Canvas	• The integrated application is web based and customizable • You need very tightly coupled UI integration • You need be aware of who the calling Salesforce user is, or what they are doing in Salesforce
FAT application automation	• The FAT application has an automation library • You need to hand off the UI to the user after some automation, and you are okay installing and maintaining code on users' individual desktops *or* you are okay with setting up an automation server that handles the automation

(*continued*)

Table 11-1. (*continued*)

Application Automation Integration

Option	A good option if
Web browser automation	• The integrated application is web based • You need to do more than navigation • The integrated application does not have any native means of integration • You are okay with the web site owner's ability to break your code at any time with no notice • You need to hand off the UI to the user after some automation, and you are okay installing and maintaining code on users' individual desktops *or* you are okay with setting up an automation server that handles the automation
Web browser extensions	• The integrated application is web based • You need to do more than navigation • The integrated application does not have any native means of integration • You are okay with the website owner's ability to break your code at any time with no notice • You need to hand off the UI to the user after some automation, and you are okay installing and maintaining code on users' individual desktops
Windows automation	• You make a deal with the devil and have no other choice

CHAPTER 12

A Library of Reusable Code

If you read any book on coding best practices, the subject of "code reuse" is bound to come up. So, it's no surprise that when we covered best practices (in Chapter 6). One of the best practices we examined (Best Practice 21 in Chapter 6) was to "Build up a library of reusable code." Having a library of reusable code will not only save you time when you next need to build a data migration or integration, but also it will improve code quality, because over time your library will become tried and true.

If you are like me and work in professional services (consulting), you have to work with lots of different ETL (or middleware) tools and lots of different RDBMSs. And, unfortunately, any reusable ETL code you write has to be either tool or RDBMS specific. As we saw in Chapter 7, when we did our sample migration, I like to keep all my transformation code in the RDBMS, because I find that it's easier to centralize it there (Best Practice 8 in Chapter 6). There are also less mainstream RDBMSs than there are ETL tools/middleware, so I get more reuse by writing code for the RDBMS than I do for ETL tools/middleware.[1]

In this chapter, I'm going to share with you (a portion) of my library of MS SQL Server reusable transformation code. This library has been built up over a few years and is updated constantly by myself or a member of my team.

The code is written as UDFs in T-SQL. A UDF is just like any native SQL function, except that its custom written. What I like about them is that they can be used inline in SQL, so they are very easy to reuse. Like most small code functions or snippets, they

---

[1]Also, for whatever reason, a lot of ETL tool/middleware vendors make writing reusable code difficult.

© David Masri 2019
D. Masri, *Developing Data Migrations and Integrations with Salesforce*,
https://doi.org/10.1007/978-1-4842-4209-4_12

often start with a Google search, then copy it and modify it, and then it continues to evolve over time. I have attempted to locate the original source for each of these snippets and, if I was able to locate it, I provide the location.

Again, I want to point out that you don't have to do this in T-SQL or use UDFs. The goal if this chapter is to give you an example of a decent (transformation) code library, show you some common transformations that you may need, and—because I already have this code written—share it with you.

Transformation UDFs and Templates

If you recall from our sample migration (Chapter 7), we used a few of these as part of that migration to do things like

- Format phone numbers

- Validate e-mail addresses

- Split out name parts (first, middle, last)

- Combine contact types into a semicolon-delimited list to be loaded into a multiselect picklist

- Base64 encode binary file data to be loaded as Salesforce files

- Split out file paths into their various parts

Here we will review the code used for these transformations and many more. A lot of this code was written to accomplish only what was needed at the time. If you decide to use some of this code, you should modify it as needed to fit your use cases. Here they are in (mostly) alphabetical order.

fn_Base64Encode

Function Description: If you recall from our sample migration (Chapter 7), we had to load file attachments to Salesforce. To do this, we needed to take the file's binary data and base64[2] encode it. In Chapter 7, we used the KingswaySoft connector, which handled the conversion for us. But, if the connector you are using doesn't accommodate the conversion, you may need custom code (such as this).

---

[2]For more information on base64 encoding, see https://stackoverflow.com/questions/201479/what-is-base-64-encoding-used-for.

Originating Source: https://stackoverflow.com/questions/5082345/base64-encoding-in-sql-server-2005-t-sql

Sample Usage:

```
SELECT
        [dbo].[Fn_Base64Encode](f.[FileData]) as [FileData64]
FROM [dbo].[Files] f
```

Sample Input: 0x255044462D312E330A25C7EC8FA20A3.......
Sample Output: JVBERi0xLjMKJcfsj6IKMzAgMCBvYmoKPD......
Code:

```
CREATE FUNCTION [dbo].[Fn_Base64Encode](@Input VARCHAR(MAX))
RETURNS VARCHAR(MAX)
BEGIN
        declare @source varbinary(max)
        declare @encoded varchar(max)
        set @source = convert(varbinary(max), @Input)
        set @encoded = cast(" as xml).value('xs:base64Binary(sql:variable
        ("@source"))', 'varchar(max)')
        RETURN @encoded
END
```

fn_Base64Decode

Function Description: fn_Base64Decode does the exact opposite as fn_Base64Encode. It takes a base64-encoded string or binary and decodes it. You can use such a function if you need to download attachments from Salesforce and load them to a database or stream them to the file system. As with base64 encoding, some connectors may do this for you.

Originating Source: https://stackoverflow.com/questions/5082345/base64-encoding-in-sql-server-2005-t-sql

Sample Usage:

```
SELECT
        [dbo].[Fn_Base64Decode](f.[FileData64]) as [FileData]
FROM [dbo].[Files] f
```

Sample Input: JVBERi0xLjMKJcfsj6IKMzAgMCBvYmoKPD......

Sample Output: 0x255044462D312E330A25C7EC8FA20A3.......

Code:

```
CREATE FUNCTION [dbo].[Fn_Base64Decode](@Input VARCHAR(MAX))
RETURNS VARCHAR(MAX)
BEGIN
        DECLARE @DecodedOutput VARCHAR(MAX)
        set @DecodedOutput = cast(" as xml).value('xs:base64Binary(sql:vari
        able("@Input"))', 'varbinary(max)')
        RETURN @DecodedOutput
END
```

fn_CamelCase

Function Description: On occasion, you will be migrating or integrating with a system that likes to store all data in uppercase (or all lowercase). Loading names or other data in all uppercase is ugly, and you may want to convert the whole thing to lowercase except for the first letter of every word (camel case). Fn_CamelCase does just that. The function makes the whole string lowercase except for the first letter of each word. It determines whether a letter is the first in a word by checking whether it is the first letter in the string or whether it comes after a "word delimiter" (a space, a comma, other punctuation, and so on).

Originating Source: http://stackoverflow.com/questions/5164201/is-there-any-sql-server-built-in-function-to-convert-string-in-camel-case

Sample Usage:

```
Select dbo.[fn_CamelCase](Name) as Name
from dbo.People
```

Sample Input: JOHN DOE

Sample Output: John Doe

Code:

```
CREATE FUNCTION [dbo].[fn_CamelCase] (@InputString nvarchar(4000) )
RETURNS nVARCHAR(4000)
AS
  BEGIN
    DECLARE @Index         INT
```

```
    DECLARE @Char              nCHAR(1)
    DECLARE @PrevChar          nCHAR(1)
    DECLARE @OutputString      nVARCHAR(255)

    SET @OutputString = LOWER(@InputString)
    SET @Index = 1

    WHILE @Index <= LEN(@InputString)
    BEGIN
        SET @Char       = SUBSTRING(@InputString, @Index, 1)
        SET @PrevChar =
        CASE WHEN @Index = 1 THEN ' '
            ELSE SUBSTRING(@InputString, @Index - 1, 1)
        END

        IF @PrevChar IN (' ', ';', ':', '!', '?', ',', '.', '_', '-', '/',
        '&', "", '(')
        BEGIN
        IF @PrevChar != "" OR UPPER(@Char) != 'S'
        SET @OutputString = STUFF(@OutputString, @Index, 1, UPPER(@Char))
        END
        SET @Index = @Index + 1
    END
  RETURN @OutputString
END
```

fn_Convert15CharIDTo18

Function Description: This function takes the 15-character Salesforce Id, calculates the three-character hash, appends it to the 15-character Id, and returns the 18-character Id.

  Originating Source: https://joelmansford.wordpress.com/2010/01/21/ function-to-convert-15char-salesforce-com-ids-to-18char-ones-in-t-sql-sql-server/

  Sample Usage:

```
Select dbo.fn_Convert15CharIDTo18('0016A00000PBUBV') as ID
```

Sample Input: 0016A00000PBUBV

Sample Output: 0016A00000PBUBVQA5

Code:

```
-- ===============================================
-- Author:        Joel Mansford
-- Create date:   Jan 2010
-- Description:   Converts 15char SF Ids to 18char ones
-- History: June 2010 - issue with over-running and incorrectly producing
--   ']' as a character with input such as '0033000000dGpDN'
-- ===============================================
CREATE FUNCTION dbo.fn_Convert15CharIDTo18( @InputId char(15))
RETURNS char(18)
AS
BEGIN
    -- Hacky way to raise an error but it works and there's no alternative!
    DECLARE @ErrorStringReally int
    IF LEN(@InputId)<>15
        SET @ErrorStringReally ='Input Salesforce Id must be exactly 15
        characters input was "'+ @InputId+'"'
    DECLARE @OutputId char(18)
    DECLARE @Hash varchar(3)
    SET @Hash = "
    DECLARE @Chunk tinyint
    DECLARE @ThisChunk char(5)
    DECLARE @CharPos tinyint
    DECLARE @ThisHashDigit tinyint

    -- Split string in to 3 chunks of 5chars
    SET @Chunk = 1
    WHILE @Chunk<=3
    BEGIN
        SELECT @ThisChunk = RIGHT(LEFT(@InputId,@Chunk*5),5)
        SET @ThisHashDigit = 0
```

```
        SET @CharPos = 1
        -- Iterate over the chunk
        WHILE @CharPos<=5
        BEGIN
            IF ASCII(SUBSTRING(@ThisChunk,@CharPos,1)) BETWEEN 65 AND 90 --
            If Uppercase -- then add a binary '1' digit in the appropriate
            position, otherwise it's still 0
                SET @ThisHashDigit +=POWER(2,@CharPos-1)
            SET @CharPos+=1
        END
        IF @ThisHashDigit>=26
        -- Digits 0-9, minus 26 as SFDC have numbers come 'after' letters
            SET @Hash +=CHAR(@ThisHashDigit+48-26)
        ELSE
            -- Letter 'A'
            SET @Hash +=CHAR(@ThisHashDigit+65)
        SET @Chunk+=1
    END
    SET @OutputId = @InputId + @Hash
    RETURN @OutputId
END
```

fn_Fix_Invalid_XML_Chars

Function Description: There are some characters that are invalid for use in XML, so if your source data include one of them, the generated XML that gets sent to Salesforce as part of a SOAP call will fail. You have to strip them out of your data first. This function replaces all invalid XML characters with what I think is the best replacement (you may disagree, and modify it as you like).

Note that this code is slow. I recommend you comment-out all the lines that replace characters that don't exist in your data. If it's still too slow, you can process your data and let the bad records fail, then use a function like fn_Fix_Invalid_XML_Chars to strip out the invalid characters from only the failed records, then reprocess only those records.

OriginatingSource:https://stackoverflow.com/questions/28365316/sql-server-replace-invalid-xml-characters-from-a-varcharmax-field

Sample Usage:

```
Select
        [dbo].[fn_Fix_Invalid_XML_Chars](LongText) as Notetext
from dbo.Notes
```

Code:

```
Create Function [dbo].[fn_Fix_Invalid_XML_Chars](@strText NVARCHAR(max))
RETURNS NVARCHAR(max)
AS
BEGIN
        set @strText = replace(@strText,CHAR(0x0),")
        set @strText = replace(@strText,CHAR(0x1),")
        set @strText = replace(@strText,CHAR(0x2),")
        set @strText = replace(@strText,CHAR(0x3),")
        set @strText = replace(@strText,CHAR(0x4),")
        set @strText = replace(@strText,CHAR(0x5),")
        set @strText = replace(@strText,CHAR(0x6),")
        set @strText = replace(@strText,CHAR(0x7),")
        set @strText = replace(@strText,CHAR(0x8),")
        set @strText = replace(@strText,CHAR(0x9),")

        set @strText = replace(@strText,CHAR(0x10),")
        set @strText = replace(@strText,CHAR(0x11),")
        set @strText = replace(@strText,CHAR(0x12),")
        set @strText = replace(@strText,CHAR(0x13),")
        set @strText = replace(@strText,CHAR(0x14),")
        set @strText = replace(@strText,CHAR(0x15),")
        set @strText = replace(@strText,CHAR(0x16),")
        set @strText = replace(@strText,CHAR(0x17),")
        set @strText = replace(@strText,CHAR(0x18),")
        set @strText = replace(@strText,CHAR(0x19),")

        set @strText = replace(@strText,CHAR(0xa),")
        set @strText = replace(@strText,CHAR(0xb),")
        set @strText = replace(@strText,CHAR(0xc),")
```

```
    set @strText = replace(@strText,CHAR(0xd),Char(10))
    set @strText = replace(@strText,CHAR(0xe),")
    set @strText = replace(@strText,CHAR(0xf),")

    set @strText = replace(@strText,CHAR(0x1a),"")
    set @strText = replace(@strText,CHAR(0x1b),")
    set @strText = replace(@strText,CHAR(0x1c),")
    set @strText = replace(@strText,CHAR(0x1d),")
    set @strText = replace(@strText,CHAR(0x1e),")
    set @strText = replace(@strText,CHAR(0x1f),")

    set @strText = replace(@strText,CHAR(0x7f),")

    RETURN @strText
END
```

fn_FormatPhone

Function Description: As we know from Chapter 2, Salesforce only formats phone numbers when its being entered by the UI. So, if we are loading phone numbers via the Salesforce API, we have to format them ourselves. fn_FormatPhone does just that (for US numbers only; for non-US numbers, it just leaves them as is). It strips out any existing formatting, then reformats them to Salesforce's standard format. It also takes into account extensions. If there is an "e" or an "x" in the phone number passed in, it only formats the phone number section (the numbers prior to the "e" or the "x") of the string.

Sometimes I feel like I have to modify this code every other week. People seem to find a million and one ways to type a phone number. If I get a dataset that doesn't have any e-mail addresses in the phone number field, I consider this a win.

Originating Source: N/A

Sample Usage:

```
Select dbo.[fn_FormatPhone](HomePhone) as HomePhone
from dbo.People
```

Sample Input: 555 555.5555 xtn25

Sample Output: (555) 555-5555 xtn25

Code:

```
Create Function [dbo].[fn_FormatPhone](@strTextFull VARCHAR(1000))
RETURNS VARCHAR(1000)
AS
BEGIN
        declare @strText VARCHAR(1000)
        declare @strCleanText VARCHAR(1000)
        declare @strTextExt VARCHAR(1000)
        select @strTextExt="

        ---
        select @strCleanText=replace(@strTextFull,' ',")
        select @strCleanText=replace(@strCleanText,'-',")
        select @strCleanText=replace(@strCleanText,'.',")
        select @strCleanText=replace(@strCleanText,'(',")
        select @strCleanText=replace(@strCleanText,')',")
        if SUBSTRING(@strCleanText,1,1)='+' ---------------- Remove Leading
        Plus
                select @strCleanText=SUBSTRING(@strCleanText,2,1000)
        if SUBSTRING(@strCleanText,1,1)='1' ---------------- Remove Leading 1
                select @strCleanText=SUBSTRING(@strCleanText,2,1000)

        -- for Extensions
        if SUBSTRING(@strCleanText,11,1)='x' or SUBSTRING(@strCleanText,
        11,1)='e'
        begin
                select @strTextExt=SUBSTRING(@strCleanText,11,1000)
                select @strCleanText=SUBSTRING(@strCleanText,1,10)
        end

        if isnumeric(@strCleanText)=0
        begin
                return @strTextFull-- No Transformation
        end
```

```
        if len(@strCleanText)<>10
        begin
                return @strTextFull -- No Transformation
        end

    select @strCleanText='('+substring(@strCleanText,1,3)+') '+substring(@
strCleanText,4,3)+'-'+substring(@strCleanText,7,4)


    RETURN @strCleanText+' '+@strTextExt
END
```

fn_Format_for_ContentNoteText

Function Description: The ContentNote.content field wants data that are formatted as HTML, but the field is very restrictive on the HTML it actually accepts. When loading data to the ContentNote object, if there is something that looks like HTML (but is really not) or uses an unsupported HTML tag, we may get the error message "Note can't be saved because it contains HTML tags or unescaped characters that are not allowed in a Note." [3] This function converts the faux HTML, so that the note displays correctly in Salesforce, and it also converts line breaks and tabs into proper HTML.

I know this is confusing, and is probably making your head spin. Sorry. It's as if two developers got into an argument over whether this field should be rich text (HTML) or plain text and came to some wacky compromise.[4]

Developer 1: This should be a rich text field.

Developer 2: What?!! It's a Notes field! Notes are plain text ONLY!

Developer 1: I said RICH TEXT!

Developer 2: YOUR MOTHER INDENTS WITH SPACES!

Developer 1: [Audible gasp] DEM'S FIGHTIN' WORDS!

Putting aside how much of a mess this is, I recommend you ignore that you ever read this and hope you never get that error message. If you do, come back and try this code (or implement something similar in your language/tool of choice).

---

[3]For more information, see https://help.salesforce.com/articleView?id=000232870&type=1.

[4]For more information, see https://help.salesforce.com/articleView?id=000230867&language=en_US&type=1.

Originating Source: N/A

Sample Usage:

```
Select
        [dbo].[fn_Format_for_ContentNoteText](LongText) as NoteText
from dbo.Notes
```

Sample Input: <<Yo!>>

Sample Output: <<Yo!>>

Code:

```
Create Function [dbo].[fn_Format_for_ContentNoteText](@strText nVARCHAR(max))
RETURNS VARCHAR(max)
AS
BEGIN
        set @strText=replace(@strText,'&','&')
        set @strText=replace(@strText,'<','<')
        set @strText=replace(@strText,'>','>')
        set @strText=replace(@strText,'"','&quot;')
        set @strText=replace(@strText,"",''')
        set @strText=replace(@strText,char(9),'    ')
        set @strText=replace(@strText,char(10),'<br>')
        set @strText=replace(@strText,char(23),'<br>')
        set @strText=replace(@strText,char(13),'<br>')

    RETURN coalesce(@strText,")
END
```

fn_GetAccountAggregation: Example for Multiselect Picklist

Function Description: In Chapter 2, we learned that multiselect picklists store multiple picklist values in a semicolon-delimited string. We also learned that this is starkly different than how a relational database would store such data. A relational database would store these data in a one-to-many child table. If we are loading this type of data to Salesforce, we need to find all child rows per Id and concatenate the values into a single semicolon-delimited field.

This code is more of a template then a reusable function. We need to modify the SQL used to get the child data. It takes an Id (or whatever needs to go into the "where" clause) and it returns the semicolon-delimited list of child values.

Originating Source: https://stackoverflow.com/questions/887628/convert-multiple-rows-into-one-with-comma-as-separator

Sample Usage:

```
Select dbo.[fn_GetAccountAggregation](CompanyID) as Companytypes
from dbo.Company
```

Sample Input: 126

Sample Output: Retail;Wholesale;e-Commerce

Code:

```
Create function [dbo].[fn_GetAccountAggregation](@companyID varchar(255))
returns nvarchar(1000)
begin
        declare @CommaString nvarchar(max)
        set @CommaString="
        select @CommaString +=rtrim(ltrim(Type)) +';' from dbo.companytype
where companyID=@companyID  -- Modify this SQL
        if len(@CommaString)>0
                begin
                        -- Drop Extra Semi-Colon
                 SET @CommaString = LEFT(@CommaString, LEN(@CommaString) - 1)
                end
        Return @CommaString
End
```

fn_GetAddressLines

Function Description: Salesforce stores every address in one multiline text field. Many other systems store addresses using one line per field. For outbound integrations, you may find the need to breakup Salesforce addresses into multiple fields. This function takes a Salesforce Address field and a Line Number parameter (formatted as "L1", "L2," or "L3") and returns the requested address line.

Originating Source: N/A
Sample Usage:

```
select
        [dbo].[fn_GetAddressLines]([MailingStreet],'L1') as
        MailingStreetLine1,
        [dbo].[fn_GetAddressLines]([MailingStreet],'L2') as
        MailingStreetLine2,
        [dbo].[fn_GetAddressLines]([MailingStreet],'L3') as
        MailingStreetLine3,
        from [dbo].[SF_Contact]
```

Sample Input: 123 Sesame Street
Suite 501
New York, NY 10001[5]
Sample Output: 123 Sesame Street
Code:

```
Create function [dbo].[fn_GetAddressLines](@Address nVarchar(3000),
@Linepart Char(2))
returns nvarchar(1000)
-- @Linepart : L1=First,L2=L3=Last
begin

    Declare @Line1 nVarchar(3000)
    Declare @Line2 nVarchar(3000)
    Declare @Line3 nVarchar(3000)
    Declare @Return nVarchar(3000)

    select @Address=rtrim(ltrim(coalesce(@Address,")))
    SELECT @Line1= rtrim(ltrim(coalesce(@Address,")))
    SELECT @Line2="
    SELECT @Line3="
```

---

[5]Yes, Sesame Street is in Manhattan, NY. See https://en.wikipedia.org/wiki/
Sesame_Street_(fictional_location).

```
if @Address like '%'+char(10)+'%'
Begin
    SELECT @Line1= SUBSTRING(@Address, 1, CHARINDEX(Char(10), @
    Address) - 1)
    SELECT @Line2=substring(replace(@Address,@Line1,"),2,3000)
end

select @Address=@Line2

if @Address like '%'+char(10)+'%'
Begin
    SELECT @Line2= SUBSTRING(@Address, 1, CHARINDEX(Char(10), @
    Address) - 1)
    SELECT @Line3=substring(replace(@Address,@Line2,"),2,3000)
    SELECT @Line3=replace(@Line3,char(10),'-')
end

SELECT @Return = case when @Linepart = 'L1' then @Line1
            when @Linepart = 'L2' then @Line2
            when @Linepart = 'L3' then @Line3
        else Null end

    Return rtrim(ltrim(@Return))
end
```

fn_GetDomain

Function Description: The fn_GetDomain function parses the domain section out of a URL. I have used this mostly for data-cleansing purposes.

OriginatingSource:https://social.msdn.microsoft.com/Forums/sqlserver/en-US/ fbafbdef-9a5e-470a-8c73-4c95bd547603/parsing-domain-names-form-url

Sample Usage:

```
Select dbo.[fn_GetDomain](url) as Domain
from dbo.Company
```

Sample Input: https://www.linkedin.com/in/davidmasri/

Sample Output: linkedin.com

Code:

```
CREATE FUNCTION [dbo].[fn_GetDomain]  (@strURL nvarchar(1000))
RETURNS nvarchar(1000)
AS
BEGIN
IF CHARINDEX('http://',@strURL) > 0 OR CHARINDEX('https://',@strURL) > 0
SELECT @strURL = REPLACE(@strURL,' ','')
SELECT @strURL = REPLACE(@strURL,'https://','')
SELECT @strURL = REPLACE(@strURL,'http://','')
SELECT @strURL = REPLACE(@strURL,'www.','')
SELECT @strURL = REPLACE(@strURL,'www','')
SELECT @strURL = REPLACE(@strURL,'ftp://','')
-- Remove everything after "/" if one exists

IF CHARINDEX('/',@strURL) > 0 (SELECT @strURL = LEFT(@
strURL,CHARINDEX('/',@strURL)-1))
    --Optional: Remove subdomains but differentiate between www.google.com
    and www.google.com.au
    --IF (LEN(@strURL)-LEN(REPLACE(@strURL,'.','')))/LEN('.') < 3 -- if
there are less than 3 periods
    --SELECT @strURL = PARSENAME(@strURL,2) + '.' + PARSENAME(@strURL,1)
    --ELSE -- It's likely a google.co.uk, or google.com.au
    --SELECT @strURL = PARSENAME(@strURL,3) + '.' + PARSENAME(@strURL,2) +
    '.' + PARSENAME(@strURL,1)
RETURN @strURL
END
```

fn_GetFileExtension

Function Description: The fn_GetFileExtension function takes a file name and returns just the extension (the part of the file name after the dot), which is generally the best way to identify the kind of file it is. (This only works for three- or four-character extensions).

Originating Source: N/A

Sample Usage:

```
Select dbo.[fn_GetFileExtension](filename) as FileExtension
from dbo.files
```

Sample Input: Dave.txt

Sample Output: txt

Code:

```
Create Function [dbo].[fn_GetFileExtension](@FileName nVARCHAR(1000))
RETURNS nVARCHAR(1000)
AS
BEGIN
    Return
    case
      when substring(right(@FileName,4),1,1)='.' then right(@FileName,4)
      when substring(right(@FileName,5),1,1)='.' then right(@FileName,5)
    else "
end
```

fn_GetFileFromPath

Function Description: The fn_GetFileFromPath function takes a full file path and returns only the file name. Like GetFileExtention, we can use the fn_GetFileFromPath function when loading attachments to Salesforce and the source data do not have a separate field for file name.

Originating Source: N/A

Sample Usage:

```
Select dbo.[fn_GetFileFromPath](filepath) as filename
from dbo.files
```

Sample Input: c:\files\Dave.txt

Sample Output: Dave.txt

Code:

```
CREATE Function [dbo].[fn_GetFileFromPath](@PathFile NVARCHAR(1000))
RETURNS NVARCHAR(1000)
```

```
AS
BEGIN
    declare @FileName NVARCHAR(1000)
    SELECT @PathFile='\'+replace(@PathFile,'/','\') -- For Unix Type Paths
    SELECT @FileName=reverse(left(reverse(@PathFile),
                        charindex('\',reverse(@PathFile), 1) - 1))
    RETURN @FileName
END
```

fn_GetNamePart

Function Description: Salesforce has three fields for contact name: FirstName, MiddleName, and LastName. If our source data only has one field for a name, we can use the fn_GetNamePart function to split it. It takes a parameter to specify which "name part" we want (F = first, M = middle, L = last). If there are more than three words in the name, the function uses the first word as the first name, the last word as the last name, and all others as the middle name.

Originating Source: N/A

Sample Usage:

```
select
    dbo.[fn_GetNamePart](FullName,'F') as FirstName
    ,dbo.[fn_GetNamePart](FullName,'M') as MiddleName
    ,dbo.[fn_GetNamePart](FullName,'L') as LastName
from People
```

Sample Input: Dave J. Masri

Sample Output: Dave

Code:

```
CREATE function [dbo].[fn_GetNamePart](@FullName NVarchar(3000),@Namepart
Char(1))
returns Nvarchar(1000)
-- @Namepart : F=First,M=Middle,L=Last
```

```
begin
    Declare @FirstName Varchar(1000)
    Declare @MiddleName Varchar(1000)
    Declare @LastName Varchar(1000)
    Declare @Return Varchar(1000)

    select @FullName=rtrim(ltrim(coalesce(@FullName,")))+' '
    SELECT @FirstName= SUBSTRING(@FullName, 1, CHARINDEX(' ', @FullName) - 1)

    select @FullName=' '+rtrim(ltrim(@FullName))
    SELECT @LastName=  REVERSE(SUBSTRING(REVERSE(@FullName), 1, CHARINDEX('
', REVERSE(@FullName)) - 1))
    SELECT @MiddleName=replace(replace(@FullName,@FirstName,"),@LastName,")

    SELECT @Return = case when @Namepart = 'F' then @FirstName
              when @Namepart = 'M' then @MiddleName
              when @Namepart = 'L' then @LastName
          else Null end

    Return rtrim(ltrim(@Return))
end
```

fn_GoodEmailorBlank

Function Description: Invalid e-mail addresses is probably the most common reason for row-level contact insert, update, and upsert errors. The fn_GoodEmailorBlank function checks whether an email is valid. If it is, it returns the e-mail address; otherwise, it returns a blank. In this way, we can still load the contact, just without the e-mail address (if it's invalid).

Unfortunately, it seems there is no real standard way for validating e-mail addresses. And even if we did find the perfect code, Salesforces e-mail validation code is not perfect. But, the following code catches the vast majority of invalid e-mail addresses.

We can also use the following code to find invalid e-mail addresses by comparing the original e-mail address to the e-mail address returned from this function. We can load the invalid email addresses into a plaintext field for user review (as we did in Chapter 7), so there is no data loss.

Originating Source: https://stackoverflow.com/questions/229824/tsql-email-validation-without-regex

Sample Usage:

```
Select dbo.[fn_GoodEmailorBlank](email) as Email
from People
```

Sample Usage to get a list of contacts with an invalid e-mail address:

```
Select
    ID
    ,Email
from People
where coalesce(email,")<>dbo.[fn_GoodEmailorBlank](email)
```

Sample Input: Dave@demo.demo

Sample Output: Dave@demo.demo

Code:

```
Create function [dbo].[fn_GoodEmailorBlank](@EmailAddress varchar(1000))
returns varchar(1000)
begin
    declare @return varchar(1000)
    declare @email varchar(1000)
    set @email = rtrim(ltrim(@EmailAddress))

    -- cannot end with apostrophe, but they are ok inside of a name: e.g.
       O'Connor
    select  @email =
        CASE WHEN
                @email LIKE '%_@_%._%'
                AND @email NOT LIKE '%.'
                and @email NOT LIKE '%@%@%'
                and @email NOT LIKE '%@%[_]%' ----- This is a Salesforce
                defect, Domains can have Underscores
        THEN @email
        ELSE "
        END
```

```
---- Validate there is no spaces or invalid Chars in the Email Address
select  @return =
CASE WHEN
        @email LIKE '% %' or @email LIKE '%,%'  or @email LIKE '%;%'
THEN    ''
ELSE @email
END

return  @return
end
```

fn_MultiSelect_DedupAndSort

Function Description: If we look back at our synchronization patterns (Chapter 9), a few of the patterns require that we compare values to determine which records have changed. In Chapter 2, we learned that multiselect picklists won't save the values in the order in which we loaded them. So, comparing multiselect picklist source values to Salesforce as a means to detect changes can result in false positives! The fn_MultiSelect_ DedupAndSort function "dedupes" and sorts picklist values so we can perform multiselect picklist value comparisons. I often use this function in conjunction with the fn_GetAccountAggregations function.

Originating Source: https://blog.sqlauthority.com/2009/01/15/sql-server-remove-duplicate-entry-from-comma-delimited-string-udf/

Sample Usage:

```
Select
    dbo.fn_MultiSelect_DedupAndSort(dbo.[fn_GetAccountAggregation]
    (CompanyID)) as Companytypes
from dbo.Company
```

Sample Input: Retail;Retail;Wholesale;e-Commerce
Sample Output: e-Commerce;Retail;Wholesale
Code:

```
Create FUNCTION dbo.fn_MultiSelect_DedupAndSort(@List nVARCHAR(MAX))
RETURNS nVARCHAR(MAX)
AS
```

```
    BEGIN
    DECLARE @Delim CHAR=';'

    DECLARE @ParsedList TABLE
    (
    Item nVARCHAR(MAX)
    )
    DECLARE @list1 nVARCHAR(MAX), @Pos INT, @rList nVARCHAR(MAX)
    SET @list = LTRIM(RTRIM(@list)) + @Delim
    SET @pos = CHARINDEX(@delim, @list, 1)
    WHILE @pos > 0
    BEGIN
        SET @list1 = LTRIM(RTRIM(LEFT(@list, @pos - 1)))
        IF @list1 <> "
            INSERT INTO @ParsedList VALUES (CAST(@list1 AS nVARCHAR(MAX)))
            SET @list = SUBSTRING(@list, @pos+1, LEN(@list))
            SET @pos = CHARINDEX(@delim, @list, 1)
            END
    SELECT
        @rlist = COALESCE(@rlist+@Delim,") + item
    FROM (SELECT DISTINCT Item FROM @ParsedList) t
    RETURN @rlist
END
GO
```

fn_StripHTML

Function Description: If we need to load HTML text into a plain text field, we have to strip out the HTML first. The fn_StripHTML function converts HTML to plain text (by stripping out all HTML used for formatting) while keeping the line breaks, and converts the commonly encoded characters.[6] It's not perfect, but it performs fairly well.

Originating Source: https://stackoverflow.com/questions/457701/best-way-to-strip-html-tags-from-a-string-in-sql-server

---

[6]You can add more easily, if needed, but this action will affect performance negatively.

Sample Usage:

```
Select
    [dbo].[fn_Format_for_ContentNoteText](LongText) as NoteText
from dbo.Notes
```

Sample Input: Dave
Sample Output: Dave
Code:

```
CREATE FUNCTION [dbo].[fn_StripHTML] (@HTMLText nVARCHAR(MAX))
RETURNS nVARCHAR(MAX) AS
BEGIN
    DECLARE @Start INT
    DECLARE @End INT
    DECLARE @Length INT
        SET @HTMLText=replace(@HTMLText,'<BR>',Char(10))
        SET @HTMLText=replace(@HTMLText,'</BR>',Char(10))
        SET @HTMLText=replace(@HTMLText,' ',' ')
        SET @HTMLText=replace(@HTMLText,''',"")
        SET @HTMLText=replace(@HTMLText,'&','&')
        SET @HTMLText=replace(@HTMLText,'&quot;','"')

    SET @Start = CHARINDEX('<',@HTMLText)
    SET @End = CHARINDEX('>',@HTMLText,CHARINDEX('<',@HTMLText))
    SET @Length = (@End - @Start) + 1
    WHILE @Start > 0 AND @End > 0 AND @Length > 0
    BEGIN
        SET @HTMLText = STUFF(@HTMLText,@Start,@Length,")
        SET @Start = CHARINDEX('<',@HTMLText)
        SET @End = CHARINDEX('>',@HTMLText,CHARINDEX('<',@HTMLText))
        SET @Length = (@End - @Start) + 1
    END
        --- For MS Dynamics or Emails
        SET @HTMLText=replace(@HTMLText,'{behavior:url(#default#VML);}',")
        SET @HTMLText=replace(@HTMLText,'v\:*',")
        SET @HTMLText=replace(@HTMLText,'o\:*',")
```

```
        SET @HTMLText=replace(@HTMLText,'w\:*',")
        SET @HTMLText=replace(@HTMLText,'.shape',")
        SET @HTMLText=replace(@HTMLText,'.shape',")
    RETURN LTRIM(RTRIM(@HTMLText))
END
GO
```

fn_StripNonAlphaNumericCharacters

Function Description: The fn_StripNonAlphaNumericCharacters function removes all characters that are not letters or numbers. The function can be used when you don't have a PK in your source data and you need to build one. (I find it better to keep junk out of my PKs.)

Originating Source: N/A

Sample Usage:

```
select
    dbo.[fn_StripNonAlphaNumericCharacters](FullName) as PK
from People
```

Sample Input: @Dave!

Sample Output: Dave

Code:

```
Create Function [dbo].[fn_StripNonAlphaNumericCharacters](@Temp
VarChar(max))
Returns VarChar(max)
AS
Begin

    Declare @KeepValues as varchar(50)
    Set @KeepValues = '%[^a-z0-9]%'
    While PatIndex(@KeepValues, @Temp) > 0
        Set @Temp = Stuff(@Temp, PatIndex(@KeepValues, @Temp), 1, ")

    Return @Temp
End
```

fn_RemoveNonNumeric

Function Description: The fn_RemoveNonNumeric function removes all non-numeric characters from the passed-in string (including spaces). It's usually used to remove formatting from numbers, from things like phone numbers, driver's license numbers, account numbers, and Social Security numbers. The fn_RemoveNonNumeric function is used in Appendix A, so I am including it here.

　　Originating Source: https://dba.stackexchange.com/questions/21166/how-can-i-strip-non-numeric-characters-outof-a-string

　　Sample Usage:

```
Select
    dbo.[fn_RemoveNonNumeric](SSN) as SSN_Clean
from People
```

　　Sample Input: (123) 456-7890
　　Sample Output: 1234567890
　　Code:

```
CREATE Function [dbo].[fn_RemoveNonNumeric](@strText nVARCHAR(1000))
RETURNS nVARCHAR(1000)
AS
BEGIN
    WHILE PATINDEX('%[^0-9]%', @strText) > 0
    BEGIN
        SET @strText = STUFF(@strText, PATINDEX('%[^0-9]%', @strText), 1, ")
    END
    RETURN coalesce(@strText,")
END
```

fn_StripSpaces

Function Description: The fn_StripSpaces function is a very simple UDF. All it does is remove all spaces from the passed-in string. It too is used in Appendix A, so I am including it here.

　　Originating Source: N/A
　　Sample Input: Dave Masri
　　Sample Output: DaveMasri

Code:

```
create Function [dbo].[fn_StripSpaces](@string nvarChar(Max))
returns nvarChar(max)
as
begin
    return coalesce(replace(@string,' ',''),'')
end
```

fn_TextToHTML

Function Description: If we have plain text that we want to load into a rich text field, but don't want to lose line breaks or characters that may be accidentally interpreted as HTML, we can use the fn_TextToHTML function to convert the plain text to HTML.

  Originating Source: N/A

  Sample Usage:

```
select
    dbo.[fn_TextToHTML](Note) as HTMLNote
from Notes
```

  Sample Input:

  Dave,

  Just spoke to Dan, he said "Hello"

  Sample Output:

```
<pre>Dave,<br>Just spoke to Dan, he said &quot;Hello&quot;<br></pre>
```

  Code:

```
CREATE Function [dbo].[fn_TextToHTML](@strText nVARCHAR(max))
RETURNS VARCHAR(max)
AS
BEGIN
    set @strText=replace(@strText,'&','&amp;')
    set @strText=replace(@strText,'<','&lt;')
    set @strText=replace(@strText,'>','&gt;')
    set @strText=replace(@strText,'"','&quot;')
    set @strText=replace(@strText,"'",'&#39')
```

```
set @strText=replace(@strText,char(9),'<br>')
set @strText=replace(@strText,char(10),'<br>')
set @strText=replace(@strText,char(23),'<br>')
set @strText=replace(@strText,char(13),'<br>')

RETURN '<pre>'+coalesce(@strText,")+'</pre>'
END
```

sp_GetDirTree

Function Description: Suppose we are given a directory of files, and the directory has subdirectories. We are then told that each directory name corresponds to an account name and we are to load all the files in the directory to the corresponding account.

This stored procedure (not UDF) will loop through a directory, all subdirectories, and give us a single record set that we can use to load the files.

The record set returned has six columns:

1. **Id:** An AutoNumber to act as an Id

2. **SubDirectory:** The directory name or file name

3. **Depth:** How many directories deep it is

4. **FileFlag:** 1 means this record is a file; 0 means it's a directory

5. **ParentDirectoryID:** The Id of the direct parent directory record

6. **Full_Path:** The full path of the file or directory, which makes it easy to mine the directory structure for information

Originating Source: https://stackoverflow.com/questions/11559846/how-to-list-files-inside-a-folder-with-sql-server

Sample Usage: [sp_GetDirTree] 'C:\Clients\'

Sample Input: c:\Clients \

Sample Output:

Id	SubDirectory	Depth	FileFlag	ParentDirectoryID	Full_Path
1	Google	1	0	NULL	\Google
2	Google Notes.txt	2	1	1	\Google\Google Notes.txt
3	IBM	1	0	NULL	\IBM

(continued)

Id	SubDirectory	Depth	FileFlag	ParentDirectoryID	Full_Path
4	ERD.txt	2	1	3	\IBM\ERD.txt
5	Notes.txt	2	1	3	\IBM\Notes.txt
6	Microsoft	1	0	NULL	\Microsoft
7	Contract.txt	2	1	6	\Microsoft\Contract.txt
8	Passwords - SHHH!.txt	2	1	6	\Microsoft\Passwords - SHHH!.txt
9	Salesforce	1	0	NULL	\Salesforce
10	Proposal.txt	2	1	9	\Salesforce\Proposal.txt

Code:

```
Create Procedure [dbo].[sp_GetDirTree](@BackupDirectory varchar(4000))    as
begin
  IF OBJECT_ID('tempdb..#DirTree') IS NOT NULL
    DROP TABLE #DirTree

  IF OBJECT_ID('tempdb..#ParentDirectoryIDs') IS NOT NULL
    DROP TABLE #ParentDirectoryIDs

  CREATE TABLE #DirTree (
    Id int identity(1,1),
    SubDirectory nvarchar(255),
    Depth smallint,
    FileFlag bit,
    ParentDirectoryID int
  )

  INSERT INTO #DirTree (SubDirectory, Depth, FileFlag)
  EXEC master..xp_dirtree @BackupDirectory, 10, 1

  UPDATE #DirTree
  SET ParentDirectoryID = (
   SELECT MAX(Id) FROM #DirTree d2
   WHERE Depth = d.Depth - 1 AND d2.Id < d.Id
   )
  FROM #DirTree d
```

268

```
DECLARE
  @ID INT,
  @BackupFile VARCHAR(MAX),
  @Depth TINYINT,
  @FileFlag BIT,
  @ParentDirectoryID INT,
  @wkSubParentDirectoryID INT,
  @wkSubDirectory VARCHAR(MAX)

DECLARE @BackupFiles TABLE
(
  FileNamePath VARCHAR(MAX),
  TransLogFlag BIT,
  BackupFile VARCHAR(MAX),
  DatabaseName VARCHAR(MAX)
)

DECLARE FileCursor CURSOR LOCAL FORWARD_ONLY FOR
SELECT * FROM #DirTree WHERE FileFlag = 1

OPEN FileCursor
FETCH NEXT FROM FileCursor INTO
  @ID,
  @BackupFile,
  @Depth,
  @FileFlag,
  @ParentDirectoryID

SET @wkSubParentDirectoryID = @ParentDirectoryID


WHILE @@FETCH_STATUS = 0
BEGIN
  --loop to generate path in reverse, starting with backup file then
prefixing subfolders in a loop
  WHILE @wkSubParentDirectoryID IS NOT NULL
  BEGIN
```

269

```
    SELECT @wkSubDirectory = SubDirectory, @wkSubParentDirectoryID =
    ParentDirectoryID
    FROM #DirTree
    WHERE ID = @wkSubParentDirectoryID

    SELECT @BackupFile = @wkSubDirectory + '\' + @BackupFile
  END

  --no more subfolders in loop so now prefix the root backup folder
  SELECT @BackupFile = @BackupDirectory + @BackupFile

  --put backupfile into a table and then later work out which ones are
  log and full backups
  INSERT INTO @BackupFiles (FileNamePath) VALUES(@BackupFile)

  FETCH NEXT FROM FileCursor INTO
    @ID,
    @BackupFile,
    @Depth,
    @FileFlag,
    @ParentDirectoryID

    SET @wkSubParentDirectoryID = @ParentDirectoryID
  END

  CLOSE FileCursor
  DEALLOCATE FileCursor
-- Populate Full Path
alter table #DirTree add Full_Path varchar(4000)

declare @minID int
declare @currPath varchar(4000)

update #DirTree set Full_Path="

Select distinct ParentDirectoryID
into #ParentDirectoryIDs
    from #DirTree
    where ParentDirectoryID is not null
    --and id<15
```

```
WHILE (select count(1) from #ParentDirectoryIDs) > 0
begin
    select @minID=min(ParentDirectoryID) from #ParentDirectoryIDs
    select @currPath=Full_Path+SubDirectory from #DirTree where id= @minID

    Update #DirTree set Full_Path=Full_Path+'\'+@currPath where
    ParentDirectoryID=@minID and ParentDirectoryID is not null

    delete from #ParentDirectoryIDs where ParentDirectoryID=@minID
end
update #DirTree set Full_Path=Full_Path+'\'+SubDirectory

select * from #DirTree

  IF OBJECT_ID('tempdb..#DirTree') IS NOT NULL
    DROP TABLE #DirTree

  IF OBJECT_ID('tempdb..#ParentDirectoryIDs') IS NOT NULL
    DROP TABLE #ParentDirectoryIDs

end
GO
```

Summary

Great! Hopefully you now have a good understanding of what I mean by a library of reusable code. It doesn't have to be anything gigantic or complex. As you code your transformations, if you are writing code that you feel you may need later, simply port it over to your library when done. Over time, you will find there are a few handfuls of functions (or classes or modules or code snippets or whatever) that you need to use repeatedly. Next time you need that code, you have it, and it has already been tested! Saves time and improves quality!

CHAPTER 13

FAQs (aka Frequently Asked Questions)

I'm sure you have a ton of questions. This chapter contains some of the more common questions I have been asked throughout the years pertaining to Salesforce data migrations and integrations, as well as a few less common but interesting ones. Most of this stuff can probably be inferred by reading the first 12 chapters of this book, and quite a bit of this stuff is stated outright in the section covering the subject at hand. Regardless, it's good to review. So, without further ado . . . .

Migration Questions

What is the difference between a data migration and a data integration?

From a strictly definition perspective, a data migration is when we need to move data from one system (legacy or source) to another (target), where the target system will wholly replace the functionality of the source system. So, after the data are moved over and the new system goes live, there is no need to work in the legacy system any more (at least for the functionality that was migrated). So, this is a "onetime" data movement.

Again from a strictly definition perspective, a data integration is when we move data from one system (source) to another (target) on an ongoing basis, generally to reduce or eliminate all the problems that come from duplicate data entry.

One of my reasons for writing this book was to dispel the very prevalent thinking that somehow data migrations, because they are onetime, can be held to a lower coding standard than data integrations. "Onetime" should be thought of as "onetime to production." And much like when building a rocket that will carry a robot to Mars one time, we need to keep to the highest of standards, and test our code thoroughly.

© David Masri 2019
D. Masri, *Developing Data Migrations and Integrations with Salesforce*,
https://doi.org/10.1007/978-1-4842-4209-4_13

Of our six attributes the only difference between data migrations and integrations is that, although migrations need to be repairable, integrations need to be self-repairing. All our best practices apply to both data migrations and data integrations.

What do I do if my source data dosen't have a PK to use as an External Id?

Make one up. We discussed how to do this in Chapter 6, Best Practice 27.

We are shutting down the legacy system. Why do I need to load legacy Ids to Salesforce?

Maintaining the legacy Ids is critical for testability and repairability, which are two of our six attributes (see Chapter 4).

As data people, we tend to test our code by querying the back end of a source system and comparing those data to the data in Salesforce. Users prefer to test by going to the legacy system UI, navigating to a record, finding the same record in Salesforce, then comparing the data displayed. For both these approaches, having the External Id in Salesforce is critical. For back-end querying, we want to be able to pass in the same Id to both queries (legacy system and Salesforce); for UI comparisons, we want to make searching the Salesforce UI as easy as possible. Remember that External Ids are searchable via the Salesforce search bar by default, so all users have to do to find their record is type the legacy Id into the Salesforce search bar and press Enter.

Regarding repairability, if we find an issue with our migration after go-live, performing a full wipe and load is probably not an option. We need to patch the data, which means we need to retransform the data points that are bad and update only those fields in Salesforce. To do this, we must be able to match the existing Salesforce records back to the original legacy system record. As our migrations get bigger (more objects) and more complex (more transformations), the odds that a defect is found after go-live increase exponentially. Fixing the data must be easy, and having the External Id in Salesforce makes it easy.

What do I do if I need to migrate data into a noncustomizable object, which means I can't create an External Id?

Here we need to focus on the goal, which is traceability. We want to make sure we can track every record in Salesforce to a record in the source system. We have two basic options:

1. Rely on a natural key.[1] Suppose we are loading a junction object that is not customizable, such as Account Contact Role,[2] in which the combination of two Ids is unique. We can then get the legacy Ids of the (two) corresponding parent records and use them to identify the legacy junction record in Salesforce. Or, perhaps we can load something unique into the Name field.

2. The second option is to save cross-reference tables outside of Salesforce. At the time of loading, include the External Id as part of the dataset. Even though we won't have anything to which to map it, the success records returned will include the Salesforce Id as well as the External Id, even though it was not mapped. If we need to repair the data, we can use this cross-reference table to match the Salesforce data back to the original legacy record.

What do I do with legacy data that are needed for historical purposes but won't be updated in Salesforce going forward?

The answer to this question really depends on whether we need the data to be accessible in Salesforce. If we only need it for auditing purposes or for reference, after we go live with Salesforce, we can backup the legacy system and make it available as read-only to those who may need it.

For data that are needed in Salesforce, I recommend making a set of legacy fields to hold these data and create a special section on the page layout to view it (read-only). If we don't want to create too many legacy fields, we can create a single large text area and load all the legacy data into it, nicely formatted with labels and line breaks.

---

[1]See Appendix A for a detailed discussion on natural and artificial keys.
[2]*Not* Account Contact Relation, which is different.

How do I migrate data from one sandbox to another, or from one Salesforce org to another?

The same exact way we would migrate from any other system. The fact that the migration is from Salesforce to Salesforce doesn't change a thing. Yes, we store the source Id as External Ids in the target Salesforce org.

I will add that there are tools on the market that can do this for you, assuming the two orgs are the same (objects and fields).

Wait! What? There are tools on the market that can replicate a Salesforce org?

Yes. Some of the tools we discussed can do this, such as Informatica Cloud and Relational Junction. There are also specialty tools that can do this, but they are marketed as Salesforce backup and recovery tools. Salesforce's Data Backup & Recovery Best Practices page[3] lists the following third-party options:

- **OwnBackup for Salesforce:** `https://www.ownbackup.com/`

- **Spanning Backup for Salesforce:** `https://spanning.com/products/salesforce-backup/`

- **CloudAlly Backup for Salesforce:** `https://www.cloudally.com/backup-salesforce/`

- **Backupify for Salesforce:** `https://www.backupify.com/salesforce-backup`

- **Odaseva for Salesforce:** `https://www.odaseva.com/`

- **Druva:** `https://www.druva.com/solutions/salesforce/`

What are the different ways I can backup my Salesforce data either on demand or on a schedule?

Salesforce has native functionality that backs up all your data to .csv files and zips them for ease of downloading.[4] This backup can be scheduled to run as often as once a week. If this solution does not meet you needs, you'll have to go with a third-party solution or custom-build one (see the answer to the previous question).

---

[3]See `https://help.salesforce.com/articleView?id=000213366&type=1`.
[4]See `https://help.salesforce.com/articleView?id=admin_exportdata.htm&type=5`.

The new picklist values don't line up with the legacy values. How do I migrate them?

You need to handle this in your transformation layer. If that's not an option, you can create the legacy values as inactive picklist values so you can load them, then let your users deal with this issue manually after go-live. More likely than not, telling them to deal with it manually will convince them that it is in fact possible to come up with a set of rules to convert the values.

What are the basic things that need to be checked before starting a data migration?

The answer to this question is covered extensively in Chapter 6, when we examined 40 best practices, and then again in Chapter 7, when we walked through a data migration together. The abridged answer is: Understand the source data. Understand the Salesforce data model. Build relationships with the right people. Plan it out.

Is it mandatory that I have External Ids for native and custom objects when migrating data?

Yes.

When migrating data, is it okay to turn off validation rules, triggers, workflows, and so on?

Yes, but only if you understand the functionality being disabled and you are okay with losing those updates, or if you plan to perform those updates as part of your migration.

What are the different tools available for migrating data to Salesforce?

In Chapter 3, we looked at quite a few tool options. At the time, I advised that you choose the ETL or middleware tool that best fits your (or your organization's) current skill set, even if it's not in the list I provided. At the time, I also noted, "Regardless of the tool you choose, because all of them hit the same APIs, the Salesforce connectors in them are quite similar."

When performing a data migration (as opposed to building an integration), you probably don't need to support the code base more than a few months after go-live (in case you need to fix a defect found), so you can be a bit shortsighted with regard to code support. If you are a third-party implementation partner performing the migration, you only need to be concerned with your skill set, because your client will never need to support (or run) the code.

When building an integration, you need to consider the skill set and coding standards of the individuals or organization that will be supporting the code after go-live.

What are the different ways to eliminate duplicates while migrating data to Salesforce?

If you use Salesforce's Duplicate Management[5] to stop duplicates from being created in Salesforce at the time of migration, you run the risk of not migrating the child data related to the duplicate records that are blocked. For example, suppose we are migrating two contacts, both with activities, and Salesforce allows the first one to get created, then blocks the second as a duplicate of the first. If this happens, for the contact that doesn't get migrated, neither will the activities associated with it. What we want is for those activities to get migrated, but they get associated with the first contact.

You have two basic options here:

1. Migrate all the data, then use some utility to detect and merge duplicates in Salesforce.

2. Detect duplicates as part of your transformation layer and migrate a single contact only, and have your transformation layer be smart enough to reparent the child records.

My personal preference is option 2, for a few reasons. The biggest is that option 1 is very hard to automate, and probably requires a lot of manual steps. It's also hard to repair if things go wrong, and it generally violates a bunch of best practices and principals outlined in this book.

In Appendix A, we walk through how to code duplicate detection logic using nothing but simple SQL code.

With the Apex Data Loader, I can import up to 5,000,000 records. What do I do if I need to load more than 5,000,000 records?

Per the official Data Loader documentation[6]: *"If you need to load more than 5 million records, we recommend you work with a Salesforce partner or visit the App Exchange for a suitable partner product."*

I agree with this answer completely. More often than not, the Apex Data Loader is not the right tool for the job.

---

[5]See https://trailhead.salesforce.com/en/modules/sales_admin_duplicate_management/ units/sales_admin_duplicate_management_unit_1.

[6]It can be found here: https://resources.docs.salesforce.com/204/latest/en-us/sfdc/pdf/ salesforce_data_loader.pdf.

Why can't I use the Data Loader? I love the Apex data loader.

Look, you absolutely can build data migrations and even data integrations using the Apex Data Loader while following every single best practice in this book.[7] It's just simply not designed to be used that way and is an error-prone process.

But if you insist, I recommend that you

1. Learn the Data Loader command line and automate it fully using Windows Script (or batch) files

2. Learn how to connect the Data Loader to an ODBC source as opposed to .csv files

3. Use some scripting language to manipulate data, which can also be called from Windows Script files and be fully automated

4. Note that even though you can connect the Data Loader to an ODBC source, the success and error files can only be outputted to a .csv file. Your scripts should be able to pick these up and process them.

I want to stress that the difficulties you face in automating the Apex Data Loader, particularly in automating your data transformations, are not an excuse to introduce manual steps.

How do I roll back updates to a record?

You can't. You need to take a backup of the records prior to updating, then use those data to perform a second update, setting the field values back to the original values.

I'm doing a small migration. Can't I just do it manually?

Yes, but you would be wrong to do so. Also, by saying "just," you are implying that doing it manually is somehow easier. And you would be wrong about that too.

I have a field that got migrated incorrectly. It wasn't discovered until a few weeks after go-live and users updated some records. How do I fix this field?

Here's what you need to do:

1. Backup your original transformation code for the object in question.

2. Fix the transformation code.

---

[7]And, in fact, I have.

3. Compare the dataset created from your new transformation code to the one created from the original code. Include only records in which the field in question has changed. This becomes the target record set to fix.

4. Now compare this new dataset to what's in Salesforce. If the record's created-date matchs its last modified date, then you know the record has not been touched since go live and you can update it safely.

5. For the rest of the records, you can generate a report for your users to fix manually. Include the following:

   - LastModifiedBy

   - The current value for the field in question (in Salesforce)

   - The original value (as it was when migrated)

   - The new value (per the new transformation code)

6. If there is too much data to fix manually, you can ask your users whether you should fix records in which the current value matches the original value set as part of the migration. For these records, it's probably safe to assume the value in field in question has not changed since the migration. Hopefully, this cuts down substantially on the number of records that users need to fix manually.

How do I set the audit fields (CreatedBy, CreatedDate, LastModifiedByID, LastModifiedDate) as part of my migration?

You can configure Salesforce to allow these fields to be set, but only on record creation.[8]

Unfortunately, this means you can't upsert data into objects and set the audit fields at the same time, because all the updates will fail. (This is true even if you are overwriting the audit data with the same values.) You have to code your inserts and updates as independent loads. If you find an error with the data that you loaded into one of the audit fields and you want to fix it, your only option is to delete the record and re-insert it. Some people prefer to load these data into custom fields, which isn't a bad option if you just need the information for historical reference.

---

[8]See https://help.salesforce.com/articleView?id=Enable-Create-Audit-Fields&language=en_US&type=1.

My migration is taking too long. What can I do?

If you have a set time to do your migration (say, an evening) but can't get all the data in because the time window is too small, you should consider coding your migration as if it were an incremental or differential integration synchronization job (see Chapter 9). Then you can preload all your data weeks in advance, and only load the updates when you are ready to go live.

Integration Questions

What do I do if I have multiple sources for the same field in Salesforce and they conflict? For example, phone number or e-mail?

I like to have one field in Salesforce for each system/field combination. So, if you have two systems feeding in phone numbers, you will have two fields: System_A_ Phone__c and System_B_Phone__c (or use two of the native fields). You can then create a formula field to choose one of them for display, or create a workflow that populates one of the native Salesforce phone number fields based on some set of rules. This allows your users to have access to the alternate number as well as the primary, just in case.

Users want to be able to update data in Salesforce and not have it overwritten by the integration. What do I do? Users only want data to be populated in Salesforce via the integration if the field is empty.

You have two basic options:

1. Implement a solution similar to what was discussed in the previous answer, but instead have one of the fields user maintained.

2. Download the existing data from Salesforce. Then, as part of your transformation layer, use the existing Salesforce data, so your code checks whether the field is blank in Salesforce. If so, it sends the source system's value. If not, it sends the current value.[9] You can code this in T-SQL like so[10]:

---

[9]This assumes there are updates needed for other fields. Obviously, we won't send an update if nothing changed. Also remember that you want your transformation code to be completely centralized (including all fields being populated by the integration), so you don't want to leave it out. That would entail segmenting your code.

[10]Coalesce returns the first non-NULL value from a list of fields.

```
Select
    ts.SourceId
    ,Coalesce(sfo.f1,ts.f1) as F1 -- If exists and is not null in SF use
    that else use TS
    ,ts.f2
    ,ts.f3
    ,ts.f4
    ,...
from Transfomed_Source ts
Left join SF_Object sfo on sfo.Sourceid=ts.SourceId  -- SourceId is our
ExternalId
```

I need to set the name on Insert, but then afterward Salesforce will own it. So, I can't update it going forward. Does this mean I can't use an upsert?

No, you can. See the answer to the previous question. If your transformation layer knows the current Salesforce value, then you can implement logic that says if the record exists in Salesforce, send the Salesforce name or else send X. [Note that if you use a Differential Synchronization pattern (see Chapter 9), you have the current Salesforce values.]

I am doing an outbound date-based (incremental) integration, but Salesforce doesn't update the last modified date when cross-object formula fields or rollups are updated. How can I get the set of updated records since the last run?

You can create a new formula field that calculates the effective last modified date by taking the max last modified date from the current record, as well as all records used in the cross-object formula or rollups. Then, use the new formula field to determine which records have changed.

Where do I store user-maintained cross-reference data? In a source system-to-Salesforce user Id cross-reference table, for example?

I would store the data on the Salesforce object that is being referenced. This approach has the advantage that you get a UI for maintaining it. Otherwise, you can store them in any location accessible by your transformation layer.

I have to sync child records (Contact) but not parent records (Accounts). The parent records are created manually, then child records are matched manually (associated) to the parents. The parent Id (AccountId) is required. How can I do this?

In general, I like to create holding accounts for this type of situation. So for inserts, when creating the contact, I set the account Id as the holding account Id. This works nicely because users can go to the holding account and see all contacts that need to be matched.

Also remember that your integration code should create the holding account for you. If you have the Salesforce contact data available in your transformation layer, you can code it to set only the account Id to the holding account if the contact is new for Insert; otherwise, it uses the current account Id. You can do this in T-SQL like so:

```
1.   Select
2.       ts.SourceId
3.       ,Coalesce(sfo.AccountId,ts.AccountId) as AccountId -- If exists
         in SF use current value, else TS
4.       ,ts.f2
5.       ,ts.f3
6.       ,ts.f4
7.       ,...
8.   from Transfomed_Source ts
9.   Left join SF_Object sfo on sfo.Sourceid=ts.SourceId  -- SourceId is
our ExternalId
```

The Account Contact Relation object does not let me modify the account Id or contact Id! How can I update them?

If you need to update the account or contact on the Account Contact Relation object, you need to delete the records and reinsert them. I will add that this makes logical sense. AccountContactRelation is a junction object, and because the account/contact combination is enforced as unique, the combination account/contact is a compound key. The only reason it's not a PK is because you already have one.[11] Bearing this in mind, there really is no reason to update this record (save it being a shortcut to performing a delete and insert). Technically speaking, the new record is not the same as the old, because it has a different PK (account/contact combination). Maybe this is why Salesforce disallows updates to the account and contact Ids, but it's probably because of other validation rules being run behind the scenes.[12]

---

[11]With relational databases, a compound key is exactly that—a key comprised of more than one field. If that key was the only way to identify the records uniquely, it would also be the PK.

[12]Namely, keeping this object in sync with contact records' account Ids. Every contact's primary account is represented automatically in this object and is flagged as Direct.

If I can't use Upsert and I have to split my load into an insert and update, how do I determine whether a record needs to be inserted or updated?

You need to check whether the External Ids currently exist in Salesforce. Just like we did in Chapter 9 with our differential patterns, you use a left join with a "where is Null" to determine which records are new. Like so:

```
1.   Select
2.        sfo.Id
3.   from SF_Object sfo
4.   left join Transfomed_Source ts on ts.ExternalSourceId = sfo.
     ExternalSourceId
5.   where sfo.SourceId is Null -- --  Record does not Exists in Salesforce
```

My legacy system uses integers for PK, as do lots of other systems. How can I make my External Ids compatible?

Just convert them to a string and load it in. You can always convert them back if/when you export it. When converting integers to strings, be sure not to include decimal places. I have seen this mistake cause an entire migration to be duplicated. The second time the migration was run, the External Ids did not match those from the original run (when comparing strings, "1" is not the same as "1.00").[13]

I only want to export records created by my ETL. How do I do this?

When writing your SOQL, you can add a "where" clause on CreatedById only to pull records created by your ETL user. If you are using the same ETL user for more than one thing, this solution may not work. Your next best option is to pull all records that have the External Id populated (of course, in theory, they could have been populated after the record was created, but what are the odds of that?). Your last option is to use the job Id (see Chapter 6, Best Practice 31), although this too may have been modified (maybe even by the ETL) after go-live. If this was a migration, you could try and use the CreatedDate field.

I am integrating two systems to Salesforce. Would you recommend I prefix the External Id with some system code to make sure they are unique? Or create two Id fields?

---

[13]I will also point out that this would never happen with an automated load. Automation ensures consistency.

Unless you know that the two systems have completely distinct datasets with no overlap, I would recommend that you use two Id fields. Having two fields—one for each system—allows you to merge records without any data loss and keeps the integration going between the surviving record and both systems. It's not uncommon to have to go back and split an External Id into two fields because record merges were needed. There was a time that Salesforce only allowed three External Ids per object. This is no longer the case. You can now have up to 25 External Ids per object, so you don't need to be conservative.

Summary

These are by far the most common questions I have been asked during the past few years regarding Salesforce migrations and integrations. Of course, the people asking them didn't have the benefit of reading this book, so you may have completely different questions! If you do, feel free to reach out to me on LinkedIn (`https://www.linkedin.com/in/davidmasri/`). Mention that you bought this book and have a question. If I'm not inundated with questions, I'll do my best to respond.[14] Perhaps your question will make it into the second edition of this book!

---

[14]Disclaimer: I reserve the right to ignore your message or any other message sent to me via LinkedIn or any other medium.

APPENDIX A

A Simple Duplicate Detection Algorithm

I prepared this appendix for you because data cleansing and duplicate management is such an important part of a data migration or integration specialist's job.[1]

The two primary reasons companies migrate off one system to another is the lack of needed functionality and missing controls to maintain data quality properly. In general, users are very resourceful and can find clever ways to overcome system limitations. They use fields or features to do things for which they were not intended, simply so they can do their job. Over time, the system's data becomes messy and inaccurate, leading to loss of system usefulness.

If we were to migrate data from such a system as is, we run the risk of frustrating users with bad data. This is not the way we want to start our users on the new system (Salesforce). Bad data puts a damper on user enthusiasm and affects adoption rates negatively.

Two Categories of Data Quality Issues

We can classify data quality issues loosely into two categories:

1. Field-level issues

2. Row-level issues

---

[1] I originally had an incredibly humorous introduction here that left everyone who read it rolling with laughter. Unfortunately, my editors vetoed it, so you are stuck with this straight-to-the-point intro sentence instead. Sorry.

© David Masri 2019

D. Masri, *Developing Data Migrations and Integrations with Salesforce*,
https://doi.org/10.1007/978-1-4842-4209-4

Thankfully, Salesforce has a lot of tools and processes for keeping our data clean after it's in Salesforce, such as Data.com[2] and Duplicate Management[3], in addition to using workflows, triggers, validation rules, and such.

Field-level Data Quality Issues

Field-level data quality issues are issues in which a field's data is sparsely populated, badly formatted, or simply incorrect. Issues arising from conflicting field values because the same data are stored in more than one place (table or system[4]) also fall into this category. In Chapter 6, Best Practice 24, I recommended we fix code not data, and discussed some common field-level cleanup tasks. In Best Practice 21 (also in Chapter 6), we looked at building a library of reusable code that can be used for data cleansing or for common transformations (and the focus of Chapter 12 was building that library).

At the same time, I also mentioned that there are some things that just can't be done in code, and that a data cleanup project may be warranted. You can do it either in the source system before go-live or in Salesforce afterward.

At the time I also warned you that, based on my past experiences, any plan to clean up data after go-live rarely comes to fruition. I stand by this statement. It's better to clean up data before it makes it into Salesforce rather than after, simply because you want your users to start off on the right foot.

Row-level Data Quality Issues

Row-level data quality issues are issues that affect records as a whole, as opposed to individual data points. Examples include

- Missing records

- Invalid records (orphaned child records)

- Duplicate records

---

[2]See: https://help.salesforce.com/articleView?id=data_quality.htm&type=5, https://www.salesforce.com/products/data/solutions/ and https://www.data.com/

[3]For more information, see https://help.salesforce.com/articleView?id=managing_duplicates_overview.htm&type=5.

[4]This is the classic data integrity issue relational databases seek to resolve as discussed in Chapter 1.

All of these issues can, potentially, be handled in the transformation layer. It's not hard to see how we can eliminate orphaned records[5] or create missing records[6] easily. So that leaves detecting duplicate records.

There are various tools on the market that have features for duplicate detection. What we want is one that can be integrated easily into our existing process, works with data outside of Salesforce, and can be fully automated. Even with these additional requirements, there are still plenty of tools on the market that can do the job, so why learn how to custom-build one?

Well, often these products are expensive, and people feel the need to buy them because they don't know how easy it is to code a simple and effective algorithm that can detect duplicates. The remainder of this chapter focuses on exactly that; it explains how to build a simple and effective algorithm for duplicate detection that can be automated and plugged into a transformation layer.

I'm not recommending that you custom-build a duplicate detection solution rather than purchase one. What I am recommending is that you know how duplicate detection solutions work, and what it takes to build one, so you can make an informed build-or-buy decision. None of the product vendors on the market will tell you exactly how their product works, but I can (almost) guarantee that their algorithm, at its core, is very similar to what I describe here.

A Simple (and Effective) Data Matching and Duplicate Detection Algorithm

Computers are very good at comparing data points and determining whether they are the same, so it's no surprise that all data management systems use Ids to identify records or objects. If we are dealing with a relational database, the Ids are not only compared when searching for a record in the same table, but also when searching for related data.

As we discussed in Chapter 1, a key is a field that identifies a record or set of records. The PK (primary key) uniquely identifies a single record and an FK (foreign key) identifies a set of records related to the PK of another table. What we did not discuss is artificial and natural keys.

---

[5]An inner join between the child table and the parent could do this.
[6]Assuming you can figure out logic that determines what is missing.

Artificial Key: An artificial key, often called a *surrogate key*, is what we traditionally think of when we think of Ids. Usually, they are AutoNumbers (for example, 25), a gibberish string (for example, 00QA000000i22fFMAQ), or a globally unique identifier (for example, 5a471428-97de-484b-a08e-6fce84a750ad).

Natural Key: A natural key is a key that exists in your data and is real data. Although the purpose of storing it is not for record identification, it can be used for that by its very nature. Natural keys are things like name, phone number, Social Security number, tax Id, driver's license Id, product SKU, e-mail address, logon user Id, credit card number, or anything else you might ask someone for when searching for a record.

There was a time when there was an active debate in the data community regarding whether it was a good Idea to use natural keys as your PKs rather than creating artificial ones.[7] Natural keys may or may not be able to identify a record uniquely. Social Security numbers or tax Ids may work well, but names probably won't.

As far as I can tell, this debate over the use of natural Ids vs. artificial Ids is over, and the artificial Id camp won,[8] but that does not mean that natural keys don't exist within your data and that they can't be used to identify entities (the thing the record represents). In case you have not already guessed, using natural keys to identify possible duplicates is exactly the approach we are going to take.

It's important to note that most natural keys by themselves probably can't identify an entity uniquely. First name and last name by themselves are far from unique. Phone numbers are often shared between household or office members. But you can combine them to give you a very strong natural key—for example, First Name + Last Name + Phone Number.

---

[7] You can learn all about this debate with a simple Google search. It's really interesting stuff, particularly for people interested in data theory (https://www.google.com/?q=artificial+vs+natural+keys+debate).

[8] I'm in this camp, so I am somewhat biased in my opinion, which is based on fact and experience. Seriously, if you decide to build a system using natural keys as your PKs, you better make sure your Ids are really unique, not just in your system, but in the whole universe. Every potential record really has a natural Id (not everyone has a Social Security number) and they never change. (Changing a record's PK is a pain, especially when there is a lot of related data.)

So here are the rules of the duplicate finding game: Identify as many natural keys as you can, build a table out of them, and then match them up to find the duplicates!

Easier said than done? Nope! Let's do it. Like the previous examples in this book, I code this solution in T-SQL on MS SQL Server, but the code is so simple (and I will explain it), you should have no issues translating the basic algorithm to the platform/language of your choice.

A Working Example

To make this easy, for our example we will use Salesforce as our data source. In this way, you are more likely to be familiar with the data structure. We are going to look for duplicates within the Contact and Lead objects themselves, as well as look for cross-object duplicates—in other words, a record that exists as both a contact and a lead.

The first thing we need to do is download all our Lead and Contact records to local tables in our database.[9] For leads, we exclude all records that have `IsConverted = True`. IsConverted is a system field that Salesforce sets to True when the lead is converted,[10] so we would expect these records to exist in our Contact object and would not be considered duplicates.

For our example, we first load the contact data into a table called SF_Contacts, and the Leads into a table called SF_Leads.

Next, we are going to build a SQL view that calculates a list of natural keys for each of our contacts. This view returns three columns:

- **ContactId:** The Salesforce contact Id

- **KeyName:** The name of the natural key, for reference

- **KeyValue:** The actual value of the natural key

---

[9]If you want to follow along using your favorite ETL tool, download the Contact and Lead objects from Salesforce into your database and name the tables SF_Contacts and SF_Leads, respectively.

[10]Also, upon conversion, Salesforce also sets ConvertedDate to the current time and ConvertedAccountId, ConvertedContactId, and ConvertedOpportunityId to the newly created record Ids. See `https://developer.salesforce.com/docs/atlas.en-us.api.meta/api/sforce_api_objects_lead.htm`.

Great! Let's look at the code:

```
1.    Create View [dbo].[Contact_DupKeys] as
2.    Select
3.          c.id as CONTACTId
4.          ,'Email' as KeyName
5.          ,dbo.fn_StripSpaces(c.EMAIL) as KeyValue
6.    from SF_Contacts c
7.    where dbo.fn_StripSpaces(c.EMAIL) <>"
8.    union
9.    select
10.         c.id as CONTACTId
11.         ,'First+Last' as KeyName
12.         ,dbo.fn_StripSpaces(c.FIRSTNAME+c.lastname) as KeyValue
13.   from SF_Contacts c
14.   where dbo.fn_StripSpaces(c.FIRSTNAME+c.lastname) <>"
15.   union
16.   select
17.         c.id as CONTACTId
18.         ,'MobilePhone' as KeyName
19.         ,dbo.fn_RemoveNonNumeric(c.MobilePhone) as KeyValue
20.   from SF_Contacts c
21.   where dbo.fn_RemoveNonNumeric(c.MobilePhone) is not null
22.   and dbo.fn_RemoveNonNumeric(c.MobilePhone)<>"
23.   union
24.   select
25.         c.id as CONTACTId
26.         ,'Phone' as KeyName
27.         ,dbo.fn_RemoveNonNumeric(c.Phone) as KeyValue
28.   from SF_Contacts c
29.   where dbo.fn_RemoveNonNumeric(c.Phone) is not null
30.   and dbo.fn_RemoveNonNumeric(c.Phone)<>"
31.   union
32.   select
33.         c.id as CONTACTId
34.         ,'HomePhone' as KeyName
```

```
35.          ,dbo.fn_RemoveNonNumeric(c.HomePhone) as KeyValue
36.  from SF_Contacts c
37.  where dbo.fn_RemoveNonNumeric(c.HomePhone) is not null
38.  and dbo.fn_RemoveNonNumeric(c.HomePhone)<>"
39.  union
40.  select
41.          c.id as CONTACTId
42.          ,'Fax' as KeyName
43.          ,dbo.fn_RemoveNonNumeric(c.Fax) as KeyValue
44.  from SF_Contacts c
45.  where dbo.fn_RemoveNonNumeric(c.Fax) is not null
46.  and dbo.fn_RemoveNonNumeric(c.Fax)<>"
47.  union
48.  select
49.          c.id as CONTACTId
50.          ,'OtherPhone' as KeyName
51.          ,dbo.fn_StripSpaces(c.lastname)+dbo.fn_RemoveNonNumeric
             (c.OtherPhone) as KeyValue
52.  from SF_Contacts c
53.  where dbo.fn_RemoveNonNumeric(c.OtherPhone) is not null
54.  and dbo.fn_RemoveNonNumeric(c.OtherPhone)<>"
55.  union
56.  select
57.          c.id as CONTACTId
58.          ,'Last+Phone' as KeyName
59.          ,dbo.fn_StripSpaces(c.lastname)+dbo.fn_RemoveNonNumeric(c.Phone)
             as KeyValue
60.  from SF_Contacts c
61.  where dbo.fn_RemoveNonNumeric(c.Phone) is not null
62.  and dbo.fn_RemoveNonNumeric(c.Phone)<>"
63.  union
64.  select
65.          c.id as CONTACTId
66.          ,'Last+HomePhone' as KeyName
67.          ,dbo.fn_StripSpaces(c.lastname)+dbo.fn_RemoveNonNumeric
             (c.HomePhone) as KeyValue
```

```
68.  from SF_Contacts c
69.  where dbo.fn_RemoveNonNumeric(c.HomePhone) is not null
70.  and dbo.fn_RemoveNonNumeric(c.HomePhone)<>"
71.  union
72.  select
73.      c.id as CONTACTId
74.      ,'Last+Fax' as KeyName
75.      ,dbo.fn_StripSpaces(c.lastname)+dbo.fn_RemoveNonNumeric(c.Fax) as
         KeyValue
76.  from SF_Contacts c
77.  where dbo.fn_RemoveNonNumeric(c.Fax) is not null
78.  and dbo.fn_RemoveNonNumeric(c.Fax)<>"
79.  union
80.  select
81.      c.id as CONTACTId
82.      ,'Last+OtherPhone' as KeyName
83.      , dbo.fn_StripSpaces(c.lastname)+dbo.fn_RemoveNonNumeric
         (c.OtherPhone) as KeyValue
84.  from SF_Contacts c
85.  where dbo.fn_RemoveNonNumeric(c.OtherPhone) is not null
86.  and dbo.fn_RemoveNonNumeric(c.OtherPhone)<>"
```

Okay. This code looks long and complex, but it's really incredibly simple. You'll notice that the same Select statement is repeated over and over again, but with a different natural key, and then is unioned together to create a single record set.

Also note that we used UDFs (see Chapters 7 and 12) to cleanse our data. In this example, we used two very simple UDFs:

- **fn_StripSpaces:** This UDF removes all spaces from the passed-in string.

- **fn_RemoveNonNumeric:** This function removes all non-numeric characters from the passed-in string, essentially removing all the formatting from phone numbers, so we can match on the number only.

So, for a single Salesforce Contact record, we would get a record set like the one shown in Table A-1:

Table A-1. *A Set of Natural Keys for a Contact Record*

ContactId	KeyName	KeyValue
003A00000016zItIAA	Email	DMasri@Demo.Demo
003A00000016zItIAA	First+Last	DaveMasri
003A00000016zItIAA	HomePhone	5558675309
003A00000016zItIAA	Last+HomePhone	Masri5558675309
003A00000016zItIAA	Last+Phone	Masri6668675309
003A00000016zItIAA	MobilePhone	9178675309
003A00000016zItIAA	Phone	6668675309

Next, we create a similar view for leads:

```
1.   Create View [dbo].[Lead_DupKeys] as
2.   Select
3.        c.id as LeadId
4.        ,'Email' as KeyName
5.        ,dbo.fn_StripSpaces(c.EMAIL) as KeyValue
6.   from SF_Leads c
7.   where dbo.fn_StripSpaces(c.EMAIL) <>''
8.   union
9.   select
10.       c.id as LeadId
11.       ,'First+Last' as KeyName
12.       ,dbo.fn_StripSpaces(c.FIRSTNAME+c.lastname) as KeyValue
13.  from SF_Leads c
14.  where dbo.fn_StripSpaces(c.FIRSTNAME+c.lastname) <>''
15.  union
16.  select
17.       c.id as LeadId
18.       ,'MobilePhone' as KeyName
19.       ,dbo.fn_RemoveNonNumeric(c.MobilePhone) as KeyValue
20.  from SF_Leads c
21.  where dbo.fn_RemoveNonNumeric(c.MobilePhone) is not null
```

```
22.   and dbo.fn_RemoveNonNumeric(c.MobilePhone)<>"
23.   union
24.   select
25.        c.id as LeadId
26.        ,'Phone' as KeyName
27.        ,dbo.fn_RemoveNonNumeric(c.Phone) as KeyValue
28.   from SF_Leads c
29.   where dbo.fn_RemoveNonNumeric(c.Phone) is not null
30.   and dbo.fn_RemoveNonNumeric(c.Phone)<>"
31.   union
32.   select
33.        c.id as LeadId
34.        ,'Fax' as KeyName
35.        ,dbo.fn_RemoveNonNumeric(c.Fax) as KeyValue
36.   from SF_Leads c
37.   where dbo.fn_RemoveNonNumeric(c.Fax) is not null
38.   and dbo.fn_RemoveNonNumeric(c.Fax)<>"
```

This code produces a similar dataset to what we saw earlier for contacts. Next, we write some basic queries to find our duplicates. Let's start with contact duplicates. Here is the basic query to identify any natural keys associated with more than one contact:

```
1.   Select
2.        KeyValue
3.        ,count(distinct contactid)
4.   from Contact_DupKeys
5.   group by KeyValue having count(distinct contactid)>1
```

Note that this query does not use the KeyType field, so if one contact's home phone number matched another contact's mobile phone number, it gets detected as a match!

Next, we want to bring in the additional contact data, so we can see the actual contact information related to these natural keys. We do this like so:

```
1.   Select
2.        cd.ContactId
3.        ,cd.KeyName
4.        ,cd.KeyValue
```

```
5.          ,c.* ---- All the fields on SF_Conatct
6.    from SF_Contacts c
7.    join [dbo].[Contact_DupKeys] cd on cd.ContactId=c.Id
8.    join (
9.          Select
10.              KeyValue
11.          from Contact_DupKeys cdk
12.          group by KeyValue
13.          having count(distinct contactid)>1
14.      ) dr on dr.KeyValue=cd.KeyValue
15.  order by cd.KeyValue,c.id
```

That's it! All we did was use standard SQL joins to bring in the additional data (joining the SF_Contact Table and the Contact_DupKeys view to our original query).

We can do the exact same thing to find duplicates within the Lead object, but what if we want to check for duplicates across the two objects? In that case, we simply check for all key values that exist in both the Contact_DupKeys view and the Lead_DupKeys view using an inner join, like so[11]:

```
1.    Select Distinct
2.        Ld.LeadId
3.        ,cd.CONTACTId
4.        ,c.* ---- All the fields on SF_Contact
5.        ,l.* ---- All the fields on SF_Leads
6.    from  dbo.Lead_DupKeys ld
7.    Join dbo.Contact_DupKeys cd on cd.KeyValue=ld.KeyValue
8.    join dbo.SF_Leads l on l.id=ld.LeadId
9.    join dbo.SF_Contacts c on c.id=cd.CONTACTId
```

That's it! It's really that simple. All that is left to do is go through a few iterations of checking our results and fine-tuning the natural keys used (removing keys that are giving us too many false positives or maybe identifying new keys or combinations of keys we can use). For example, we didn't use address at all. Maybe we want to use Last Name + Zip Code + House Number. The possibilities are endless.

---

[11]In general, using Select * in production code is a bad idea. I only did it here for code brevity. See https://stackoverflow.com/questions/3639861/why-is-select-considered-harmful.

The vast majority of the work here was identifying our natural keys and the combinations of them that can identify our entities uniquely.

We may have to get creative. If needed, we can do things such as the following:

- Bring in data from other systems. For example, we may have an order processing system that has credit card information and every address to which a contact has ever shipped.

- Use data from outside services to enrich our data or clean it up. For example, we may decide to use the US Postal Service's service for normalizing address information.[12]

- Use a nickname database for variants of first name, so if we create a natural key for David Masri, it also creates a key for Dave Masri

- Use a "sounds like" algorithm to create keys based on how they sound, rather than how they are spelled[13]

- Add a weight score to each of our key types. In this way, we can calculate a match "confidence score" based on what key (or keys) was used to identify the match. We may score a match on first name and last name with 15 points, but a match on Social Security number with 50. A match on both would score 65 (50 + 15).

Summary

In this appendix we covered the basics of data cleansing and learned the difference between field-level and row-level data quality issues. We learned what a natural key is and how natural keys can be used to identify an entity uniquely, even though that may not be their intended purpose. Last, we a reviewed a very simple but supereffective algorithm for using natural keys or natural key combinations to identify duplicates, either within a single dataset or across two or more datasets.

Happy cleansing!

---

[12]For more information, https://postalpro.usps.com/address-quality.

[13]Most programming languages have this built in, so it's very easy to implement. For example, T-SQL has the SOUNDEX function. See https://docs.microsoft.com/en-us/sql/t-sql/functions/soundex-transact-sql?view=sql-server-2017.

APPENDIX B

Reference Cards and Core Concepts

I provided this appendix for you to use if you ever need a quick refresher on the core concepts covered in this book. Some topics are formatted as reference cards, so you can copy them and post them on your desk. Everyone knows that people with lots of reference cards posted on their desk are the coolest chaps around.

299

© David Masri 2019
D. Masri, *Developing Data Migrations and Integrations with Salesforce*,
https://doi.org/10.1007/978-1-4842-4209-4

The Six-Attributes Reference Card

THE SIX ATTRIBUTES OF A GOOD DATA MIGRATION/INTEGRATION

1. **Well Planned:** Data migrations/integrations must be planned well. Failure to meet any of the other five attributes can be mitigated by planning, but nothing can mitigate for a bad plan or, worse, no plan.

2. **Automated:** Automation enables us to redo our migration/integration with minimal effort and with complete certainty that the results will be the same. Automation eliminates the possibility of human error.

3. **Controlled:** There must be fine control over what data are to be migrated or integrated. The control must be centralized. Control allows for rapid code, test, and fix cycles.

4. **Reversible:** Reversibility allows us to undo a data migration/integration, either fully or partially, in a controlled way.

5. **Repairable/Self-repairing:** Repairability means we can fix data in a very targeted way when a mistake is found. Mistakes happen. There are *always* mistakes. Although it's acceptable for migrations only to be repairable, integrations must be self-repairing.

6. **Testable:** Testability refers to the ease with which we or users can test the data. Ease of testability must be baked into our design.

Think of these attributes as goals—something you should strive for. You may not be able to accomplish them 100%, but some is better than none. Incremental improvements make a big difference.

Good Relationships Reference Card

GOOD RELATIONSHIPS MAKE EVERYTHING EASIER

Aim to be warm and competent.

1. **Warm:** Show concern for users' problems and demonstrate eagerness to help them.

2. **Competent:** Show your ability e to execute as a result of having the right combination of skills (both hard and soft), knowledge, and commitment.

Warmth	**High**	**Well Liked But Pitied** (No one wants to work with you, but may help you)	**Well Liked and Admired** (You want to be here)
	Low	**Hated** (People are openly hostile toward you)	**Envied** (People want you to fail and won't help you succeed)
		Low	High
		Competence	

Dave's Nonscientific Data Specialist Version of the Stereotype Content Model

All 40 Best Practices

#	Best Practices
1	Have a Plan
2	Review Your Charter and Understand Your Scope
3	Partner with Your Project Manager
4	Start Early
5	Understand the Source Data, Ask Questions to Understand Intent, Analyze Data to Know the Reality
6	Understand the Salesforce Data Model and the Hierarchy
7	Document Your Transformations
8	Centralize Your Data Transformations
9	Include Source-to-Target Mapping for Transformation Code, Not Just Transformation Logic
10	Don't Hard-code Salesforce Ids; They Change with Environments
11	Store Cross-reference Data in Salesforce
12	Load Your Data in the Order of the Object Hierarchy
13	Delete Child Records First, Then Parents, When Deleting Data
14	Create All Necessary Holding Accounts in Code
15	Don't Forget about Owners and Record Types
16	Don't Bury the Bodies; Expose Them
17	Partner with Your Business Analyst
18	Automate When Possible
19	Limit the Number of Intermediaries (Layers of Abstraction)
20	Use Proper Tools
21	Build a Library of Reusable Code
22	Turn off Duplicate Management
23	Have Some Way to Control/Limit Which Data Get Migrated
24	Fix Code, Not Data

(continued)

#	Best Practices
25	Fix Errors with Parent Objects before Moving on to Children
26	Modulation Is Also a Form of Control
27	Every Record You Insert Should Have an External Id
28	Standardize External Ids and Always Enforce Uniqueness
29	Don't Use the External Id for Anything Except the Migration or Integration
30	Use Upsert When Possible
31	Every Record You Insert Should Have a Job Id
32	Real Users Must Perform UAT on Data Migration and You Must Set Sign-off before Going Live
33	Plan for an extended UAT Period
34	Build a Relationship with the Users
35	QA and UAT Are Processes Too
36	Start Fresh for Each Round of QA and UAT
37	Log Everything and Keep Detailed Notes
38	Get a New Cut of Data for Each Round of QA and UAT
39	Record Runtimes
40	When Defects Are Found, Patch the Code Then Rerun It

Synchronization Patterns Reference Card

SYNCHRONIZATION PATTERNS

Data synchronization jobs are by far the most common type of integration job, during which we take data from one or more systems and move it into another (keeping the data in sync).

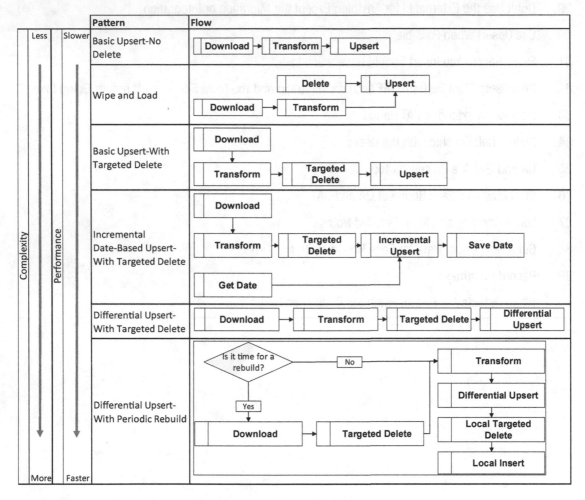

Performance Gains Come at the Expense of Code Complexity.

Other Integration Patterns

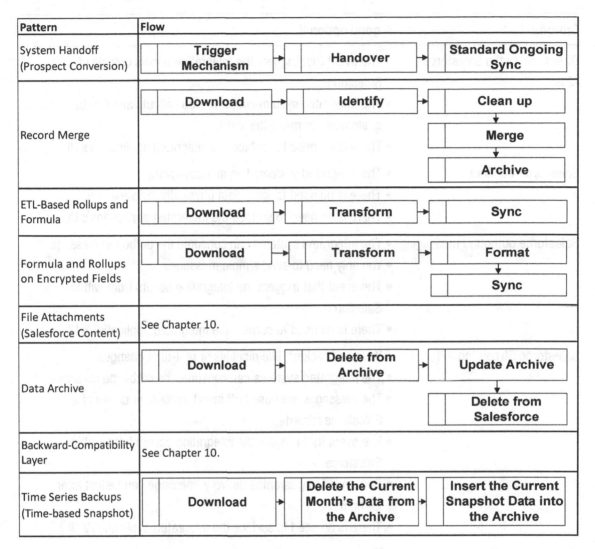

Pattern	Flow		
System Handoff (Prospect Conversion)	Trigger Mechanism	Handover	Standard Ongoing Sync
Record Merge	Download	Identify	Clean up
			Merge
			Archive
ETL-Based Rollups and Formula	Download	Transform	Sync
Formula and Rollups on Encrypted Fields	Download	Transform	Format
			Sync
File Attachments (Salesforce Content)	See Chapter 10.		
Data Archive	Download	Delete from Archive	Update Archive
			Delete from Salesforce
Backward-Compatibility Layer	See Chapter 10.		
Time Series Backups (Time-based Snapshot)	Download	Delete the Current Month's Data from the Archive	Insert the Current Snapshot Data into the Archive

Real-time Data Integration Options

Option	A good option if
Direct call to the Salesforce APIs	• The event that triggers the integration occurs outside of Salesforce • The integrated system supports web callouts and can be customized to make this call. • There is no need to surface the integrated application's UI
Salesforce Connect	• The integrated systems has an oData point • There is no need to store data physically in Salesforce • There is no need to surface the integrated application's UI
Salesforce outbound messaging	• The integrated systems can consume the outbound message • You only need to send simple messages • The event that triggers the integration occurs from within Salesforce • There is no need to surface the integrated application's UI
Salesforce Streaming API	• You need "ticker"-like displays or real-time changes • The integrated systems can consume the outbound message • The messages are based off insert, update, or delete of a Salesforce record • The event that triggers the integration occurs from within Salesforce • Don't need to guarantee delivery (message can be lost after 24 hours) • There is no need to surface the integrated application's UI
Salesforce platform events	• You need "ticker"-like displays or real-time changes • The integrated systems can consume the outbound message • The event that triggers the integration occurs from within Salesforce • You don't need to guarantee delivery (message can be lost after 24 hours) • There is no need to surface the integrated application's UI

(continued)

Option	A good option if
Apex callout	• The integrated systems can consume the callout • You need to send complex messages and, potentially, process replies • The event that triggers the integration occurs from within Salesforce • There is no need to surface the integrated application's UI
Apex web services	• The event that triggers the integration occurs outside of Salesforce • The integrated system supports web callouts and can be customized to make this call • There is no need to surface the integrated application's UI • Message to (or reply from) Salesforce is too complex to use the native Salesforce APIs
Web-to-Case	• You need web forms that can be used to create Salesforce cases
Web-to-Lead	• You need web forms that can be used to create Salesforce leads (and match them to a campaign)
Email-to-Case	• You want to support creating Salesforce cases from an incoming e-mail
Apex e-mail service	• You want to support doing anything (other than creating a case) in Salesforce from an incoming e-mail
Web service triggered ETL	• The event that triggers the integration occurs outside of Salesforce • The event that triggers the integration occurs from within Salesforce • There is no need to surface the integrated application's UI • The integrated application has no API to hit or is closed off to the Web (So, you need a back-end integration, but want to be real time.)
SOA middleware	• You currently have this infrastructure in place and want to be consistent with what your organization is doing elsewhere

Application Automation Integration Options

Option	A good option if
Native Apps	• The integrated application has a native Salesforce app
Embedded iFrame	• All you need to do is automate navigation • The integrated application is web based
Hyperlink	• All you need to do is automate navigation • The integrated application is web based
Canvas	• The integrated application is web based and customizable • You need very tightly coupled UI integration • You need to be aware of who the calling Salesforce users are, or what they are doing in Salesforce
FAT application automation	• The FAT application has an automation library • You need to hand off the UI to the user after some automation and you are okay installing and maintaining code on users' individual desktops *or* you are okay with setting up an automation server that handles the automation.
Web browser automation	• The integrated application is web based • You need to do more than navigation • The integrated application does not have any native means of integration • You are okay with the web site owner's ability to break your code at any time with no notice • You need to hand off the UI to the user after some automation, and you are okay installing and maintaining code on users' individual desktops *or* you are okay with setting up an automation server that handles the automation
Web browser extensions	• The integrated application is web based • You need to do more than navigation • The integrated application does not have any native means of integration • You are okay with the web site owner's ability to break your code at any time with no notice • You need to hand off the UI to the user after some automation, and you are okay installing and maintaining code on users' individual desktops
Windows automation	• You make a deal with the devil and have no other choice

Further Reading and References

Salesforce, and the Salesforce Ohana,[1] do a great job providing lots of wonderful content and resources (specifically with the Trailhead and Developer sites) for self-training and learning. When I was in the process of deciding to write a book, I knew that what I absolutely did not want to do was simply to organize and rehash information that was available elsewhere. If I was going to write a book, it was going to be one of original content, but at the same time, I did not want to ignore all the great content available online. I feel I accomplished that goal via the aggressive use of footnotes. In this way, I could introduce a topic, give you a resource for deep technical information, then dive into practical usage, where I feel there is lack of good content available.

This appendix lists the URLs referenced in this book and a few more.

Note I excluded all URLs from Chapter 11 as well as the "originating source" URLs from Chapter 12 because including them seemed redundant.

General Salesforce Training Sites

Salesforce Developer: API Documentation, Developer Forums, and More: https://developer.salesforce.com/

Salesforce Developer Integration Page: https://developer.salesforce.com/page/Integration

---

[1]What is the Ohana anyway? See https://www.salesforce.com/blog/2017/02/what-is-salesforce-ohana.html.

© David Masri 2019
D. Masri, *Developing Data Migrations and Integrations with Salesforce,*
https://doi.org/10.1007/978-1-4842-4209-4

Salesforce Integration Patterns and Practices White Paper:
https://resources.docs.salesforce.com/sfdc/pdf/
integration_patterns_and_practices.pdf

Salesforce Trailhead, the Fun Way to Learn Salesforce:
https://trailhead.salesforce.com/en/home

Salesforce Architecture and Technical Information

Architecture

Multitenancy: https://developer.salesforce.com/page/
Multi_Tenant_Architecture

Salesforce ERDs: https://developer.salesforce.com/docs/
atlas.en-us.api.meta/api/data_model.htm

Record Locking Cheat Sheet: https://developer.salesforce.
com/blogs/engineering/2014/07/record-locking-cheat-
sheet.html

Salesforce Shield (Encryption and Event Monitoring):
https://www.salesforce.com/products/platform/products/
shield/

Salesforce Standard Object Reference: https://developer.
salesforce.com/docs/atlas.en-us.object_reference.meta/
object_reference/sforce_api_objects_list.htm

Salesforce APIs

API Basics: https://trailhead.salesforce.com/en/modules/
api_basics/units/api_basics_overview

API Explorer: https://developer.salesforce.com/docs/api-
explorer

Bulk API

- **Developer Guide:** https://developer.salesforce.com/docs/
  atlas.en-us.api_asynch.meta/api_asynch/asynch_api_
  intro.htm

- **The Salesforce Bulk API: Maximizing Parallelism and
  Throughput Performance:** https://developer.salesforce.
  com/page/The_Salesforce_Bulk_API_-_Maximizing_
  Parallelism_and_Throughput_Performance_When_
  Integrating_or_Loading_Large_Data_Volumes

Metadata API: https://developer.salesforce.com/docs/
atlas.en-us.api_meta.meta/api_meta/meta_intro.htm

REST API Developer Guide: https://developer.salesforce.
com/docs/atlas.en-us.api_rest.meta/api_rest/intro_what_
is_rest_api.htm

SOAP API Developer Guide: https://developer.salesforce.
com/docs/atlas.en-us.api.meta/api/sforce_api_quickstart_
intro.htm

Streaming API: https://trailhead.salesforce.com/modules/
api_basics/units/api_basics_streaming

Usage Examples:

- **Consuming Force.com SOAP and REST Web Services from
  .NET Applications:** https://developer.salesforce.com/page/
  Consuming_Force.com_SOAP_and_REST_Web_Services_from_
  .NET_Applications

- **Sample Java & C# Code:** https://developer.salesforce.com/
  docs/atlas.en-us.api.meta/api/sforce_api_quickstart_
  steps_walk_through_code.htm

- **Python and the Force.com REST API: Simple Simple-Salesforce Example:** `https://developer.salesforce.com/blogs/ developer-relations/2014/01/python-and-the-force-com- rest-api-simple-simple-salesforce-example.html`

- **A JavaScript/jQuery Example:** `https://developer. salesforce.com/blogs/developer-relations/2015/08/ creating-jquery-application-using-rest-api.html`

Workbench: `https://workbench.developerforce.com/ login.php`

Performance Tuning

Best Practices for Deployments with Large Data Volumes: `https://resources.docs.salesforce.com/sfdc/pdf/ salesforce_large_data_volumes_bp.pdf`

Managing Lookup Skew in Salesforce to Avoid Record Lock Exceptions: `https://developer.salesforce.com/blogs/ engineering/2013/04/managing-lookup-skew-to-avoid- record-lock-exceptions.html`

The Salesforce Bulk API: Maximizing Parallelism and Throughput Performance: `https://developer.salesforce. com/page/The_Salesforce_Bulk_API_-_Maximizing_ Parallelism_and_Throughput_Performance_When_Integrating_ or_Loading_Large_Data_Volumes`

Governor and API Limits

API-Supported Calls: `https://developer.salesforce.com/ docs/atlas.en-us.api.meta/api/sforce_api_calls_list.htm`

DELETE_OPERATION_TOO_LARGE Error: `https://help. salesforce.com/articleView?id=000149021&type=1`

File Size and Sharing Limits: https://help.salesforce.com/
articleView?id=collab_files_size_limits.htm&type=5

Governor Limits: https://developer.salesforce.com/docs/
atlas.en-us.apexcode.meta/apexcode/apex_gov_limits.htm

Report Limits, Limitations, and Allocations: https://help.
salesforce.com/articleView?id=rd_reports_limits.
htm&type=5

Data Types and Field-level Information

Address as a Compound Field: https://developer.salesforce.
com/docs/atlas.en-us.api.meta/api/compound_fields_
address.htm

Attachments Using the Data Loader: https://www.shellblack.
com/administration/import-attachments-using-the-data-
loader/

Content Note Unescaped Characters:

- https://help.salesforce.com/articleView?id=000232870&
  type=1

- https://help.salesforce.com/articleView?id=000230867&
  language=en_US&type=1

Data Types

- **Primitive**: https://developer.salesforce.com/docs/atlas.
  en-us.api.meta/api/primitive_data_types.htm

- **Field**: https://developer.salesforce.com/docs/atlas.en-us.
  api.meta/api/field_types.htm

Date Formats and Date Literals: https://developer.
salesforce.com/docs/atlas.en-us.soql_sosl.meta/soql_
sosl/sforce_api_calls_soql_select_dateformats.htm

Enable Audit Fields: `https://help.salesforce.com/articleView?id=Enable-Create-Audit-Fields&language=en_US&type=1`

Managing Salesforce Multicurrency: `https://help.salesforce.com/articleView?id=admin_currency.htm&type=5`

Record Id Prefix Guide: `https://help.salesforce.com/articleView?id=Standard-Field-Record-ID-Prefix-Decoder&language=en_US&type=1`

Rich Text-Supported HTML: `https://help.salesforce.com/articleView?id=fields_using_rich_text_area.htm&type=5`

SystemModStamp vs. LastModifiedDate: `https://help.salesforce.com/articleView?id=When-is-SystemModStamp-different-from-LastModifiedDate&language=en_US&type=1`

Salesforces Data Backup Information

Salesforces Data Backup and Recovery Best Practices Page:
`https://help.salesforce.com/articleView?id=000213366&type=1`

Third-Party Backup Solutions:

- **OwnBackup for Salesforce:** `https://www.ownbackup.com/`

- **Spanning Backup for Salesforce:** `https://spanning.com/products/salesforce-backup/`

- **CloudAlly Backup for Salesforce:** `https://www.cloudally.com/backup-salesforce/`

- **Backupify for Salesforce:** `https://www.backupify.com/salesforce-backup`

- **Odaseva for Salesforce:** `https://www.odaseva.com/`

- **Druva:** `https://www.druva.com/solutions/salesforce/`

Other Technical Information

Bulkifying Your Code: https://developer.salesforce.com/
page/Best_Practice%3A_Bulkify_Your_Code

Considerations for Relationship Types: https://help.
salesforce.com/articleView?id=relationships_
considerations.htm&type=5

Duplicate Management and Data Quality:

- **Salesforce Data Quality:** https://help.salesforce.com/
  articleView?id=data_quality.htm&type=5

- **Duplicate Management Trailhead:** https://trailhead.
  salesforce.com/en/modules/sales_admin_duplicate_
  management

- **Data.com:**

  - https://www.salesforce.com/products/data/solutions/

  - https://www.data.com/

- **Manage Duplicates Globally (within Salesforce):** https://
  help.salesforce.com/articleView?id=manage_duplicates_
  globally.htm&type=5

Monitoring Data Storage: https://help.salesforce.com/
articleView?id=admin_monitorresources.htm&type=5

Sandbox License and Storage Information: https://help.
salesforce.com/articleView?id=data_sandbox_environments.
htm&type=5

Salesforce Native Backup (to .csv's): https://help.salesforce.
com/articleView?id=admin_exportdata.htm&type=5

Salesforce Storage Calculation: https://help.salesforce.com/
articleView?id=admin_monitorresources.htm&type=5

Shared Contacts:

- **Contacts to Multiple Accounts:** https://help.salesforce.com/
  articleView?id=shared_contacts_overview.htm&type=5

- **The Account Contact Relation Object:** https://developer.
  salesforce.com/docs/atlas.en-us.api.meta/api/sforce_
  api_objects_accountcontactrelation.htm

Shared Activities: https://help.salesforce.com/articleView?
id=activities_enable_shared_activities.htm&type=5

SOQL Documentation: https://developer.salesforce.com/
docs/atlas.en-us.soql_sosl.meta/soql_sosl/sforce_api_
calls_soql.htm

Triggers and Order of Execution: https://developer.
salesforce.com/docs/atlas.en-us.apexcode.meta/apexcode/
apex_triggers_order_of_execution.htm

Recover or Restore Lost or Deleted Records and Data: https://
help.salesforce.com/articleView?id=000004037&type=1

Recycle Bin (Viewing and Purging): https://help.salesforce.
com/articleView?id=home_delete.htm

Reporting Snapshots: https://help.salesforce.com/
articleView?id=data_about_analytic_snap.htm&type=5

Relational/Traditional Databases

Edgar F. Codd: https://www.britannica.com/biography/Edgar-
Frank-Codd

Optimistic vs. Pessimistic Locking: https://stackoverflow.com/
questions/129329/optimistic-vs-pessimistic-locking

SQL Tutorial: https://www.tutorialspoint.com/sql/sql_
tutorial.pdf

**Should I use NOT IN, OUTER APPLY, LEFT OUTER JOIN,
EXCEPT, or NOT EXISTS?:** https://sqlperformance.
com/2012/12/t-sql-queries/left-anti-semi-join

Big Data/NoSQL

NoSQL Keeps Rising, But Relational Databases Still Dominate Big Data: https://
www.techrepublic.com/article/nosql-keeps-rising-but-relational-databases-
still-dominate-big-data/

Middleware and ETL Tools

Apex Data Loader: https://resources.docs.salesforce.
com/216/latest/en-us/sfdc/pdf/salesforce_data_loader.pdf

Azure Data Factory:

- **Azure Data Factory:** https://azure.microsoft.com/en-us/
services/data-factory/

- **Azure Data Factory Salesforce Connector:** https://docs.
microsoft.com/en-us/azure/data-factory/connector-
salesforce

DBAmp: https://forceamp.com/

Dell Boomi: https://boomi.com/solutions/salesforce/

Informatica:

- **Informatica Web Site:** https://www.informatica.com/

- **Informatica PowerCenter:** https://www.informatica.com/in/
products/data-integration/powercenter.html

- **Informatica Cloud:** https://www.informatica.com/in/
products/cloud-integration.html

- **Informatica Salesforce Connector:** https://www.informatica.
com/products/cloud-integration/connectivity/salesforce-
connector.html

Jitterbit: https://www.jitterbit.com/solutions/salesforce-
integration/

MuleSoft:

- **MuleSoft Web Site:** `https://www.mulesoft.com`

- **MuleSoft Anypoint:** `https://www.mulesoft.com/platform/enterprise-integration`

- **MuleSoft Salesforce Connector:** `https://www.mulesoft.com/integration-solutions/saas/salesforce`

- **Dataloader.io:** `https://dataloader.io`

- **Salesforce Acquisition:** `https://www.mulesoft.com/press-center/salesforce-acquisition-completed`

- **Salesforce Integration Cloud:** `https://www.salesforce.com/products/integration-cloud/overview/`

Relational Junction: `http://sesamesoftware.com/relational-junction/salesforce-integration/`

Salesforce Excel Connectors:

- **Xappex XL-Connector:** `https://www.xappex.com/#Enabler4Excel`

- **Salesforce Excel Connector:** `https://code.google.com/archive/p/excel-connector-quickinstaller/`

Scribe

- **Scribe Web Site:** `https://www.scribesoft.com/`

- **Scribe Salesforce Connector:** `https://www.scribesoft.com/solutions/crm-integration/salesforce/`

SQL Server Integration Services (SSIS):

- **About SSIS:** `https://docs.microsoft.com/en-us/sql/integration-services/sql-server-integration-services?view=sql-server-2017`

- **SQL Server Developer Edition:** `https://www.microsoft.com/en-us/sql-server/sql-server-downloads`

- **SQL Server Management Studio:** `https://docs.microsoft.com/en-us/sql/ssms/download-sql-server-management-studio-ssms`

- **SQL Server Data Tools (the SSIS IDE):** `https://docs.microsoft.com/en-us/sql/ssdt/download-sql-server-data-tools-ssdt`

- **Third-Party SSIS Salesforce Connectors:**

  - **KingswaySoft:** `http://www.kingswaysoft.com/products/ssis-integration-toolkit-for-salesforce`

  - **TaskFactory:** `http://pragmaticworks.com/Products/Task-Factory/Feature/Salesforce-SSIS`

  - **CozyRoc:** `https://www.cozyroc.com/ssis/salesforce`

Miscellaneous, Technical

Amazon EC2 for Microsoft Windows: `https://aws.amazon.com/windows/products/ec2/`

Base64 Encoding: `https://stackoverflow.com/questions/201479/what-is-base-64-encoding-used-for`

Left Join Antipattern (for "where not in" logic): `https://sqlperformance.com/2012/12/t-sql-queries/left-anti-semi-join`

Premature Optimization Debate: `https://www.google.com/search?q=premature+performance+optimization+debate`

SSIS: SQL Server Destination vs. OLE DB Destination: `https://social.msdn.microsoft.com/Forums/sqlserver/en-US/9f9208ad-6371-4cdf-aed4-778b8b7eea4c/sql-server-destination-vs-ole-db-destination`

Why Does Null Not Equal Null? https://stackoverflow.com/questions/1843451/why-does-null-null-evaluate-to-false-in-sql-server

Why Select * Is Bad: https://stackoverflow.com/questions/3639861/why-is-select-considered-harmful

Miscellaneous, Nontechnical

Albert Einstein, Clock Synchronization, Space, Time, and Patents: https://www.telegraph.co.uk/culture/books/3601647/Space-time-and-patents.html

Stereotype Content Model:

- http://journals.sagepub.com/doi/pdf/10.1177/0963721417738825

- https://www.cos.gatech.edu/acultyres/Diversity_Studies/Fiske_StereotypeContent.pdf

What Is the Salesforce Ohana Anyway? https://www.salesforce.com/blog/2017/02/what-is-salesforce-ohana.html

Index

A

© David Masri 2019
D. Masri, *Developing Data Migrations and Integrations with Salesforce*,
https://doi.org/10.1007/978-1-4842-4209-4

X, Y, Z

Printed in the United States
By Bookmasters